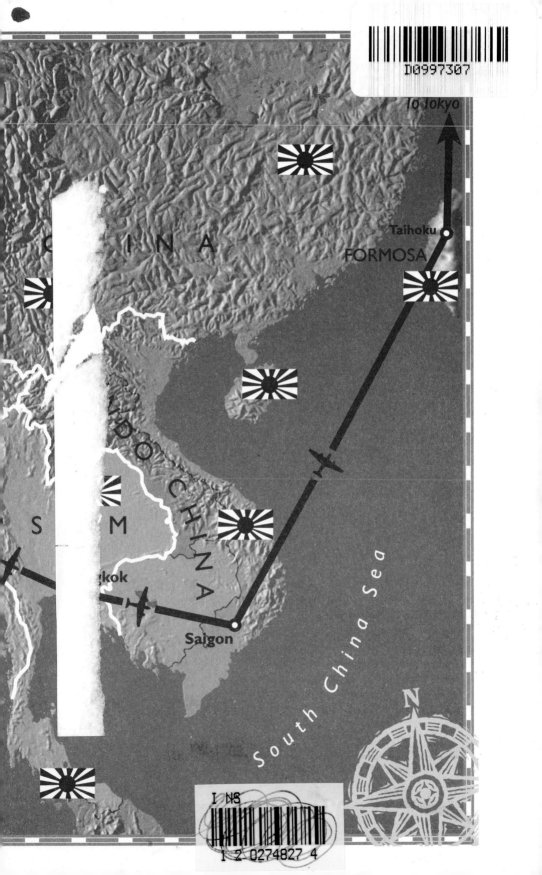

To Tokyo

Taihoku
FORMOSA

CHINA

INDO CHINA

SIAM

Bangkok

Saigon

South China Sea

N

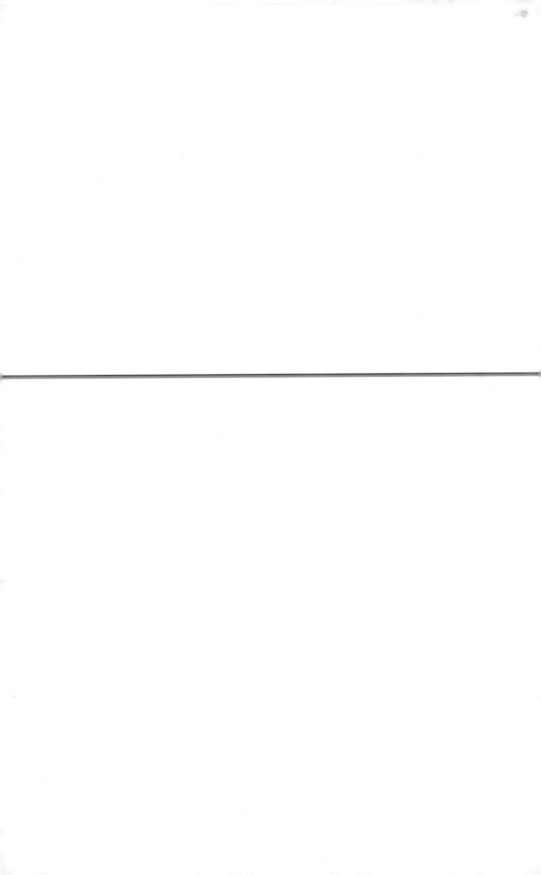

OUR CHANCES WERE ZERO

OUR CHANCES WERE ZERO

Rolf Magener

LEO COOPER

First published by Ullstein, Vienna, in 1954
Second German edition published in 1963, third edition 2000

First English language edition *Prisoner's Bluff*
with translation by Basil Creighton,
Rubert Hart-Davis, London, 1954

Published in this format in 2001 by
Leo Cooper
an imprint of Pen & Sword Books Limited
47 Church Street
Barnsley, South Yorkshire
S70 2AS

A CIP record for this book is available from
the British Library

ISBN 0 85052 844 5

Typeset in 10.5/12.5pt Plantin
by Phoenix Typesetting, Ilkley, West Yorkshire

Printed in England by CPI UK

CONTENTS

INTRODUCTION
by
Jürgen Strube
Chairman of the Board of Executive Directors
BASF Aktiengesellschaft

Dr Rolf Magener would have celebrated his ninetieth birthday in August 2000. Publication of a new edition of his book was planned to honour the occasion. Sadly, Dr Magener died on 5 May 2000.

He rated the chances of a successful escape from the camp for civilian internees at Dehra Dun in India during the Second World War as zero. In spite of the odds against the enterprise, he was bold enough to try and escape. Magener overcame all the dangers he encountered on the journey and reached Tokyo. The adventure was a success, despite the fact that he never really believed it would come off!

My first meeting with Dr Magener was in autumn 1968. It led to my joining a comprehensive trainee programme in the Finance Department at BASF Aktiengesellschaft. For a lawyer like myself, the desire to start off my career in Finance and not Legal Affairs and Tax was not an escape. It was a risk, perhaps even an adventure. The desire to get out into the world and do something, the lust for creative opportunities, the drive to climb to the top were the things that motivated me.

If you had asked me back in 1968 how I rated my chances of one day becoming Chairman of the Board of Executive Directors at BASF, my reply would have been exactly the same: zero!

If the escape had not succeeded, Dr Magener would never have become Chief Financial Officer at BASF. In this capacity he played a leading role in shaping a phase of expansion that placed exceptional demands on finance and transparency. He was convinced that a company can only grow on the international stage if it recruits the next generation of managers from those individuals who like to create opportunities, yet limit risks. It then has to promote such people at the right time. His personality and cosmopolitan approach engendered a fascination that touched the lives of many people. His great gift was winning people over and creating a sense of loyalty in them.

Dr Magener was one of those people who possesses both the art of good fortune and the art of longevity. Golden Age Jesuit teacher Baltasar Gracián has left us some helpful maxims on these two subjects in his *Pocket Oracle*:

'The Art of being Happy. There are Rules of Good Fortune; and Happiness is not always Prosperous, in regard of a Wise Man. His Industry must sometimes help it forward. Some think it enough to stand at the Gate of Fortune in a good Posture, and to wait till she opens it. Others do better, and trusting to their Confidence or Merit advance farther on, so that by the cajoling of Fortune, one way or other, they obtain her.

'The way to Live Long is to Live Well. There are two things which shorten the Life of Man: Folly and Wickedness. Some have lost it, because they knew not how to keep it; others, because they would not.'

This book shows how these rules can be applied to real life, in exceptional situations, at the very boundaries of human endurance.

Dr Magener will live on in the hearts and minds of the many people who were close to him.

Chapter One

DEHRA DUN

Dehra Dun is a town in northern Hindustan. The frontier of Nepal is not far away, and the ice-clad summits of the Himalayas would be visible but for a long line of delicately modelled foothills which curtain them off and form its background.

Its tumultuous life surges up to the edge of silence: the life of India, seething, overflowing humanity, clamour of the bazaar, jostling of narrow streets, Hindu and Moslem, pungent eastern spices, holy cow-dung and lingams.

The British had a camp for internees outside the town, where the jungle met the inhabited world, on a site which had once been a tea-plantation and had partly gone back to jungle. There were rows upon rows of reed-thatched huts, with such low eaves that a murky gloom surrounded them. Beyond the shadow blazed the tropical sun. Vultures on the look-out for garbage perched in the branches of the few trees. There was nothing else in sight but shrubs, allotments, open drains, and long rows of latrines. No women or children were to be seen in this City of Despair, but the population showed great variety; besides Germans, who came from every country from Iraq to Hong Kong and were by far the most numerous, there were Italians, Bulgarians, Hungarians, Rumanians, Finns, all engaged in the common occupation of wasting time.

Whenever people are herded together, penned like cattle and fed like cattle, an immeasurable and inhuman boredom descends; but although a brooding vacancy marks the concentration camp, mere dullness some-times conceives. Then when the time is ripe, there is a birth.

The moment I set eyes on Have I had the definite impression that he would be the right partner for an escape. We first met as opponents on the camp sports-ground, and after the event we retired to my hut to rest; it was a sultry afternoon during the monsoon, and we had better have kept still. He was dripping with sweat and sat down on a stool made out

9

of packing-case wood under a self-planted grove of papaya trees, a tree the fruit of which bursts straight out of the stem like a young girl's breasts. He was panting, but he laughed at the same time. His laugh, light-hearted with a note of daring and an undertone of scorn, was altogether typical of Heins von Have. I took him to be a little older than I; so he was, but we were both in our early thirties. There was something clear and firm and sharply defined about him which his hard blue eyes emphasized. We were each taking big gulps of tamarind juice out of large thick tumblers.

At the outbreak of war Have was engaged in trade in Batavia. The Dutch interned him, but when the Japanese landed in Java he was sent to India with all the other Germans in Indonesia. That is how he joined our crowd, who had been shut up ever since the 3rd of September, 1939. He was known for his daring escapes, and nothing pleased him better than to outwit the Indians and defy the English. When he arrived from the East Indies he was confined in a camp near Calcutta, and his first attempt at escape was made when he was being taken with a batch of other prisoners to a transit camp in the west of the country. He jumped from the moving train with another Hamburger, Hans Peter Hülsen. The attempt failed in spite of a very promising start; and so did the second, soon after. It was made with the same companion, who in the course of it lost his life.

Have gave his account of it in staccato sentences, in a manner equally nonchalant and precise. He stuck to the facts, and they were quite surprising enough. As he spoke he measured off his sentences in the air, and the cadence of his voice had a soft and dangerous quality.

"Rotten show, that last time. Don't like to think of it now," he said to wind up his brief and rapid account.

"I expect the death of the other fellow has about sickened you."

"On the contrary. It makes me much more restless than ever."

"Do you still think of—" I jerked my head in the direction of the wire.

"It has never been out of my mind since the first day I was interned. And now that Hülsen's died in the attempt, I'll damned well get out or die too. I've got to, and that's all there is to it."

He wiped his moist face and sandy-coloured hair, still wet from his exertions, with the inside of his arm, took another swig and laughed.

"Must have a breath of fresh air now and then, if it's only to annoy the English. It's a bit too close in here, don't you think?"

"Of course, but not just for a breath, for good and all if possible. The only trouble is being captured and ending up where you started."

"You're right there, but it must click sometime, and I'll pull it off next time, I tell you. Laugh if you like."

He said it in a tone of truculent assurance, and with a characteristic gesture swung his right arm across as though sheathing a dagger at his side.

"You'll take your Bible oath—"

"Believe me, it can be done. I know how far you can get, particularly if you can speak a bit of English. Look here . . ."

He drew on his experiences to sketch out a tempting plan of operations. It had its gaps and rash assumptions, but from the cradle I have always been conservative in my estimate of chances. For example, I mentioned the tender concern which would certainly be shown by the military police. But he only said: "My dear fellow, if you treat the MPs with the contempt they deserve you can fool them every time." And with that my objections were disposed of.

"But you seem to take an interest in the question," he went on after a pause. "You're not one of those who mean to put up with it, if there's any other way out."

"Perhaps not."

We got some more drink and then I casually told Have that I had been to college in England and had had a lot to do with its inhabitants from youth up. I also let fall that my firm, the I.G. Farben Industrie, had more than once sent me to London, also to India and other eastern countries, and that this had given me opportunities for an exhaustive study of English life and habits. I was gratified by the attention he paid.

April and May were always the escape months. Winter at Dehra Dun, owing to the proximity of the ice-covered mountains, was cold. The foothills, though they acted as a break against the winds from the upper heights, sent cold winds of their own down the valley, and the temperature fell to freezing-point. It was too cold to pass the night in the open. Summer began with moist heat and a sky obscured in a milky haze. The whole plain steamed and the blanket of vapour was heated mercilessly by the invisible sun. There was no let-up, no cooling off, not even by night when the prisoner lay panting inside his mosquito-net. Later came the monsoon, when the clouds discharged their burden for weeks on end, and we sat in our huts as though in submarines – surrounded by water on every side. It was no weather for a fugitive. In early spring, on the other hand, the air was dry and sparkling and the heat bearable; the earth, not yet parched, provided ample water. The country was refreshed and lent itself to hopes of escape.

Internment in India meant a double imprisonment; there was first the barbed wire; and then the country, owing to the mere physical obstructions, was a prison in itself. India is a triangle with the Himalayas as its base and the ocean as its two sides. Deserts bar the way out in the northwest; jungle in the north-east. The road to Afghanistan is blocked by the forts which guard the Khyber Pass, and the whole territory is made impassable for white men by the wild Afridi tribesmen. South of Bombay there is the small Portuguese possession of Goa. It was neutral, and at first the difficulty of other outlets made it the goal of escapers. But it was merely a stage, and the journey had to be continued from there by sea – an almost impossible proceeding because all the coasts opposite, whether in Africa or Arabia, were in British hands. Later on, when Japan invaded Burma, the thoughts of prisoners turned eastwards; and as the direct approach across the plain of the Ganges and Bengal seemed quite impracticable, we came upon the truly grandiose idea of by-passing the whole of India by a break-through into Tibet. The attempt could only be made in late spring because the Himalayan passes, over 15,000 feet high, are not clear of snow until then.

We owed these bold thoughts to the small and select body of mountaineers, members of various Himalayan expeditions, who had been caught by the outbreak of war and interned at Dehra Dun with other Germans then in India; their one desire ever since had been to get back to their beloved mountains, and it was naturally a great temptation to have the best the world can offer in that line within reach and before their very eyes. It worried them very little that insuperable barriers lay between them and Tibet – the lynx-eyed watch on the wire, desert wastes, marauding nomads, starvation, death. It seemed hopeless. How could a German fugitive possibly survive in the wild highlands of Tibet, which was then under English influence? But it was the very impossibility of it that spurred them on. Besides, they had all been in it as instigators, abettors or participants, when, the year before, eight men in pairs set out for Tibet. All had been captured, and after the usual twenty-eight days' solitary confinement restored to our society.

It is characteristic that disappointments – and so far all attempts to escape from internment in India had failed – do not damp the ardour of those who mean to escape. And this is true above all of the recaptured. When a man has once tasted freedom for a few days after years of imprisonment, when he has breathed the air beyond the wire and known

12

the thrill of the hunted, he will never again rest content, no matter how often he has failed. Many of the runaways were regular addicts with two, three and even four break-outs to their credit. And even the new hands, who were making their first attempt, were not in the least deterred by the disasters of their forerunners. Each failure taught a lesson and added to the common stock of experience. Sources of failure were sealed off, blind alleys and false directions known.

On the other hand, all these failures did seem to show how foolish and apparently ill-advised it was to think of escape from India. Those impassable frontiers, those continental distances, the oppressive climate, the native population against which every white man stood out, were all strongly dissuasive, and in practice the country seemed to have rubber walls from which every fugitive bounced back into the camp again. To flout all this time after time was crazy, let alone foolhardy; and it is not surprising that two schools of thought arose among the 1500 German internees. One found in constant failure a challenge to ever-renewed and more desperate endeavour; the other maintained, more prudently, that the attempt was hopeless from the start and should therefore be abandoned. Each failure gave the prudent added proof of the correctness of their view, and also was a salve to their consciences, for all felt the urge and many recognized the duty to escape. If the impossibility were proven, their consciences would be absolved. Thus the one school of thought aimed high, but lacked proof; the other had proof, but was conscious of having a less exalted view.

Also, statistics were against the foolhardy; in both wars about seventy attempts had failed. In face of such clear evidence even the English camp commandant was inclined to look on each fresh delinquent as a silly fool rather than a desperate criminal.

And though the majority were for sitting it out, they derived pleasure from the active minority. Every prisoner's heart leapt when a fellow-victim burst his bonds and got away. There were the sergeants' puzzled faces when they discovered at roll-call that someone was missing. Then the guards were hauled up and got a punishment. And the commandant blew up. Even the most exalted quarters in Delhi heard about it. Thus an escape meant change and excitement for all.

It was not easy to keep preparations secret. You could not move a finger in camp without every eye being on you. But for very good reasons it had to be concealed when or by whom an attempt was to be made. The British might hear of it, and the other fellows also might put the sentries on the alert by their eagerness to stand by and give their help when the get-away took place. Above all, other aspirants to freedom must be kept in the dark; otherwise they would try to get out first. That was every-body's aim, because circumstances favoured the first attempt. The later your turn, the worse your prospects; one alarm followed another until the sentries and the whole system of control were on edge. Consequently, there was a grim and secret struggle for the first place.

It was exactly this that worried Have and me, after we had finally come together.

Have knew from previous experience how much depended on a good start and was therefore determined to make the date an early one. So we made D-day the 15th of April; the year was 1944. By that date our equip-ment had to be complete, and on any day after we might be off, in which case we might surely count on being the first. But we were not ready yet. In spite of all our efforts, we had not succeeded in smuggling in a compass, torches and a railway time-table. Also it had taken longer than we had bargained for to procure money. And now we observed with mounting anxiety that others showed signs of putting their plans into immediate execution.

For months past we had devoted ourselves with the passion and the patience of which only a prisoner is capable, to the problem of getting away. He has unlimited time and the boundless fury which incarceration inspires; and as he gives all his wits, his inventiveness and will-power to the task, he is bound to prove that the watcher is no match in the long run for the watched. Routine and reliance on material superiority go well with duty and discipline, but not with the monomaniacal fervour and meticulous patience devoted by a captive to the sacred duty of escape. It follows that we had studied the whole system of guarding the prisoners at Dehra Dun to the very bottom, and separated with almost scientific accuracy those projects which had promise from those which had not.

The camp was surrounded by a double barbed-wire fence, eleven feet high, giving an alley-way for the sentries, who were posted at intervals of eight paces. They were Gurkhas, belonging to one of the warlike tribes of Nepal, who provided one of the regiments in Britain's Indian army. They were small, stocky fellows, yellow-skinned and Mongol-eyed. They wore wide-brimmed hats on their round, bald heads; wild hill-folk as ready to shoot as to slit a throat. They would shoot without mercy a fugitive who got caught in the wire, and that might well happen, as the strands were only a hand's breadth apart, and strengthened besides by a tightly coiled concertina-wire running along the surface of the ground. By night the alley-way between the double fence was brilliantly lit up and the sentries marched up and down; it was therefore suicidal to think of forcing a way through the fence. We had calculated by stop-watch that the average time taken by a sentry to turn round was a mere matter of seconds, which would not afford the least possible cover for passage through the wire. And the other alternative of getting over instead of through, using the strands as the rungs of a ladder, was turned down because the topmost strand came inward.

So we gave up all thought of negotiating the wire. Even though it was not an entirely insuperable obstacle, it could not be forced without raising the alarm, and that meant losing the start. Also experience had proved that it was particularly difficult for two to get through at the same attempt, not to mention the encumbrance of their packs. Finally, the English had grown wise by sad experience and were on the alert during the escape season; they sent out night-patrols, who could not be seen from within, because they operated beyond the lighted zone. They were a very serious danger. For all these reasons we decided not to attempt a way out via the wire unless there was no alternative; and we adopted a quite different plan.

The camp was divided up into sections, or wings, as they were called, and there were seven of them in all. They were separated by a high double fence, with an alley-way, as in the outer fence. It was only occasionally, and only by night, patrolled by sentries, with the object of preventing prisoners in one wing visiting those in another, a punishable offence which had often cost a delinquent fourteen days' solitary confinement. Now and then the orderly officer would patrol these alley-ways, which were all connected, and examine the wire for faulty places. One of these alley-ways might better be described as a wide thoroughfare, because it bisected the rectangular camp-site and was used for a lively traffic of English and Indian soldiers and servants employed in the camp. Both exits were guarded and both were kept open during the day; those who went in or out were not stopped and asked for passes, because they could only be authorized persons and not internees. This fact we very carefully noted.

On the inner side of our own section ran an alley-way which separated us from the section occupied by citizens of the Balkan States, and led into the wide intersecting thoroughfare.

On this fact, carefully weighing every circumstance and calculating every step in advance, we based our bid for freedom. The project, though it hung by a hair, attracted us; it had the elegance demanded by the

15

etiquette of escape, but unfortunately we had rivals – rivals who were in a hurry, who might hit on the same idea, and anticipate us in carrying it out, or else muff it and so spoil our chances.

D-day was already a week behind when Have invited me to take a turn on the sports ground, the only place where a consultation could be held without being overheard.

"I say, I've just been given a hint. There is to be a getaway tomorrow night."

"Who are they?"

"Aufschnaiter and Treipl."

"Tomorrow?"

"Yes."

We knew that they were making their preparations, but not that their zero hour was so close. Aufschnaiter was a professional climber, Secretary of the German Himalaya Committee, and last year he had been well on his way to Tibet. Earlier he had taken part in several Himalayan expeditions, and he was no longer young: his long, lean skull showed the first signs of age; but he was leathery and experienced. Treipl was a mere beginner, a downy, lighthearted fellow. They made a good pair.

"What's their scheme?"

"No idea."

"I've a hunch that Hanne Kopp is on the move too, though he swears not. If he hears what Aufschnaiter is up to, he'll try to get the start of him."

And Kopp was no sluggard when the hour struck. He came from Berlin and had been captured in Iraq, where he was superintending the erection of machinery when war broke out. He was brought from Baghdad to India with a batch of fellow-captives: he had a tremendous chest on him, and he was popular because he was always full of humour, and his mad stunts kept our spirits up. He had the look of a removals man always on the look-out for some object of great bulk.

"Well, Hanne, where's that grand piano?", we used to say.

His heart was in the right place and he was ready with his tongue. He was knowing too.

"Kopp won't be going alone, that's sure. I'd like to know who his partner is."

This was the very devil, because besides those already named, Heini Harrer, the irrepressible escaper, was going to try again. Harrer already had some astonishing exploits to his credit. He and his companion were

16

the first to climb the north face of the Eiger and he was in the first rank as a skier. He was a close friend of ours and we had long been in his confidence. So that made six; perhaps seven, ourselves included.

"We must try to talk the others into a week's postponement, and at once," I counselled. "By that time we shall be all set."

"We want Harrer's opinion on this," Have replied.

Harrer, whom we went after right away, raised objections. It wasn't so much a matter of the few days, but of priority. Nobody, he said, would stretch a point there, and it would not be fair to ask it.

We therefore decided to go to Ede Krämer, the strongest man in Dehra Dun.

He was known also as 'von' Krämer, at the suggestion of his manager in India; it helped the box office; Ede was not only a wrestler, but a gentleman-wrestler, and the prefix helped to make this clear. But you would not, to look at him, have taken Krämer for a wrestler; he was neither a mountain of flesh nor had he cauliflower ears. His solid frame was far from being clumsy. There were deep furrows round his mouth, engraven there doubtless by many an obstinate bout on the matting. His appetite equalled that of several persons, and he had been put on double rations. Nevertheless he was always hungry.

We found Ede in his dwelling. He had built a lean-to against the stone wall of his hut and furnished it to his own requirements. He had his bed in there, a large, clumsy table and a chair or two. A six-spiralled expander hung from a nail, and what else there was – empty bottles, clothing and crime stories – lay about the place. The one wall was plastered over its whole extent with studies of the nude, edge to edge. Here we found the mighty champion, winner of many titles, victor in every class, seated in all his glory. He was happily chewing a piece of meat of which some admirer of the Graeco-Roman style had made his idol a present. Although it was evening, the atmosphere was stale and heavy with the heat of the tropical day and the next day would take it on almost unaffected by the night.

"Well, chaps, what's on?" Ede said in greeting, while he wiped his greasy fingers on his dark blue bath-wrap. We sat down on the bed and a chair.

Krämer was the very man for our purpose. He was captain of the stalwarts and also the key-man in the camp. All threads to the outer world were in his hands; he was the darling of Tommies and Indians alike, and he had unseen control of all the camp workshops, from which he obtained many secret tips and where many a plot was hatched. He got early news of forthcoming escapes, because shoemakers, tailors and smiths were all employed in producing the necessary equipment.

And then Krämer had been out himself, and had actually reached Tibet, with Kopp as his companion. They had made their way into the interior of the country, but then hunger and unfortunate incidents with ill-disposed monks forced them to turn back into India, where, disguised as holy men, they kept going for some time. Their visionary and saintly features went excellently with their religious dress, and their muscular stride served them well as servants of God whose way led on through town and village. Then in Delhi the comedy came to a sad end; the police stripped the wolves of their sheep's clothing and all India echoed with laughter. The newspapers gave the full story of the pilgrimage of such a popular favourite as Krämer, the renowned wrestler. I have never been able to understand how he was able to carry on for so long; the only English expressions of which he was quite sure were "I'll fix it" and "O.K."

Krämer was therefore a master of escape technique; he wielded the required authority; he had his hand on every lever, and he was well disposed to both of us as well as to the way we proposed to tackle the business. He had complete faith in its success.

"Now listen to me, Ede. You've got to get us out of a jam."

"What's the matter, then?"

"We hear that Kopp, Aufschnaiter and Treipl mean to be off tomorrow night."

"Well, and—"

"Wouldn't it be best if we all came to you so as to stop us spoiling the show for each other? If there's no other way out of it, then let us all try it on together. In that case we should have a proposal to make."

"Bring 'em along," Ede commanded one of his followers in the hut.

We used the interval to explain to Ede that a week's postponement was essential if we were not to be left in the ruck. He promised his un-conditional support, even to the extent if required of exerting his physical pressure.

When the brotherhood had assembled, the memorable session opened with Ede in the chair. Laying his sledgehammer fists on the table, he put the reasons for calling the meeting very forcibly. He said nothing as yet of our proposal, but merely observed that we must all get together and say what our plans were.

"So now, friends and sportsmen, down with your cards on the table."

The answers came very stickily. It was not the custom to divulge plans except to one or two chosen persons.

"No business of yours what I'm up to," Kopp said.

But as Aufschnaiter had already come clean, Kopp had to reconcile himself to it whether he liked it or not. And so it was finally known that all except us two were going northwards over the mountains.

"Perhaps now you'll have the kindness to tell us who you're going with," Ede said to Kopp.

"Steady on. Not so much of your hustling."

"Well, get it out slowly," Krämer said to encourage him.

"I'm flitting with Sattler of Wing 6, if you must know."

We saw now that the others had not tumbled to the importance of the actual date, and that the moment had come for requesting a postponement. Have brought it up. Uproar followed. Flat refusal on all sides. Every man insisted on absolute freedom of movement. Krämer looked like getting tough, when Have interrupted him with the proposal we had to make. Its basic idea was – a common break-out. Working on our scheme, it would be possible, if necessary, to include seven. True, the risk of failure would be increased, but not unduly, not so much as to wreck the show; and our plan was far more hopeful than any other hitherto mentioned even if stretched to include us all.

"We're ready to take you in, and so compromise our own prospects, on condition that it does not happen for a week."

The room was unbearably hot; the air was moist and stale. We all took off our shirts except Krämer, who was only wearing his wrap, which he threw open. And now I tried my hand at persuasion, but even so we were no further. I whispered to Have, and we played our last card.

"Well, just to let you know what it is you're mucking up, cast an eye on these."

I produced two small books out of my pocket, two authentic British soldiers' pay-books, which it had cost us untold pains to procure through Krämer. No one so far had ever achieved that. Our plan was to cross India as Englishmen, and we now possessed an invaluable proof of identity which greatly increased our chances. To spoil them would be an outrage. Our friends were impressed. Krämer seemed to be feeling more conciliatory. Harrer came back to our proposal, as he had a good amendment to suggest.

"That alters the case, I'll allow," Kopp agreed. It had occurred to him meanwhile that our plan offered a favourable opportunity of including his partner from the other wing.

19

And suddenly the opposition gave way to enthusiastic agreement. We discussed every detail, allotted each man his part, and decided to kick off a week hence, which was a Saturday.

As a token that the business of the evening was concluded, Ede pulled a great jar from under his bed. At the sight of it Aufschnaiter was off; it contained spirits of high alcoholic content, distilled by the internees. Each had to drink half a tooth-glass, which was then instantly replenished. There were several stills in camp, but they had to be kept very dark. Discovery would have meant confiscation. They were profitable, and the various distillers fought a relentless battle for the market. They threatened to smash each other's stills and the threats were not always idle. Then one of the sufferers had the bright idea of putting himself under Ede's protection, which Ede was delighted to afford – for payment in kind.

It was late, and sleep had descended on the camp. There was not a breath of air; the conspirators' torsos gleamed with moisture. The shouts of sentries relieving each other on the wire could be heard in the distance. The glass was kept on its rounds, while we jumped fitfully from one topic to another. The last football match was discussed noisily, but we agreed in praising the centre-forward for his dash up the field and his clever footwork.

Then Harrer took a jump into the future. What should we say if anyone asked us what we had done in the war?

"'Ask a tinned pea what it's done in the tin.' That's what I'd say to the blighter," Kopp replied, and Ede was so delighted by his ready wit that he laughed until all his gold teeth flashed like the sun.

The party had now reached the stage all such parties arrived at sooner or later, when the absence of the feminine element struck its sad, responsive note; and the conversation took that inevitable turn. Someone obliged with experiences from his past, new ones, what was more; we had heard most of them dozens of times by now. Ede listened with only half an ear. He was lost in rapturous contemplation of the orderly officer's blanching face when one fine morning at roll-call he was informed of the mass escape.

"I'll walk right past him and grin in his face. And then get blotto."

Suddenly he let out a shout, whereupon a silent presence came in from the darkness. Ede had his runners on their toes all right.

"Go and haul little Müller out of bed. We want some music."

The messenger hurried off to a distant hut.

Meanwhile Ede showed us some card-tricks he had picked up from select colleagues of the ring. He had taught Kopp his best ones before their escape to Tibet. They hoped thereby to acquire an aura of the occult in the land of superstition. But it did not work out like that. The Tibetans took note of the magic of the cards, but none the less relieved them of all they had of value. Such people were not to be trusted.

Harrer felt a vehement urge to sing, and gave vent to it. Have laughed without stopping. Treipl had fallen asleep.

The musician did not turn up. He sent word to say that he had recently been strictly warned not to disturb the camp at night. We had great difficulty in restraining Ede from dealing at once with the miserable wretch who had dared – and never mind if it was late at night – to disregard his order.

"I'll smash his fiddle over his head for him, and then throw it over the fence."

He calmed down more or less at last, and stood up, a portentous figure in his bath-wrap, and, getting hold of a stick, turned to the wall where his nudes were displayed. He wished now to rise from lower things into the exalted sphere of art. Like a lecturer with slides and a pointer, he commented judiciously on each picture in turn, praising each according to its merits.

"You've been to college, we know," he said, turning on me. "But you can learn from me all the same."

True enough. Beside him, any professor might feel small.

Lack of money often held up an escape which had so far gone well, and we were determined that this should not happen in our case. Have impressed on me what unnecessary risks he had run merely to get cash for some valuable or other, or because he could not buy a railway ticket or a meal. We therefore made a particular point of procuring an ample supply of money.

There was no money in the camp. There were only camp-tokens which formed a sort of internal currency which had no value outside. Internees were credited with the money they had on them when arrested and were allowed to draw a limited sum monthly in camp-tokens.

But in spite of all search, prohibitions, and threats, Indian currency notes were to be found in the camp, though the Lord only knows how they got there. The total amount must have been small and its survival under constant threat. For safety's sake these notes had to be buried, and it was always uncertain what would be left when they were dug up again. We almost wept tears of rage when we dug up a tin box to which we had entrusted a hundred-rupee note and found that white ants had eaten all but a narrow edging. Nothing was safe from these termites. In a single night they would consume a box, or a bath-wrap hanging on the mud-wall of a hut. We mourned our loss and went to our friends for sympathy. And they felt for us until somebody remarked on the folly of the ants in devouring money on which they could have lived for years.

There were also opportunities of buying small quantities of gold. Gold stoppings were a recognized merchandise in camp, and Have bought some which he carefully sewed into the seam of his trousers.

But we were still a long way short, and there was only one way to procure money in ample quantity. This was to withdraw from our credit accounts – and mine, thanks to the forethought of my firm, was considerable – as large a sum in camp-tokens as we could possibly find excuses for without exciting attention, and then to exchange them for Indian notes.

This we managed to do, and once we found the way it was not particularly difficult.

The camp was provisioned by Indian contractors. They had access to the camp, but only to the kitchen quarters, which were in German hands. It was possible to improve upon the monotonous rations by buying extra provisions through these contractors, and the meat, or whatever it might be, was brought into the camp and the bill presented to the kitchen staff. It was paid by them in camp-tokens, which were then exchanged by the British paymaster for Indian notes on the demand of the contractor.

We hit on the idea of bribing one of the men regularly employed by the contractor to present a bill for goods he had not delivered. He succumbed to temptation.

A pig would be ordered, for which I would pay the kitchen in camp-tokens, but which was never delivered. These notes were exchanged by the paymaster into Indian currency, which the Indian collected. He took twenty per cent and smuggled the balance in to us on his next visit. This was repeated several times on various pretexts until we had collected about nine hundred rupees and an English gold sovereign.

Saturday drew nearer. There were still lots of things to do: borrowed articles to return, debts to pay, arrangements to make for the disposal of possessions left behind; in fact, dispositions to make as though for a death.

Although we had in our own minds cut loose from the camp, we still had to carry on as usual up to the last moment. We took our place on the treadmill of daily life, but with the feeling that it might be for the last time.

On kitchen-fatigue I said to myself: "If it comes off, you'll have no more potatoes to peel, no more stinking onions to slice up." There they all sat at their tasks – priests and planters, directors and engineers, scraping carrots with vacant, staring eyes. Not one of them answered any longer to his past or believed in his validity for the future. It had gone on too long for that. A busy stillness prevailed, broken only by the small thumps of vegetable-peelings as they struck the sides of the crock. Conversation was discouraged by common consent: it broke the rhythm of group-labour. A joke, on the other hand, might be got across now and then. Scraping and peeling, rubbing and scrubbing – on it went as though we had done it all our lives. Would the gates of the camp ever open again? No one could imagine it. We could only curse that wire.

Perhaps we might be breathing the stagnant air of the hut for the last time. . . . It was as hot as an oven in there. Doors and windows were kept shut all day to exclude the hot air outside. The sweating bodies of the other fellows were dimly seen in the semi-darkness of the long room, some bent over small tables they had nailed together themselves, others sprawling on their beds. Some read, some played patience, some dozed. One was darning. Somewhere in the distance the same bars were being played over and over again on a piano for hours on end. Great spirals of dust came eddying down from the thatch. Somebody brought in an English newspaper. The news was eagerly read and then discussed. "In a month's time we shall see more clearly." That was our consolation as month followed month. How we hated the sight of the filthy, fly-blown strings over which at night the mosquito-nets were draped. We made half-hearted attempts to direct our thoughts into a cheerful channel. In vain. They circled round once or twice and returned to their starting-point. Resignation to the old gloom came down again.

"Man alive, I'm sick of this," someone might shout in desperation. Yes, yes, so were we all. Who wasn't sick of seeing the same faces day after day, however much the persons in question might be esteemed? Who wasn't fed-up with the everlasting repetition of roll-call in the morning; roll-call at night, of "left of your beds", "right of your beds", of issue-food, issue-plates and issue-tables. You knew today what would happen tomorrow, and what happened tomorrow would happen next year and the year after that.

But was it happening at all? Time was emptied and chronicled no change, induced no experience. Nothing whatever occurred. And yet this emptiness of time ran on and devoured year after year. And since it knew no term, it gave its victims the additional torture of uncertainty.

The convicted criminal at least has his sentence and can start marking off the days from the moment he enters his cell. But none of us could say how long it might go on.

When I had been put under arrest over four years ago I had been given a number. Since then I had been 1775. It was marked on all my possessions and was entered on the list in the Orderly Room. Thousands of times I heard this number called out at roll-call, and each time I took three paces to my front and bawled, "Here!" As long as my number appeared in those long columns in the Orderly Room all was well. I was one of the "bloody internees", the numbers added up correctly and the commandant was satisfied. The question was whether numbers 1775 and 55826 (that was Have's number) would have the luck to upset those columns and erase themselves from the roster once and for all.

Tomorrow at this time we should be putting our fortune to the test, and either demons would thrust us back into the purlieus of hell or the gods lead us out to freedom.

I did not find it easy to go to sleep that night – I was facing my first attempt at escape. And now that the moment had come I was a prey to anxieties and doubts. Why challenge Fate, why expose oneself wilfully to danger? Why be harried and hunted as a criminal and run head-first into privations? Camp after all gave security. Custom made the daily routine tolerable and the essentials of life were provided in a settled framework. I had my occupations and my friends.

Anyone of sense could see that our project, every stage of which was incalculable, was bound to fail. It might end on the wire itself, or at the next road-crossing, after a few hours, or at latest within a few days.

True enough, Have was coming too, but they had always brought him back. And this time, after Hülsen's death, he was in a thoroughly dangerous mood. I had often had secret qualms over his habit of deliberately courting danger. He was like a desperate gambler, ready to stake all on a single throw. He would run too great risks. Wasn't it madness to be in with him on it? If I had been left to myself, and no one had known of my plan, I might have quailed. But there were Harrer and Have to put me to shame, and all the other valiant ones whom I wasn't going to admit as my superiors in courage. I had, in fact, nailed my flag to the mast, and that was a great insurance against the temptation to surrender.

My fellow-captives slept on both sides of me, each with his mosquito-netting like a rectangular cage resting on his bed. Each cage enclosed a life which for an indefinite time was to be stunted and shut off, condemned to exist in a hiatus of false security, while the world without was in a hideous uproar. They tossed and turned restlessly in their sleep, carrying over into their dreams, for nights without number, the never-ending sorrow of each day.

A sleeper cried out on my left. Perhaps it was a name, the name of a woman. He muttered something, sighed and slept on.

There was another point. How should I behave in the face of danger? It was not a thing you could know in advance. I had no experience of danger. Have had told me how he had been fired on at close quarters by an Indian army patrol, and how he had run on and got away. Should I have the courage for that? And if not, what then? It didn't bear thinking about.

I had better have gone to a late poker-party in the canteen instead of laying myself open to an attack of nerves by going early to bed. Good idea, even now, to join in a game and break the thread of my thoughts. I crept out from beneath my mosquito-net and crept silently out of the hut.

The canteen was in darkness and the card-players gone. I walked slowly back. The jackals howled in the distance. Nothing depressed me more, even from my earliest days there, than the sight of the camp by night, when I stood alone between the dark huts, each occupied by sleeping prisoners. I saw the sentries and the harsh light along the wire, and heard the foreign tongue and felt the foreignness of the Indian soil, where even the stars in the sky were foreigners too, and I used to feel an almost overwhelming melancholy.

Yet I was never in doubt about coming to the right decision. It was high time it was put into practice. I had to get out of a rut as well as out of an unpleasant situation. Otherwise I might become addicted to the poison. I had already adopted a philosophy according to which a meaning could be discovered in the meaningless – but it was a sophistry. I was pursuing my studies and pretending to pursue them for their own sake – but it was not the truth. I studied merely to fill a void, the ever-yawning abyss of dead time.

What profit was there now in weighing the merits of a course of action already decided upon? To go back on it, instead of standing fast from the beginning, led only to stultification. I had long ago grasped that sometimes common sense had to be defied for wisdom's sake. Action alone could decide. And action must be resolute.

Chapter Two

BLUFF

In the south-west corner of our section there was a henhouse abutting on the inner alley-way, among a number of hutches and sheds. Its inmates were witnesses of strange doings at about 1 p.m. on Saturday, the 29th of April, 1944. They were visited first by two persons who, to judge from the tackle they carried, must have been a make-up artist and a theatrical dresser. Immediately afterwards, two others joined them, who were at once taken in hand by the fancy-dress experts: these were Aufschnaiter and Treipl.

According to our programme, Harrer and Kopp were to follow at about 1.20 p.m., and after another interval of twenty minutes, Have and I. We were all to be fixed up by two o'clock and ready to move off.

There were only a few minutes to go before we were to make our way to the henhouse. I had everything ready to hand and was only waiting for Have, who had disappeared. At the last moment he rushed in with a cloth full of enormous chops in his hand, a very timely haul. It might be our last meal for many hours, and we devoured them without delay, and threw the remains under the bed with the callousness of those who leave behind them a place they hate. Then we hurried off to the starting-point.

Meanwhile, a transformation had occurred in the henhouse. Indian coolies were crouching beneath the low roof, complete with correctly wound turbans, shirts hanging down under their jackets, the dhotis – a cotton garment rolled round the hips and caught up between the legs – and swarthy faces. Their complexions had been obtained by rubbing a solution of permanganate of potash into their faces. When one of them addressed us in Kopp's familiar Berlin accent we nearly shouted with laughter. And now we set to work ourselves; but we turned into British officers, not into Indian coolies. With the originals daily before our eyes we were able to produce an exact copy, khaki shirts and trousers, solar topi and the rest. Have had an officer's swagger-stick under his arm and I a roll of tracing-paper.

"You look the real thing and no mistake," the Indian coolies whispered, and we repaid the compliment. It helped to keep our courage up.

Time to be off. But Harrer reported from his spy-hole that two Indians were at work shovelling soil on the other side of the alley-way in the Balkan wing just opposite us. We should have to wait for them to go. Probably it would not be long. Two o'clock, when the midday heat settled down over the whole camp and drove inmates and staff alike into the gloom of the huts, was the best time for our attempt; but those labourers took their time and kept shovelling happily on. The henhouse became a reeking oven and, owing to its low roof, a torture-chamber as well. Aufschnaiter glared at his watch. He was getting impatient.

"If we can't make it now it'll be too late. The camp will soon get lively again."

The others got jittery too. Kopp felt excusable anxiety over his rendezvous with Sattler, who was to join us farther along the alley-way, also in Indian disguise. Delay might wreck the show. Have and I were particularly upset while the prospects of success sank rapidly, because we were responsible for the plan. And we could not simply call it off. How in that case were the others to get back into camp with their coffee-coloured faces? Harrer had even shaved his head.

Then at half-past two Harrer signalled that the way was clear.

In a moment we were out and through the wire into the alley-way. As they left the henhouse Kopp and Aufschnaiter took up a ladder between them on their shoulders and buckets containing their packs in their hands. Harrer and Treipl each took one end of a long bamboo-pole which was stuck through a bulky package wound round with barbed wire, and both carried a bundle. Harrer balanced his on his head. They had detached the wire from the inner fence the night before and wound it up.

Once in the alley-way the coolies went ahead, with the officers following at a short distance – an ordinary repair-gang with their gear, such as was often to be seen along the fences. But none of us to his life's end will ever forget that procession.

When it moved off, we had the feeling of being launched through space at a mark, as well as the exhilaration of perpetrating an outrageous leg-pull. First we had to pass along the whole length of our own and the Balkan wing; as playing-fields separated us from the huts to left and right, we were unobserved. How I relished the festal, fairylike solitude of this alley-way! How sweet and Eden-like the air! The rank grass was like a soft carpet and the wire fence on either side seemed to keep all danger from us. . . . At the farthest corner of our wing stood Ede Krämer, with

27

thumbs up and a grin of encouragement. Next our alley-way led us through two new wings, one on the left in which all the Jews were collected, and on the right the Vatican City, populated by Italian priests; it was parted from us by a stretch of grass on which some of them were promenading in white cassocks.

The distance began to seem endless; post after post receded in perspective, and the strands of wire seemed to be slipping past us while we stood still. An optical delusion, of course: the coolies could be seen walking ahead, the ladder wobbled up and down on their shoulders, the roll of wire danced on the pole. Have tapped the fence with his stick as he went along and examined it with a searching eye.

I tried to look unconcerned, preoccupied though I was with the thought that a Gurkha might well loose off at us. A man emerged from the hut we were now passing, gave us a sharp look at a range of six yards or less, turned round, gave another look back at us and then walked away without displaying further interest.

We were now approaching the corner where our alley-way led into the wide thoroughfare through the middle of the camp. From here the Gurkha posted at the outer gate was visible at a distance of 140 yards. If he observed us emerging from the side-alley, his suspicions might be aroused. We looked at him anxiously. No, he had not seen us. And not even after we had emerged into the main thoroughfare. His eyes were on a tonga which was being driven along the road outside.

But where was Sattler? This was the spot at which he was to have joined the column. It had been agreed that he was to scale the inner fence and carry on with tarring the posts until we appeared. There was no sign of him. But some initiates in his wing were cautiously making signs, from which it might be deduced that Sattler had gone ahead. We drew dangerously near the gate. The Gurkha gazed up the track and become aware of us. Instantly I saw what a threadbare, chicken-witted show it all was. Harrer's calves were far too big for an Indian's and his eyes far too blue. And imagine Kopp as a Hindu! Look at his heavy, athletic frame and his massive stride! And now was the moment for Treipl's dhoti to come unstuck! But Aufschnaiter was every inch the Indian, and Have's yellow moustache was English beyond all doubt. Perhaps we might make it.

We were now so strung up that nothing which had the faintest bearing on our situation could escape our notice, whether it was near or far on the flickering expanse around us. Consequently we were all simultaneously aware of a sergeant-major bicycling along the road outside. If he turned in at the gate he would see through our fancy-dress at the first glance. For one heart-throb we all gave the show up for lost. But without so much as giving us a look he rode straight on past the gate.

The Gurkha was on the right of the gate, and so the other four swerved to the left so as to pass him at the greatest distance possible, while we two as officers were to distract his attention and so swerved slightly to the right. The Gurkha gave a lowering look . . . a suspicion seemed to cross his mind. I walked on like a puppet with a numb feeling in my joints. Three yards in front of the gate Have stopped, and I, as agreed, unrolled the sheet of tracing-paper, which he tapped with his stick, and then we loudly and excitedly discussed our building-plans. The Gurkha still had the look of a wild mountain-cat ready to spring. We were near enough to see the yellow in his eyes. His motionless pupils might hide his feline purpose. But now the rest were through the gate. We followed without deigning to give the sentry another look. Our bluff had worked.

The next twenty yards across the road and into the jungle path were, according to previous arrangement, traversed at leisure, lest sudden haste might give us away. But Harrer, who led the way, overdid it. He slowed down to a crawl. The short distance seemed endless, and all the time I imagined the sentry's rifle aimed between my shoulder-blades. Any moment he might press the trigger. But at last we were in the cover of the jungle. The camp was behind us. We were free.

The peaks of the Himalayas rose blue and distant above range upon range of mountain heights. We gave ourselves up to the sight in our mountain hiding-place, awed by the unearthly aloofness of the glaciers which climbed the empyrean on the shoulders of mountains struggling one above the other. The air was sharp and the light dazzled our eyes.

The first delicious moment of liberty had been submerged in a tumult of sensations and the onset of danger. Staggering in its suddenness, unbelievable and yet starkly real, it lasted only a few seconds, and then gave way to the sensations of the hunted.

As soon as we had reached the jungle path we were out of sight of the sentry, but directly afterwards we had to turn into another road which was guarded by a two-man patrol of Indian road-police. So we had to keep together until the first bend in the road. Then we rushed up the bank and chucked the ladder, the roll of paper and the other gear in all directions to express the release of the tension our nerves had been under since the start.

Suddenly Kopp gave the alarm. He had caught sight of someone. We charged downhill and over the fields to the river-bed, and must have made a funny sight, staggering, jumping, running pell-mell down the slopes in a most unmilitary manner. But our headlong flight made such a noise that some peasants at work took fright. We darted in among the sugar-canes, the best cover we could see. One of the peasants tried to bar our way, but we ran round him and charged across the river-bed. Harrer, Have and I ran lefthanded, the others diverged to the right. It was the last we saw of them.

We leapt from boulder to boulder of the dried-out bed as fast as we could, and when we were across I turned round and called to the other two in anguish: "They're after us; look, they're forming up."

"Rot, it's only those peasants."

"No – Tommies."

"You're seeing ghosts. It's the peasants we saw just now."

I would have sworn they were soldiers, I was so overwrought.

There was no time to lose. As soon as the alarm was given, search-parties on bicycles would be on the road which crossed the river below us, and we should be cut off. So on we pounded. Harrer led. I came last and stayed last, cursing under my breath the whole way, because I could not see the point of keeping up such an absurd pace once we were well out of sight. We soon came to the great jungle which ran on as far as the foothills, the first goal we strove for. Harrer set the pace without mercy. He gave us no time to look about us. On we went through scrub and thicket, along nullahs, over boulders, down sudden drops. Once he allowed us a brief rest by a spring. Then on again, always at the double.

We were now approaching the region where the plain ends and the mountains begin. Here we had to skirt the edge of a village and slack-ened our pace. Some Sikhs came out of their houses and looked with astonishment at the three mad Englishmen – Harrer had meanwhile abandoned his Indian dress – who were hastening up the uninhabited mountain-side at that late hour of the afternoon. After a steep climb, we came, as evening drew on, to a gorge down which a stream descended in cascades. Here Have and I resolved to spend the night.

Harrer went on alone towards Tibet.

It was a hard parting. We weren't happy about him. He had set himself a task which exceeded what any human being could accomplish. Not even his untamable will, his steely frame, his incredible capacity for enduring hardship, his sheer indestructibility could suffice, or come near to sufficing, for the perils of Tibet. He had often described them to us: murderous cold, hunger, savage Tibetan dogs which sprang straight at any stranger's throat, the immense distances between one habitation and the next, where no white man had ever set foot. . . . If he only had someone with him. But there was no one in the camp who suited him; so he preferred to go alone. He meant to make his way as an itinerant doctor, and for this purpose he had procured forceps for extracting teeth, and had also rolled hundreds of laxative pills. If he saw the chance on the way, he thought of marrying a Tibetan girl; he thought it might help. What help would that be? But no dissuasions were the least use.

He had his way and off he went.

Darkness drew on in the thickets, and when it was night we left our hiding-place by the stream and climbed on to a promontory of rock which gave us a distant view over the plain. Far below us lay a quadrangle marked out in narrow strips of light: the illuminated barbed wire of the camp.

By dawn we were on our feet again in search of a better hiding-place. As soon as we were on the ridge of the foothills, which had so far hidden the main Himalayan range, we looked up, and there above towered the glaciers and ice-clad peaks, and in the far, hazy distance a twenty-five-thousander, Nanda Devi. Through the delicate filigree of green foliage we saw the azure light of glistening snow. At our feet the warmth of life, and there the deathly cold. Rhododendrons were in bloom.

On the slope facing the mountains we found a nook which completely hid us. A cascade had hollowed out recesses beneath slabs of rock, and in one of these we made ourselves at home. We dropped into it from above as though into a manhole, and could then lie at full length with a patch of sky to look at. We remained here without stirring for five days and four nights. Have had great trouble with me. I longed to emerge into the open, and he relentlessly insisted on my remaining below. There was a military training-camp somewhere in the neighbourhood and it was possible that a party of soldiers might pass by. We only made three short excursions to survey the country around. Trackless jungle extended on all sides – the home, one might think, of beasts of prey of every kind. We saw birds with dark blue plumage, long curved tails, and undulating flight. Every evening we ventured out to have a bathe in an ice-cold mountain stream, while a waning moon feebly illumined our narrow gorge. Then we sat down on a boulder and discussed our future movements in whispers.

I ought to explain why it was that we took refuge in the mountains, which were quite out of our way, and remained there for several days without

31

moving. Our goal was Burma, and our purpose was to join up with Japanese troops at some as yet unknown point on the Indo–Burmese frontier, the Japanese being our allies and now at the gates of India. The only hope of traversing that vast distance – it was about 1500 miles from Dehra Dun to Burma – lay in making use of fast transport. And for this it was essential to pass ourselves off as British officers. We had to rely on cool bluff.

Our plan was to travel by railway as far as we could, in the first place to Calcutta. But it would have been a blunder to start on our journey immediately after getting out, because as soon as an escape was detected, the so-called little alarm was put into operation; it lasted for only twenty-four hours and was confined to the region of the camp. All police stations and railway stations within thirty miles were informed and search parties sent out. If these measures were without result, the big alarm came into force. This affected the whole of India, and warrants were issued for the arrest of the fugitives. It was just as well, then, to give the excitement a few days to die down. In our case, with a record getaway of seven men, it might last longer than usual. We also reckoned on the commandant's assuming that Have might take to his old tracks; and in this case he would pay particular attention to the line to Calcutta. But if nothing came of that, he would conclude after a few days that we had gone off towards Tibet. For these reasons we decided to spend a few days in the mountains.

Although all previous attempts at escape had failed, we felt we had a good chance of success. We had unbounded confidence in our magic weapon of bluff. It had already served us brilliantly in getting us out of camp, and we were convinced it would get us out of many another tight corner. It is the function of bluff to redress the balance between one's own inadequacy and the other man's superiority, and as this cannot be done in actual fact, but only by psychological means, which are independent of tangible resources, it is a weapon peculiarly fitted to a man on the run. We had to give the impression of complete invulnerability and so disarm our opponent from the start. This would not be easy with the British for opponents. But we hoped at least by bluffing our way along to reduce our physical fatigue to the minimum and to enjoy an eventful and varied career. There is a fascination in the titillation of the nerves caused by deliberately incurring risks and throwing prudence to the winds. Success is always in the balance, and up to the last moment the outcome cannot be guessed.

Much depended on impeccable performances as Englishmen. In

32

appearance we both came up to the mark. In speech also we were fortunate; Have had spent years in Malaya and spoke excellent English. Soldiers' slang and common phrases were quite familiar to us. Lest we should drop into German from carelessness or excitement, we decided always to speak English to each other, and made this a rule from the time we occupied our nook in the mountains.

But appearance and speech were not all. We must also be silent and reserved in the English manner. The characteristics of the English were pretty well known to us; after all, we had both lived among them long enough. Finally, we had all the required proofs of identity, made out by ourselves to the last detail and including certificates of vaccination. Have's were made out in the name of Harry F. Lloyd, and mine in that of John Edward Harding, wife's name Enid Iris, *née* Thornton, resident in Calcutta. She was a worthless baggage; and the excuse for my journey to Calcutta, in case I were asked for it, was to deal with matters arising out of the break-up of our marriage owing to her loose behaviour. I hoped that the mere mention of these painful matters would deter any Englishman worthy of the name from making tactless and unfeeling enquiries.

We both endeavoured to live our respective rôles. Have was assumed to have been born in Singapore, and I to be a native of Exeter, which I knew fairly well from having been at college there for a short time. Our military background presented peculiar difficulties. How were we to answer questions about our regiment, our depot and the name of our commanding officer? This was a ticklish question. We had no idea what units were serving in north-west India, and should give ourselves away instantly by hesitating to answer or by answering wrongly. Fortunately, we had discovered, in an English illustrated periodical which found its way into the camp, some groups of regimental officers in India, giving the name of the regimental association as well as the names of the officers, all of which we committed to memory.

But it was all very well to arrange all this in our own minds. We had to incorporate it in our very flesh and blood; and so we used to fire off questions at each other, such as "Where are you stationed?" or "Who the hell are you?" to which we had to give the right answer without a pause or a tremor.

In the matter of dress we were fairly well off. British officers on a journey are not very particular about uniform; as long as we were in khaki, badges of rank were not of great importance. Have knew that from his previous escapes. To complete our equipment we had made ourselves military haversacks out of old rucksacks, and in them we had stowed a spare khaki uniform, iron rations, first-aid outfit and one or two other things. Unfortunately, we had hidden these haversacks at the spot where our party split up. We had taken them from our coolie companions and left them behind in a bush, because they were too much of an encumbrance in our wild career. All we had taken on with us was some provisions. At the time it had seemed a good plan. Now we looked back on it as a grave blunder, since we had to risk going back almost to the camp.

Like criminals who feel compelled to leave their hiding-place and return to the scene of their crime, we came down from the mountains on the sixth day of our escape. It was early in the afternoon and a last view of the great panorama was denied us; the throne of the gods was veiled in mist.

It made our predicament worse to have to face it by daylight; but we could never have found our haversacks in the dark. After coming out of the mountain jungle we were close to the river-bed and the road; here we had a consultation and decided that one of us should go on alone. We tossed for it, and just because I had no desire whatever to perform this risky exploit, which I considered a provoking of Providence, I lost the toss. I set off with the worst forebodings. Have was to lie concealed until dark and then meet me at an agreed spot a few miles south of the camp.

As I left the cover of the jungle I saw the camp not far away. In the evening light I could see the wire running like threads round the huts, washing hanging on a line, and crows flying rapidly over the thatched roofs.

It gave me a very queer feeling to see it from the outside after having been obliged to live inside it for so long. It was just the time when the inmates, with their tin spoons in their hands, lounged against the door-posts of their huts, awaiting the supper-bell. Then they would all flock into the repulsive dining-hut, where the meal was eaten on cheap enamel plates decorated with red flowers. It was not a week since I had been one of them, and yet I felt far-removed from it all. It had been the same when I was first put inside, only in reverse. There was in both cases the same abrupt change from one life to another.

I crossed the river bed and noiselessly climbed the steep bank we had charged down at such a pace. It brought me on to a level with the camp, and also into the immediate danger-zone. The slightest oversight now would set the whole apparatus in motion. I kept hidden in the scrub and peered through the foliage; a Gurkha sentry was slowly pacing his beat inside the wire not far from me. The sight of him warned me to be cautious. I slid to the ground and decided to wait for dusk before approaching the hiding-place.

Time went on. Then I heard the camp bell ring. Was it supper or roll-call? On pain of being incarcerated all over again, I had to lie motionless, however much my limbs ached. To pass the time I counted the leaves on a branch, followed the wanderings of an ant, watched the second hand of my watch and finally tried to detect the motion of the minute hand. How farcical it all seemed! We might be on the right side of the wire now, but only for a short time. We should soon be back in the net.

When night was falling I recovered the haversacks and had to leave the camp behind me with all possible speed in order to keep my appointment with Have. He would naturally assume the finding of the haversacks to be an affair of minutes, and would now be seriously worried over my long absence.

I had to be on my guard in the precincts of the camp, where night-patrols might be out. Later, my way led through extensive tea-gardens, crossed by many roads and bordered by villages. It is impossible to go anywhere in India without continually coming up against the inhabitants. They occupy every hand's breadth of ground, jump up out of any ditch, step out from behind every bush, appear in what you took for the deepest solitude of the jungle, and rise up out of the bare soil at your feet. As for the tea-gardens that night, they might have been a bazaar. A religious festival in honour of the Moon-goddess, the Goddess of Love, was in progress; and at that hour of the night I had continually to avoid ox-wagons laden with girls chanting discordant melodies, and from every village came the thud of drums. It would have been very foolish of me to show myself on the road; Englishmen were not seen at night in the fields or in the villages. Every Indian for miles around must have heard of the break-out and would send word to the camp at the first hint of a suspicion; there was a tempting reward for information received. So it took me a long time to get through the plantations in their state of nocturnal revelry, and when at three in the morning I at last joined Have, he had made up his mind I had been caught.

South of Dehra Dun are the Siwaliks, a range of low mountains running parallel to the Himalayas, of erratically folded strata, which run up into jagged peaks. They are thickly clothed in jungle and quite uninhabited. Behind them lies the north-eastern plain, which, beginning in the Punjab, extends along the Himalayas as far as Bengal. This is the plain upon which, thousands of years ago, the Aryans descended and wrote the hymns of the Veda in the dawn of the human spirit; Gautama Buddha, the son of a king, made known here his teaching of the four truths, and here the Moguls broke in, to ravage Islam with fire and sword and to build up and down the country their fairy-like palaces of flashing marble. Roads have traversed this plain since earliest times, and today railway-lines run alongside them. The northernmost of these links Lahore and Calcutta. Saharanpur, about fifty miles south of Dehra Dun, is on this line, and it was there we intended to take the train.

There was a road to Saharanpur, with a service of buses, but it would have been too foolhardy to make use of one of these. There was no alternative to crossing the jungle-barrier of the Siwaliks; and as we had with all speed to put the greatest possible distance between us and the camp, it was necessary to walk on all day. This we were fortunately able to do, because there were at that time several training and convalescent camps in the neighbourhood of Dehra Dun, and so the inhabitants were accustomed to the sight of British soldiers.

We left our hiding-place early in the morning, and in full uniform, with our haversacks slung from our shoulders, set off in the direction of the Siwaliks. It was hot even then, and the heat increased steadily. We had scarcely started before we were streaming with sweat. Our bottles, only just filled at the stream, were empty in a moment. The heat of India is unspeakably trying; it breaks the will, drugs the brain and may cause a heat-stroke which dangerously impairs the functions regulating the temperature of the body. There was no escaping it. All round were fields on which not even a bush was to be seen. Here and there the bleached skeletons of superannuated oxen lay in the fields, and the vultures hovered above on the look-out for more recent deaths. Little clouds of dust raised by the naked feet of Indians on their way to work in the fields hung and drifted above the road.

We should have been thankful to avoid the villages of cube-shaped huts which appeared now and again on the quivering horizon, but they were now the only means of procuring water. Our approach was never unannounced; as soon as we reached the outskirts of a village the children playing in the roadside-dust ran in terror to warn the inhabitants of our arrival. The women timidly withdrew and the men stood in the doorways as though to keep us out. Mangy dogs, as thin as skeletons and as hairless as if they had been flayed, slept in the sun, apparently unaware of the flies which clustered in black clots on their sores. There was a smell of burning cow-dung, the only fuel these wretched people had; and innumerable hand-made dollops adhered to the walls in various stages of drying in the sun. We entered one of those miserable clay-built dwellings, where, thanks to the small windows and thick walls, it was a little cooler than outside, and asked a listless Hindustani for a drink, half afraid that they might be too poor to have even water to offer. We had no need to bother about our ignorance of their language. Very few British soldiers could speak it.

In many villages the untouchables occupy a quarter of their own in a state of such dirt and dilapidation, and in such a sorry companionship of misery and hopelessness, that one turns away in horror, unable to bear these scenes of eternal damnation, or to conceive how human beings can survive such a fate as they have for thousands of years.

We reached the Siwaliks and struck a road which kept to the fringe of the forest and only occasionally came out into the open. It was midday, and the sun bored into our bones and burned there like a fever. The leaves of the forest trees were coated with dust. Grotesquely furrowed, sulphur-coloured ant-hills rose within the dark shadow of the forest. We panted along forlornly as though scarcely able to breathe the thick air. Have, accustomed though he was to life in the tropics, seemed to be more exhausted than usual.

As we rounded a bend we saw through the trunks of the trees a sight that aroused our suspicions – yes, they were soldiers. It was too late to slip into the undergrowth and hide. We had to keep straight on. Fortunately, they were Indians, out on a field exercise. We hoped there was not a British officer with them. As we passed they smiled, showing their white teeth in shy friendliness. So Have went up to one of them and asked unconcernedly for a drink of water. It was willingly given and turned out to be cold tea. Have loved such exploits. He fairly revelled in them, whereas they made all the blood run out of my veins.

We walked on. After a time Have complained of a headache. What was the matter with him?

"We'll go on a bit and then have a rest," I said to encourage him.

"Not for me. I'm all right. Let's keep on."

I saw now from his eyes that he was feverish, his old trouble.

"My dear chap, it's malaria!"

We turned off the road into the jungle and lay down in the dense undergrowth. There was no doubt about it. Have had an attack of malaria. His temperature was rushing up. Our thermometer registered 104 degrees. I began to feel anxious.

He had covered his face with his pith helmet and fallen asleep. I was in despair. What rotten luck! So close to the camp, scarcely ten miles from it, and now this blow! It meant the loss of precious time and perhaps the wreck of our whole adventure. Have had already had more than fifteen bouts of malaria and was on intimate terms with it, but I remembered that bad attacks had left him unconscious for hours on end. Would he have the strength now to drag himself through the mountains and endure all the privations an escape always entailed? If the double dose of atebrin he had just taken – we had procured it from the camp hospital – did not quickly bring down his temperature, we should be in a fix. My reflections were interrupted by a little white-spotted jungle deer. I threw a stone at it and it crashed through the undergrowth. Have woke at the noise. Some symptoms of the fever were less acute, but his temperature was no lower.

"Don't get ideas," Have said when he saw my anxious face. "I'll be fit again first thing in the morning. I'm used to this. It's quickly over."

"Let's hope you're right. But will you be in any state to cross the Siwaliks?"

Have did not reply at once.

"We shall have to alter our plans," he said after a pause. "We must stay here until the fever goes and then take the bus to Saharanpur instead."

Now, the commandant had always insisted that no escaped prisoner could possibly travel by bus, because the passengers were too closely scrutinized. I therefore demurred.

"Better chance it than get stuck here in the mountains," Have replied. "We'll bluff them, police or spy."

"Right then. Let's try it."

Next morning the fever had nearly gone, and Have felt strong enough by midday to walk to the road along which the buses ran. Luckily the attack had been a light one.

We gave our disguises a brush-up before stepping out into the big world. So far we had kept in seclusion and shunned all encounters. From now on our operations would be conducted in the open and in constant touch with the enemy.

A bus came along just as we reached the road. Ought we to stop it, considering that it had proved the undoing of others before us? After wavering between hope and fear, we recklessly took the risk, signalled to the driver and climbed in. We found no suspicious passengers; there was only a veiled Mohammedan woman and her child. The white robe these women wear has a round headpiece sewn on to it, in which there is a narrow slit pierced like a sieve to look through. They look just like milk-cans.

The Indian driver seemed to be impressed by the high military honour paid to his rattling bus. He asked politely what our destination was. And when we replied Saharanpur, he said he would have to step on it to ensure that we did not miss our connection. We gave a start at the sight of a police station; a sentry in uniform with brilliant red turban and fixed bayonet was planted in front of it. But he did not hold us up. On we went.

We only just made it. The other bus was there, full to the roof with Indians. They were all as thin as laths and swathed in cotton; their head-coverings formed a close medly of turbans, felt hats, fezzes and peaked caps. Peasants and coolies, with the ascetic-looking heads of theological students and a sad, pleading expression in their eyes. We asked the driver to make room for us in front and he promptly chased some Indians out of the better seats. Have sat immediately behind the driver with me beside him. At the last moment an intelligent and educated Indian squeezed his way in and sat down beside me. I felt sure he was inquisitive and wondered whether he might be a spy. So to be on the safe side I rehearsed a few suitable replies. Sure enough, soon after we started he asked whether we had come from Dehra Dun. There were troops as well as internees at Dehra Dun, but the question might be a trap all the same.

"No; I have not come from Dehra Dun," I answered shortly. "I came here with a motor transport column and am travelling to Calcutta on duty."

He seemed satisfied and my polite tone did not invite further comment.

"I say, John, how it stinks in this old bus," Have called out to me cheerfully. He was obviously as delighted as I was not to be footing it over the Siwaliks; the road's hairpin bends showed what we were missing. It was a grim and gruesome sight, every ravine a fiery crucible, dense undergrowth armed with piercing spikes, not a drop of water.

Suddenly we braked hard. Two military lorries blocked the road as we rounded a bend. They were locked together – one full of Indians and one of Australians. The Australians wore their slouched hats and were stripped to the waist. They were covered in dust and running with sweat from an exercise in the open. They were cursing unmercifully and only

39

making the Indians more and more helpless and confused; so at last they had to turn to themselves, at which they cursed all the more. Their proximity made me gush with wave after wave of sweat. One of them passing the front of our bus remarked that a bottle of beer would go down well. My God, I thought so too. At last the lorries were parted and on we went. When we reached the top of the pass, the driver gave the bus its head in the reckless way native drivers have. We took our corners at hair-raising speed.

"If you don't drive more carefully, I'll throw you out, you fool," I shouted to him. If I had been more ceremonious he would never have taken me for a British soldier.

When we were down on the plain we stopped at a camp of motorized troops. There were extensive car-parks among the tents, and at the edge of the road a bar where you could buy milk or lemonade. Although we were tortured by thirst, we did not dare get out because there were British soldiers lounging against the counter. After this there was no stop before Saharanpur, where the driver said we should arrive at half-past four – much too early for us, as the train for Calcutta did not leave until half-past seven. How should we ever get through those three hours? This tormenting thought spoiled the rest of the journey. The last part of it was through irrigated country. On all sides canals, sluices, cuttings and ditches were to be seen. Water-wheels scooped the water up on to the fields. Long-horned white cattle with humps and hanging dewlaps drew carts soberly along the rough roads without rousing the prostrate driver from his blissful sleep.

As we approached the town we met a great many military vehicles, which alarmed us owing to the prospect of much military activity in Saharanpur. And so it proved. When we got out in front of the station, we found it alive with soldiers and many other people too. Chattering natives squatted in groups beside their bundles, spitting red betel-juice in wide arcs. Porters shouted their way along. Sturdy Gurkhas with short, curved kukris at their sides, tall Punjabis and freckled Tommies were standing about; and we had our first sight of the red-banded caps of the military police. Ugh – what a terrifying sight! We stood uneasily in the midst of the crowd, dazed by all the pushing and shouting, uncertain what to do next. Then the station-master came past. Have, getting back to his usual form, coolly asked him to show us the way to the waiting-room. He took us through the barrier, past two MPs, and we sat down at a vacant table in the farthest corner of the room. It was not large and almost unoccupied. We bought a newspaper to take cover behind, and two lemon squashes to slake our burning throats. Every time the door opened we peered over the top of the newspaper to see whether our hour had come.

"It won't do here," Have said under his breath. "We must get out into the streets. To be stuck here for three hours is madness."

I flatly disagreed. Now we were safely in the station, we ought to stay there. I succeeded in convincing him and, just as we were starting to read the paper through for the second time, the door opened and two MPs came in, one British and one Indian. The tension was terrific as they walked straight towards our table. We sat motionless, awaiting annihilation. We couldn't have made it easier for them. They only had to get to work.

They sat down two tables off. The white 'MP' on their red arm-bands, the heavy revolvers at their belts, were threateningly close. What were they up to? They took off their caps, wiped their foreheads and ordered lemonade. They had found the heat too much for them and had come in for a moment's refreshment. The Englishman made himself comfortable and put his feet up on the edge of the table. Then he turned his head and while he fanned his face with his handkerchief gave us a long and searching scrutiny. Nothing seemed to strike him – we sat quietly in our corner and his professional eye was pleased with what it saw. To us it was very different. My nails tingled at the thought of my pay-book, the value of which as a proof of identity seemed to me now, just when I might have to show it, highly questionable. It might take in an Indian, but would any Englishman fall into such a trap? I certainly needed a leave-pass. If I could not produce it, I should lie under the imputation of being absent without leave. If the truth came out, my pay-book would only make matters worse. Better push the beastly thing under the tablecloth. I could always recover it if they went out again. And in fact after a short time they got up and left. My relief was even greater than Have's. My self-reproach, after having obstinately insisted on sitting tight, would have been bitter.

As Have was as dubious about the pay-books as I was, we saw that we should have to consult on each occasion whether to show them or not. But it would be impossible to do so openly before a third person; so we resolved to give the books code names, Zoja for Have's, Simone for mine, these being the names of girls from whom the war had separated us.

We kept looking at the clock, but time stood still. Gradually the room filled up with Indians and soldiers. For a time a tall Sikh sat at our table. He did not address us. He merely fondled his long silken beard dreamily.

41

It was parted in the middle, and the ends, which by stern command of his sect might never be cut, were cunningly wound in under his chin. We could not but feel uneasy in the presence of this pale-cheeked, mysteriously smiling man, whose turban suggested that he might be a conjurer or a thought-reader. I shouldn't have been surprised if he had addressed us by our right names and told us off the reel what we were about.

When the Sikh departed, Have went out to buy tickets. They had to be ordinary tickets, as we should have needed a railway-warrant for Service ones. He returned with two second-class tickets to Calcutta. To have travelled third would have been beneath the dignity of two British officers. On the ticket it said 1,026 miles to Calcutta – what a distance!

"Harry, wait a bit! Here comes a woman—" I almost gave a shout of joy.

The first woman we had seen for years! She went softly past and sat down at a table near us. She had the milky skin of a red-haired beauty, and her eyes – I saw later they were greenish – were full of warmth to their depths. She seemed to make poetry of the very air.

"Don't upset the table in your enthusiasm," Have said rather dampingly.

"My boy, it's a great moment," I said, feasting my unaccustomed eyes on the lovely apparition. And it really was an event to be aware of a woman's presence after years of raw male existence behind the wire, where the absence of women had been not only one insult the more, but a calculated torture. We were thankful to providence for sparing us any disillusionment; she was no discredit to her sex and breed. That was assuredly a good omen. Fugitives, for whom all hangs on chance, grow superstitious and begin to look everywhere for signs and portents.

Time began to move.

We ordered supper. When it came it included beer.

For us, who had been shut away in darkness, all this seemed like an overdose of life – trains roaring past, strange faces, children, white tablecloths, service, bright red lips. Such thronging life raised us to a higher level of existence, and when at last the express thundered in we were in the best of form and would have had it out, if necessary, with the Devil himself.

Chapter Three

"PASSES, PLEASE"

The wind of the incoming train caught up the stale air of the platform and brought in its place something of India's vastness and immeasurable distances. Passengers surged out of the carriages, but while brown arms, tin trunks, children, bedding and poultry were still emerging, the doors were stormed by those wishing to get in. We kept on the edge of the surging throng in order to have a better view, and then when the tumult began to subside we walked along the coaches looking for a suitable compartment. But there was none as far as we could see in the second class. At last, as the train was already moving, we found one full as we thought of Indians, but when we had got in we saw with consternation that there were two Englishmen in uniform in the farther corners. One was a lieutenant and the other a pilot. If anyone had told us at that moment that we should travel for over forty hours in that compartment, we should have jumped for it at the next curve.

We rapidly and distrustfully inspected the other passengers. There was nothing about them to arouse suspicion at first sight, but nothing either to inspire confidence. There was an Anglo-Indian, a Parsee, the usual Indian babu tradespeople. They and their packages took up a lot of room, but we did not complain of that as long as they formed a block between us and the Englishmen. After a time my neighbour began rummaging in his pack and pulled out a bottle of Indian whisky. He offered us a drink. We accepted with thanks. We could do with a pick-me-up. Would the other two gentlemen have a drink also? They declined with a shake of the head. The pilot gave us a passing glance, and said something to the other man while he stroked the barrel of the automatic between his knees.

We had least to fear from the fat and oily babus; they looked soft and good-humoured. They were in European dress, but with the character-istic difference of wearing their shirts outside their trousers. They had a spot of red between their eyebrows, the Hindu caste-mark. They were obviously well provided with the riches of this world, and yet a Hindu such as they were might give away all he possessed overnight and live a life of solitude and poverty to the end of his days. The Anglo-Indian made us uneasier; he was sure to be in the public service, as most Eurasians were, and might quite likely be a police-agent. In spite of an infusion of English blood, he looked feeble and listless. The Parsee had the beak of a bird of prey, and wore a brimless, lacquered top-hat, dotted all over with innumerable little stars. He sat bowed over his leather case, gripping the handle in both hands. As a descendant of Persian immigrants, who still profess the religion of Zoroaster, he was a fire-worshipper, and when he died, if he adhered to the burial rites of Parsees, his corpse would be laid out on one of the towers of silence to be devoured by vultures. Up to that moment, however, his sole preoccupation would be the accumulation of money. We were unlikely to discourse about the rate of interest and real estate, and so he would probably pay us no attention.

For a time the railway ran parallel to the Himalayas. We could just see the silhouette of the foothills in the failing light. Long shadows lay along the ground and soon would swallow the outlines of the hills.

Our compartment got emptier, and luckily the Anglo-Indian was among those who got out. We now had seats obliquely facing the Englishmen. The lieutenant was tall, leathery and hollow-eyed; the pilot had a complexion of milk and roses. So far we had avoided speaking to them. It was getting late now and preparations for sleep were made by degrees. By pushing up the seat-backs, each seat became two bunks. Two Indians climbed into the upper bunks, and one began to pray at great length, without being in the least put out by the presence of strangers. Indians have an astonishing power of abstracting themselves at any moment from the world around them. In the noise and bustle of railway platforms, bazaars and narrow thoroughfares, they can often be seen sitting with limbs folded and eyes glazed, lost in contemplation.

Sleep in our case was not to be thought of. The noise of the train, the uncomfortable seats, the anxiety lest an inspection of passes might take place at the next station, the presence of the British officers, all made us restless. Even the rattle of the windows kept us on tenterhooks. The shades were pulled down over the lights and the carriage was lighted only by a blue and ghostly glimmer. We marked every movement of the two Englishmen through the slits of our closed eyes. Pushing this way and pulling that, they were making a sleeping-place for themselves. We were looking in silence at the darkness racing by outside the window, and I

44

was getting my feet free of a kitbag an Indian had put on the floor to sleep on, when the pilot woke up. The Indian had lain down on his feet and now started up at a kick. I could see only the white of his eyes and their expression of a beaten hound. After stammering his excuses, he stood in the middle of the compartment like a schoolboy who had been punished.

The pilot met my eye and held out his cigarettes. "They're so damned submissive. And the worst of it is, it works." I nodded in assent.

"Don't stand there. Lie down again," he told the man.

We smoked our cigarettes and said no more. I pretended to be tired, yawned, leaned back in my corner and shut my eyes. The Englishman went to sleep again. For the moment the danger had passed.

Next morning we were plunged into a conversation. It was impossible to avoid it. All we could do was to keep it as monosyllabic and as non-committal as possible.

"Are you for Calcutta too?" we were asked.

"Yes."

"Anything going on there now?" they wanted to know.

"We haven't been there for some time now."

"How long have you been out?"

"Oh, a long time."

All true enough.

The lieutenant ordered breakfast for four at one of the stations we stopped at, and a boy brought tea, eggs, rolls and fruit along to our compartment. The Englishman wouldn't hear of our paying our share and insisted on treating us. We thanked him and submitted. We would gladly have accepted breakfasts from him for the rest of our lives if he would only leave our military record alone. But he was bound to wonder who and what we were – officers, privates, NCOs? Our uniforms did not answer the question. And what peculiar haversacks we had! Could we possibly belong to front-line troops, or were we from base? Very odd. What saved us no doubt must have been the notice in each compartment which, besides warning troops that long trousers were to be worn at night because of the risk of malaria, also forbade all mention of military affairs.

The train was now crossing the plain of the Ganges, old used-up country which had all turned to barren dust. A deadly sameness every-where, sapless, colourless, spent. The wretched inhabitants clung to a pitiful existence. Beggars, emaciated, verminous, filthy, were on the platform at every little station we stopped at. Many were blind, many had their noses eaten away with disease; the children's stomachs were swollen from starvation. They pressed up against the windows wherever they saw Europeans, always making the same pleading gestures – first patting their empty stomachs and then pointing with their fingers down their throats. This stricken multitude is the curse of India, and it increases at a terrible rate.

By ten o'clock we were approaching Lucknow, famous for its siege during the Mutiny of 1857, when the English were shut up there by the Sepoys and only relieved after great loss of life. Today Lucknow is a large city and an important railway junction. As we ran in I had a presentiment that trains would be checked here; so retired to the lavatory to wash and shave. When the train stopped I was surveying my lathered face in the glass. Suddenly something occurred which went through me like red-hot needles. I distinctly heard a voice say, "Gentlemen, your passes, please."

Military police in our compartment! I went limp. In a few seconds I should be hustled out of my temporary retreat, arrested and hauled back to camp in handcuffs – before the eyes of all. I held my breath and listened. Unquestionably our last hour had come. Any moment Have would be asked to show his pass. But wait – I had nearly forgotten. I must hide "Simone" at once. But where? Up there in the ventilation shutter. Again I saw my face: it was distorted, and my soap-surrounded lips quivered as though trying to form words. Would my fervent prayer be heard? At first nothing, nothing whatever happened; no commotion in the compartment, no bangs on my door – and then as though a hand from on high had averted the inevitable, I heard, "Thank you, gentlemen, good morning." I could not believe my ears. The danger was undoubtedly past, but how had Have managed it? After a pause I ventured to open the door. There was Have, rather pale, but composed and able to speak. I was devoured with curiosity, but I had to curb it. We could not say a word about it during the journey, and it was only when we reached Calcutta that I heard the story.

Have had seen the MP approaching our carriage along the platform. There was no time to get out and mix with the crowd, and to have got out on the other side on to the track would have aroused suspicion immediately. There was therefore nothing to do but sit still and let the catastrophe run its course. He had no reason to thrust himself forward; so he let the two Englishmen go ahead. They produced a whole sheaf of documents, beside which our pay-books would have made a very paltry show. Just as the MP was turning to Have, who was now resigned to capture, the lieutenant hastily produced another pass and with a wave in Have's direction said, "And this is my batman's." The MP gave a fleeting glance, saluted and went out without another word. He must have taken Have for the batman – there was no other explanation. There was a batman, but he was an Indian, who was travelling in another coach, and it was in his direction that the lieutenant was waving his hand. As the MPs were only making a sample check and had not visited the coach in which the batman was travelling, the error was not detected.

It took a long time to get the fright out of my bones. It was all very well to have escaped the clutch of the Provost Marshal, but would chance come to our help a second time? Human calculations ruled that out. The miracle had happened, and now the normal course of events would be resumed. I felt certain that we had now had our run of luck. There was little time to pursue my thoughts, for the lieutenant opened up on the topics then uppermost in India – Gandhi's release and the Bengal famine. We nodded at intervals, murmured our agreement and smoked his cigarettes.

By noon it became intolerably hot. The wind of the train only brought fresh waves of hot air in at the window. We travelled through the invisible fumes of a conflagration. The villages and small towns burned without flames. The dust seemed to have changed to hot ash. White darts of light had abolished refraction, and with it colour. The plain was like a huge burning-glass trying in vain to throw back the invading sunbeams. In such heat as this, one should confine the bodily functions to the task of evaporation and resign oneself limply to the motion of the train. Passivity, total relaxation, a vegetative daze were the only answers to such thermometer-readings. But we were keyed up by circumstances to a state which was very unsuitable to the climate, because we sweated for mental as well as for physical causes. There was the unceasing stab of apprehension over the next stop; each time we anxiously scanned the crowd for the first glimpse of a red-banded cap. If we saw one we got out on to the step on the other side of the train. We were harassed also by the fear that fresh passengers might get in. Our luck had held so far, but it might change and send us a spy, or someone of an inquisitive turn of mind. We had to be constantly on our guard lest conversation with our present fellow-travellers – the Parsee was getting more talkative – might unexpectedly take an awkward turn.

Yet by degrees familiarity with danger drugged the sensations of fear – though not our watchfulness. It was useless to await the next blow in a constant state of suspense. In that case one would be sure to parry it badly.

The rails droned sleepily as the train held on its undeviating way across

47

the plains. They seemed to stretch on for ever without a change, and the country was equally monotonous; it was sunk in the heart of a continent, where no water reflected the sky, where the horizon was lost in vaporous dust and all was earthbound. I felt melancholy as well as bored – it was all so vast and so unvarying and the end of our journey was so distant, and so pointless. But the vastness of India has a special characteristic – the haunting and depressing note of suffering. It was in the very air, and you could never escape it. It was in the faces of the natives, waiting in crowds on the platforms, in the look they had of belonging to another world; and its burden was felt throughout the whole country. For generations it has been their fervent desire to annihilate all joy in living and to escape from this earthly vale of tears; and this spiritual atmosphere has by now invaded the whole of India. Before I saw India I imagined it as a tropical paradise of palm-happy, carefree people. I found it half a desert, a land of tribulation, where human life is a torment, which inspires only the wish to leave it behind as soon as possible.

"Half an hour's stop at the next station," the guard called in at the window. "Dinner will be served in the refreshment-room for members of the Forces. Shall I reserve places for you, gentlemen?"

The two Englishmen reserved two places for officers. We could not very well have got out of doing the same.

But first we came to Benares, the stronghold of Hinduism on the sacred Ganges. The railway skirted the town, and we saw nothing of its teeming life. But as the train slowly crossed the river by the heavily guarded bridge we had a view of the river-front, which gives the most characteristic view of the city. It is built entirely for the river, and on the river-front is crowded all its architecture. The river-bank is closely occupied in terraces by temples, spiked cupolas and narrow-fronted houses. A repulsive smell of floral offerings and cow-dung fills the narrow lanes. Ornamentation sprouts exuberantly from the temple walls, and the multiplicity of the monstrous symbols which express the worship of the divine is distressing – phallic, or in the form of ape, serpent, cow or elephant deities, and also in human shape – many-armed, grotesque and often obscene, all showing the influence of the darkest devil-worship. At the river's edge there is a bewildering huddle of gangways, landing-stages and platforms built out into the water. Brahmins sit under disc-shaped parasols with long handles, lost in motionless contemplation. Pilgrims stand in groups in the water to be cleansed in the sacred river; curls of smoke rise up from the funeral pyres on which corpses are being burnt.

I remembered being present at a cremation before the war. It needed strong nerves to stomach it. It was obviously the head of the family's obsequies, and the eldest son officiated at the pyre, while the rest of the family stood round it as spectators. The fire had consumed all but the head and feet of the deceased, and the son pushed the two ends together and broke up the skull, as the ancient ritual required, with a bamboo pole. The ashes were scattered in the Ganges, which flowed slowly and broadly on past the greatest of its holy places.

The evening fires were alight in the villages when the train stopped at the station where we were to dine. We walked to the small station building, which stood in the open country, with the lieutenant and the pilot, who took his heavy automatic with him. The small dining-room was full of officers and most of the tables were occupied. There was a crowd at the bar, where flasks were being filled with gin. A waiter led us to our reserved seats at a table where a major and a captain, both Englishmen, were already seated. We sat down in a stupor beside the two from our carriage, and the meal began in silence. We are never likely to forget our table-companions. The major looked severe and thoroughly dangerous – sharp features, black hair and penetrating blue eyes. The gold crown on his epaulettes shone out. The captain was shy; he had a fine wide forehead and a large childlike face; it was lit up by the low, hanging electric light, which made it seem all the larger. The war might very likely have interrupted his studies at Oxford or Cambridge. These two sat opposite us, our train-companions covered our flank, and all round the main body threatened in overwhelming numbers. Complete encirclement. We were alone in the midst of the enemy, protected only by the flimsiest of camouflage. If our table-companions only knew with whom they were having dinner! We felt suffocated at the thought, and dared not look up from our plates. A large drop of sweat fell from my forehead on to my as yet unfolded napkin – the air felt charred. Have, who had observed, as I had, that the captain was trying to enter into conversation with us, took the bull by the horns by beginning one with me.

"Oh dear," he began. "It's chicken again," just as though we had had nothing else in camp. As I could think of nothing interesting to say about roast chicken, I switched over to tennis, and Have branched off into a story about a girl as soon as his games-vocabulary gave out. The captain gazed at us with large, enquiring eyes while we leaped nimbly from one topic to the next. How many more courses still to go? Then we caught it; the major started up over the cheese, mercifully with the lieutenant first. Where was he going? Aha! To Calcutta. His voice was like thin steel.

Before he could proceed to further interrogations, the station-master came in to request all passengers to take their seats in the train. We bowed coolly to the table and hurried out.

When we were outside the whole nightmare vanished like smoke. We were as exultant as if we had won a battle.

"We only have to survive a flirtation with the Viceroy's daughter," I said.

"Now that we've got through that, I don't see what's to stop us. With all those officers taking us for one of themselves." Have was not behind-hand in drawing foolhardy conclusions.

"Anyway," I said as I climbed up into our compartment, "I shall be less anguished in future. Getting too het-up is detrimental to the best prospects of escape."

The night was hideous. Everything conspired to make a martyrdom of it. The heat alone! It was impossible to close an eye in such damp, enervating and fantastic heat. It was like being steamed over a fire. At every station people pushed their way noisily in or out. Once an Indian came in with a basket such as snake-charmers put their snakes in. We kept our eyes on the lid, expecting to see the head of a cobra emerge at any moment. The stops at the stations seemed to last for ever. We were tortured by thirst and got out at every station to drink water. The religious cleavage between Hindu and Mohammedan comes out even in drinking-water. In all stations separate taps are provided, with a notice to say for which variety of throat it is intended. Modern methods of transport, however, have tended to lower the barriers of caste. Even a generation ago in South India the pariah had to have a bell to warn the Brahmin, lest the unclean shadow fell on his person. Today both travel in the same trams and trains.

When dawn came at last the landscape had altered. We were approaching the great delta formed by the Ganges and the Brahmaputra, the fever-haunted Sunderbund. The land was as flat as ever, but its thirst was appeased. Ponds and watercourses became more frequent. Rice succeeded to millet. Primeval-looking water-buffaloes wallowed in mud pools, showing only their nostrils and horns. Occasionally a patch of green showed up. Palms now came into the landscape; they stood as a rule in groups among the houses, which were becoming more numerous: the railway traversed one of the most thickly populated regions of over-populated India. Besides tall palmyra palms, there was the arching foliage of bamboos falling in green fountains, and the broad-leaved banana gave shade. Now and then a temple glided by; they were built round square pools with steps down to the water, which was mantled with green slime. The pyramidal towers over the entrance-gates were covered with a welter of fantastic forms. Priests, who wore the holy thread round their naked torsos, guarded the sacred precincts.

The old underlying uneasiness was still there. What would the next hour bring forth? And Calcutta, which we were to reach at midday? And the days after that? From what quarter would the wind come next? When would the blow fall? We were only cradling ourselves in false security if we believed that past luck ensured us against future danger. It had gone well long enough; the end was rapidly approaching. These I knew were not Have's thoughts. When the lieutenant again offered us breakfast, he took it as proof that our luck must hold. I took it only as a brief respite from the gallows.

At one of the stops we saw our first Americans; a train-load of engineers and service troops went past. Military transport was now more frequent, a sign that we were nearing the base for the eastern theatre of war.

We had one more unwelcome intrusion. The prayerful Indian was the cause of it. His wife was travelling in the train, in the coach reserved for women, which we were not allowed to enter. He had flouted this regulation and travelled with her for part of the way, but the guard hauled him out at one of the stations, and he became abusive. The two came along the platform in hot debate and were quickly joined by a policeman, who demanded proofs of identity before going any further. We both withdrew discreetly to the lavatory.

Lunch was again provided at one of the stations. This time the pilot went with us, and the company was sadly below the standard set by the evening before. We had to put up with a quite ordinary tank-driver. To show our recognition of past hospitality, we treated the pilot to a gin.

The long journey, the heat, the agitation and the sleepless nights had racked our nerves and worn us down; yet we could not let up for a second. There was Calcutta to face next. We should be there any moment now; the train was passing through the outer suburbs already, and as its speed gradually diminished we felt that it was drawing us slowly and surely into the jaws of a huge trap. It was the tenth day of our escape, and we were a thousand miles from the camp, no mean exploit. If we were fated to be nabbed at that dangerous defile, the barrier of Howrah Railway Station, and restored to captivity, we should not need to feel ashamed of ourselves. I thought of Harrer, whom it would take many months, perhaps a year, to cover an equal distance. Where would he be at this moment, I wondered.

51

But this was no moment for comparing times. Arrest seemed very probable when we finally drew up at the terminus. Although our thoughts were not on polite acknowledgements, we did not wish to incur the imputation of ingratitude. We therefore said good-bye to our two Englishmen very cordially; after all, it was only owing to their reserve that we had been able to survive two days in the same compartment. Hope and anxiety, subdued by a dash of fatalism, made up our state of mind as we got out of the train. Have was immediately swept from me in the crowd and carried along among a mob of British soldiers, from whom, I was glad to note, it was impossible to distinguish him. Red-caps shone out menacingly behind the barrier. Have walked straight past them surrounded by his bodyguard. When my turn came, they were busy with soldiers asking where their units were and where they were to doss down; and so I could slip by unobserved. The crowd was far too great for checking each man singly.

Without knowing quite how it had happened, we had arrived in Calcutta, the second largest city of the British Empire.

In spite of all our efforts, we could not get hold of a taxi. But then Have pulled off one of his stunts. He went briskly up to the policeman on traffic control and ordered him to find us a taxi at once. The policeman held up an empty one which was hurrying past and told us to get in. He was graciously tipped, and there we were. It was a comfortable open taxi, and we set off on an extensive tour of the town to get our bearings and find out what Calcutta had to offer to two Germans on the run.

Chapter Four

CALCUTTA SPREE

"Talk a bit louder," Have said in the taxi. "I can't hear what you say."

"How shall we ever survive Calcutta?" I repeated.

"We shall soon see – don't know yet myself."

We had emerged into the station square on one of those waves of exhilaration which dangers leave behind them, but now the exhilaration was momentarily over and we had a feeling of helplessness, a sense of doom, which never left us while we were in Calcutta. So far we had acted on a plan which we had thought out in advance; but now we had come to a point where improvisation set in; we had to take our fences as we came to them. It had been utterly impossible in camp to look beyond Calcutta. Calcutta was like a dense mist blotting out a view. And now here we were in the mist itself, without a map or a course laid down. Was it sense to stay there at all and lose our impetus? Wouldn't it be wiser to take a train on at once? But in what direction? The Burma front was long. We felt in our bones that we had come to the critical parting of the ways. Everything might turn on the choice we now made.

Calcutta was like the base camp of an army. Military transport and columns of lorries rattled without a pause along the large main streets. The ground shook and the hot air stank of petrol fumes. Khaki was the only colour. Nearly every pedestrian wore it and nearly every vehicle was camouflaged with it. The Allied Command had turned the city into a supply and reserve base for the Burma front and China. The pulse of war could be felt.

Our taxi had difficulty in getting through the congested traffic in the Chowringhee, the main street. We had to fall in at walking pace behind columns of heavy lorries; but this really suited our purpose for finding out whether we should be able to put up at any of the large European hotels. It was not from overweening self-confidence, but because we believed we should be less noticed if we openly mixed with the British than if we hid ourselves and shrank away. We were not to be daunted by high prices; we had money at our disposal. But registering would be a difficulty. We were passing the Grand Hotel at the moment. Notices proclaimed that it was reserved exclusively for officers. Undoubtedly the reception desk would be very particular – even if there were any rooms free. This ruled it out for us. We told the driver to take us to the Great Eastern, but there it was the same story. We could not venture to spend the night in an Indian hotel. Have knew from his first escape that the native hotels of Calcutta were under very strict police surveillance.

To gain time, I told the driver to take us to Fort William.

"If we can't find anywhere, we must spend the night in the open," I said under my breath to Have.

"No go. We should be nabbed."

"Right, then what about the red light quarter?"

"Out of the question."

"Why?"

"MPs."

Yes, he was right there. The MPs would naturally have their eyes on every brothel.

"What on earth are we to do, then?"

"I've got it," Have whispered. "Hey!" he shouted to the driver. "To the bazaar."

Have had a dim memory from his last visit of having seen a YMCA hostel near the Indian University quarter. Perhaps it might have shelter to offer. The driver knew of it, and took us along past the large new commercial buildings of Central Avenue, which glare up into the sky like gigantic white posts. The largest appeared to have been commandeered by the Army. For a time we kept on along this wide and busy thorough-fare, and then turned off into the native quarter and plunged abruptly into the East. There was no sign here of war; nothing but bargaining and shouting, sleeping and begging. The sour smell of rotting garbage and human exhalations hung about the streets. There was the usual con-gestion. The pavement was crowded and the passengers hung like grapes from the flame-coloured trams which almost filled the narrow streets. Our taxi drew up at a crossing. There was the YMCA I sat where I was while Have got out and entered the shabby old building. He asked to see the secretary and enquired for a room.

"I am sorry. Our hostel is full. Also we only let rooms to Indian members, and then only to permanent residents."

Have was not going to be put off so easily. His face hardened, "I am an old member."

"No doubt. But you should apply to the British hostel."

"That's just why I am here. It is full."

"I am sorry, sir, but you must apply to some other organization for a billet."

"Well, I am here now and I mean to stay here."

"Sir, as I have said already, we are full up."

"Think it over – perhaps you have a dressing-room or something—"

"I do not see why you as a British soldier must insist on being put up in this Indian hostel. Perhaps you have some particular reason?"

"What do you mean by that?" Have asked angrily, and turned to go.

"Nothing at all, sahib. Nothing whatever. I meant nothing," he cried out as he ran after Have. "Wait one moment. I think I might be able to help you. Wait."

A refuge was found for us. We were given the sitting-room. It had no beds. We slept side by side on the long table used for committee meetings. We were not asked to register or to fill in a form for the police.

Next morning we joined the throng of soldiers in the Chowringhee.

The whole boulevard quivered in the blinding glare, and the heat struck us as though it issued in breaths of fire from a thousand brazen throats. The Chowringhee looks on the Maidan, that large expanse of grass like a racecourse in the heart of Calcutta, but this does not make it any the more airy. The excessive heat is the same everywhere, and rests in heavy swathes in the open spaces as well. People walked in a daze through the bath of fire, striving instinctively towards the next oasis of shade, economizing on every movement, holding their arms at a slight angle to let the air circulate between, and now and then freeing their skins from the moist clasp of their shirts. The crowd was on the built-up side, where hotels, cinemas, bars, warehouses and shops were the attraction, and like grottoes and shady recesses offered an escape from the sun. The mark of a mercantile empire and overseas trade was on these buildings; they spoke of rich returns and high colonial dividends.

At that time war was the prevailing note. The shop windows were sandbagged against blast, and on the Maidan side there were huts, car parks, dumps, special fun-fairs for the troops, and stalls where they could buy solar topis, medal-ribbon clasps and identity discs. The pavement seethed with soldiers in streams which met or passed or crossed or jammed. Most were on leave and wanted only relaxation and distraction and quick ways of spending their back pay. But there were a few busy people who had to dodge their way through the strolling mob.

To mix with so many foreign soldiers was like secretly attending a meeting of one's enemies and finding out with bated breath who they all were who had sworn to destroy you. In the Chowringhee all nations which had joined in the war against Japan, Germany's ally, were represented. The whole Empire was called up. There were not only Englishmen and Scotsmen, but all those adherents of Britain – Australians, New Zealanders, Canadians, with members of the Indian Army interspersed. We avoided looking the British in the face and preferred to keep our eyes on their knees, which showed between their shorts and stockings. The Indians were fine specimens from the warlike tribes of the north-west; they were true warriors with beak-like noses, flashing eyes and high foreheads. The large number of Americans surprised us, and their Negro transport-drivers and Chinese training-troops. The Yanks stole the picture. They barged around in cheery gangs, bought up whole shops, mobbed the stalls, whistled after the girls and took them for joy-rides in Service vehicles. The GIs blew in on Calcutta like a breath of fresh air. In contrast with the dignified bearing of the British, they seemed to be out for fun and nothing else. They wanted to make a spree out of everything and anything, on duty or off duty, in the bars or on the razzle – in fact, to paint the whole town red.

I looked furtively at the advertisement pillars. It always struck me as a particularly exciting moment in crime stories when the criminal stood unobserved in front of his own police description. I wanted to experience the thrill myself, but was disappointed; I could not find a proclamation with our portraits anywhere. The whole country must have been alerted on our account, and yet there was nothing to show for it. The hand that was closing on us was unseen.

We kept on walking about, merely because we were flummoxed. We were really marking time. The urge to get forward, to get out, to get to work, was strong. But in what direction were we to hurl our weight? We were like incendiaries with flaming tow in their hands, desperately looking for the doomed house they cannot find.

We diligently searched all the kiosks and bookshops in the Chowringhee for a serviceable map of the region which now formed the front line, but in vain. So we were thrown back on the two small sketch-maps we had cut out of a newspaper in camp, and these gave only very vague indications of where the line ran. When we came to the Army and Navy Stores we gave up the search and went in to buy some articles we needed to complete our outfit. It took some time, because Have found the sales-girl attractive.

When that was done he wanted to have his shoes shined. There was a

56

row of shoeblacks at the next corner, and as soon as we had been taken in hand an American fell in beside Have. He jerked his elbow in the direction of a miserable group of beggars standing on the kerb behind us and turned his flabby, red-blotched face to Have.

"Say, listen. You British ought to be ashamed of yourselves to let that kind of thing happen."

"No business of mine—"

"Why don't you do something about it? With us back home such wretched sights wouldn't be allowed."

"Why do you pick on me? Take over the whole cursed country for all I care. You can have it, with all its beggars included, and Gandhi thrown in," Have answered in annoyance.

"That would suit you – to have us drag your cart out of the muck."

"If you don't want to accept the responsibility, you needn't criticize."

"Oh, yeah – that's you Britishers all over. If your attention's drawn to any little thing that's wrong, you get crabby."

With this parting shot, the reformer tossed the beggars a coin and went his way sweating profusely and cursing to himself.

The British had put two or three captured Japanese tanks and armoured cars in the square at the end of the Chowringhee, to instigate a profoundly pacifist public to buy war loan. They attracted the attention of only very few and very uninterested bystanders. And really it was a waste of time to incite to violence people whose religious horror of killing goes to such lengths that there is a sect among them, the Jains, who wear a gauze veil in front of their mouths in case they inadvertently swallow a fly.

Our special friends, the MPs, patrolled the streets indefatigably. They strode smartly along two by two in white anklets. We were apparently so entirely in keeping that they never gave us a look. In fact, the Chowringhee and the strolling soldiers were our chosen refuge when elsewhere we found the ground too hot for us.

All the same, we had to take a risk. We could not go on marking time for ever. We must start the ball rolling somehow; and we needed information, something to go on.

I suggested to Have that we should go and have a drink in the exclusive Great Eastern Hotel. He agreed.

In spite of notices on all sides restricting entry to the elect, we marched straight through to the bar and sat down at an unoccupied table in the corner. After the glare of the streets we were in a cool twilight. Some officers, a colonel among them, were seated not far from us. No need to worry. Not one of them would get up and demand our passes. And when the bar-waiter brought us our gimlets – a mixture of gin and lemon and water, well iced – we almost forgot that we were escaped prisoners at all.

An Anglo-Indian girl was sitting at a table opposite us with two elderly American officers, whose backs were turned to us. She had a mass of black hair above the perfect oval of her face. Her lips were full and blood-red, and when she smiled – but she did not appear to be greatly taken with her companions – she displayed flashing white teeth. She had looked up when we came in and had since given us a quick glance now and then. The years behind the wire had left us a little uncertain of our sex-appeal, and the fleeting attention she paid us was very helpful; we felt an almost adolescent excitement tingle in our veins. Pity! She'd just got up and gone out with her escort.

I summoned the waiter, "Boy, two more of the same." Over our second gimlets, we put together all we had been able to gather about the Burma front. We knew from reports in the newspapers that the Japanese were at that time engaged in an offensive near Manipur on the border of Assam, in the course of which they had crossed the Indian frontier. Imphal, the residence of the Maharajah of Manipur, was threatened. Before getting out of camp, we had decided that this scene of operations would suit us particularly well, because in a war of movement there is always a good deal of confusion and it would be easier for us to get through to the advancing Japanese. We knew nothing at all about the physical features and railway communications of Assam, but we feared they might present peculiar difficulties. On the other hand, Have from his previous attempt knew something of the hinterland of the southern-most section of this front on the Bay of Bengal, and thought we might find our way through better in that region.

"That's far too vague," I told him. It was gradually getting on my nerves that we could do nothing but grope about in the dark.

"Don't be impatient."

"I'm not; but do let's consider sensibly who there is we might make use of. First of all, there are the Tommies. We might go about among them and listen to what they said—"

"Better not – that wouldn't work—"

"Secondly, the Indians. There might be someone—"

At that moment the door opened and there was the Anglo-Indian girl back again. Alone this time. She sat down against the wall opposite us – with a faint note of invitation, I thought. Perhaps her feminine instinct told her that we were marked out as her prey. She took a cigarette from her case and held it to her lips without lighting it. I went over, gave her a light and invited her to have a drink with us. When she was sitting between us, we felt like monks whose wits Satan was leading astray and who might find that their virtue was not as impregnable as they had thought it. I was tormented by self-reproach; anything might follow from such thoughtlessness. It was inexcusable to invite any stranger to share our table, let alone an attractive woman. It offended against the first law of escape – never to draw attention to yourself.

"My name is Muriel. What are yours?"

"He's John," Have told her. "And I'm Harry."

"Have you come from the Burma front?"

"No. That's where we're bound for."

"What section?"

"We don't know yet. Soon find out!"

"Not to Assam, let's hope."

"Let's hope not. That's where the worst fighting is."

"Yes. Those two Americans were telling me just now."

"The Japanese seem to be bad people to come up against."

"Bad isn't the word—"

Ought we to question her? She was pretty enough and well-read in men, but she obviously had no knowledge whatever of the military situation. Have apparently had come to the same conclusion; he spoke of other things and then prepared to wind up the occasion.

"Oh, tell me, Muriel, what's on in Calcutta nowadays? We've come from the north-west and are quite out of it—"

"Firpo's is the place to eat, and there are the films."

"Do you know of a good one?"

"There's *Stormy Weather*, a Negro film, on at the Roxy. They say it's good."

We got up.

"Would you like to come and see it with us?" I suggested.

Have frowned.

"Your enthusiasm is fine, John. But you seem to forget that we have military duties this afternoon."

"Why do you always think of military duties at the most inappropriate moments? I'm afraid he's right, Muriel. Sorry. We must meet another time. May I have your telephone number?"

She gave her address and we parted. "Don't forget to ring me," she called after us.

When we were in the street Have told me off. How could I be so damned silly? Didn't I know the prejudice of the British against Anglo-Indian girls? And what more glaring folly could there be than to be seen about with one?

"Yes, yes. I know. You're quite right. But just imagine their faces in camp when we tell them about it."

"They won't believe a word of it."

In reality the incident depressed me. We had made a bold step forward in contempt of prudence, and yet it had led to nothing.

"We shall have to try the Indians," Have decided.

The house was in Central Avenue. I walked up and down, waiting impatiently for Have, who was up on the third floor, visiting an Indian dentist. He had got to know him on his first escape and hoped to get some information out of him. It was a very odd acquaintanceship, which dated from the days when he and Hülsen had been on the loose together in Calcutta.

They had no money and could not think how to procure any. Then they had an idea – a very clever and original one. Indians who took degrees at foreign universities always liked to add the town and the letters after their name. It gave prestige. Hülsen and Have searched the telephone book until they found the name of a man who had taken his degree at a German university. "D.M.D., Heidelberg," rewarded their search. They agreed that a man who had spent long years in Germany was the most promising man to borrow from. Having come to that decision, they presented themselves and took seats in his waiting-room. After a time one of them was summoned, but both went in together. Have sat down in the chair and Hülsen remained standing. The Indian dentist bent over Have with his little looking-glass and his instrument and asked him what was wrong. Have pushed his hand gently aside and said with a smile, "Nothing – with my teeth, Doctor."

The dentist was very much surprised at this. Have asked to speak to him alone. His secretary then left the room.

"Doctor," Have began, speaking in English, "I have something to say which will surprise you."

He paused.

"We are not Englishmen at all and we have not got toothache. We are Germans."

The Indian nearly collapsed and dropped his instruments as if they had given him an electric shock.

"Germans?" he stammered, letting his arms fall to his sides.

"Yes; Germans. Escaped prisoners."

That was more than he could stand. His face went pale, and he could only just speak.

"Then leave this room at once."

"Not before you have given us some money."

"You want money? They want money too! I cannot give you any money. Please go."

He gripped his forehead in desperation.

"We don't want much. Make it what you please."

"I implore you. Leave me in peace and go. You force me to summon the police."

Have now resumed in German: "You've been in Heidelberg, so you must as an Indian have an understanding of our situation. We need the money to carry out our escape."

The Indian was silent. Then he burst out: "Gentlemen, I have had much experience of the CID, but this is by far the most cunning trap they have laid for me. I shall not do you the favour of falling into it."

"Then you are on our side after all. You are at war with the English," Have said delightedly.

"You need not say another word," the Indian answered resolutely. "I see through your plot to the very bottom."

"But do believe at least that we are Germans who have escaped from prison."

"You cannot deceive me. I must make an end of this and call my assistant. My patients are waiting."

He walked to the door.

"Wait just one second," Hülsen implored him, horrified at having hit on the right man and yet being unable to convince him.

"You need not tax yourselves any further. I have had enough of your investigations. You have put me to untold miseries because my wife is a German—"

"What? Your wife is a German? Then there is the solution. Confront us with her, and we'll soon prove we are fellow-countrymen of hers."

The Indian hesitated. Then he went out quickly, shutting the door.

"He's fetching the police, man—"

After a minute or two the door opened again. A European woman in Indian dress looked in cautiously and asked in Bavarian German:

"Are you German really?"

"Of course we are. Your husband won't believe us. But perhaps you can convince him."

"Yes, you do speak like Germans. Like North Germans at least," she added with a smile, and quickly retired and shut the door.

A few more minutes passed before the dentist returned. He was in great agitation, torn between fear and resolution. He went close up to Have, took a hundred-rupee note out of his coat pocket and gave it him without a word. At the same time the door opened once more and they heard:

"But you're a couple of rogues."

So this was the Indian whom Have was now visiting. Since the ice had been broken, their talk this time might go more smoothly. It certainly was not long before he rejoined me.

"He nearly passed out at the sight of me."

"Not surprised."

"Unfortunately he hadn't much to say. And he was so rattled he couldn't collect his thoughts."

"What did he say?"

"When he found his tongue he told me that the line to Chittagong is not confined to troops. Civilians can travel by it too."

"Well, and what else?"

"Nothing else very definite. He said that there was the strictest watch everywhere."

"Did he say whether we should make for Assam or keep to the coast?"

"How should a poor devil know—?"

"Quite right. How should he?"

Firpo's, Calcutta's most elegant restaurant, is in the Chowringhee. It was the place Muriel had recommended. We could accept her recommendation with a clear conscience, because it was in accordance with our principle of being seen where we were least expected – that is, where the British congregated. It was also according to programme to eat as often and as well as possible. Calcutta would certainly be the last place where we should find European food.

"Come along," I said to Have as we ascended the wide staircase to the first floor. "We'll mix once more with the lords of the land."

There was a regular scrum of officers and men round the bar. Iced drinks were handed out without a pause. We sat down beside two Englishmen at a table and ordered John Collinses, a long gin drink. Our first concern was to engage a table for two in the large dining-room next door, to avoid unwelcome table companions, and I went out to see about it. The Englishmen got up soon after and we followed them.

The large luxurious room, capable of seating two hundred, quickly filled up. Everyone was in uniform, excepting a few Indians and white-haired elderly Europeans. The Americans stormed in by gangs as usual and occupied the larger tables without giving a thought to their sweat-soaked shirts. They brought Anglo-Indian girls with them. The British looked priggish and wooden beside them, but they had the cooler heads and were more mature and composed. A small orchestra started playing soft and subdued music, mostly Viennese waltzes. Turbaned waiters in spotless white sped to and fro. The fans whirred above our heads. As gatecrashers we experienced the delight of secretly mocking at the inno-cence of the rest of the room. Little did they think who were lunching in their company! It was an added thrill to sit down with our enemies in such sumptuous surroundings. We had an excellent lunch – crab mayon-naise, cold turkey, and ice-cream. The bill only came to two rupees, eight annas. In Bengal, according to the papers, hundreds of thousands were dying of starvation.

Everybody has felt the wild impulse to jump up in a crowded room and shout something in an interval of silence. I suddenly felt this longing at Firpo's. I wanted to get up and roar out unequivocally in German that we were escaped prisoners, and then vanish before the astonishment and the tumult had died down.

"You're a neurotic," Have said when I confessed this singular temp-tation. "And that's the fellow I've taken up with!"

We sat in silence over cigars and coffee. The moments as they passed seemed incredible. First, prisoners for years, mere numbers, objects to be kicked about, and then at one blow masters of our fate. Yet what a ticklish balance there was between the situations as they came to meet us and our power to deal with them. Here in Calcutta the circle within which we could act freely was very restricted. We could only wait with patience for the right moment to come.

"Well, what now?" Have said, breaking in on my meditation.

"Now? Now we go to the cinema," I replied.

"I say, are we escaping or travelling for pleasure?"

"I don't argue about words, but as we shan't be out very much longer we may as well enjoy what Calcutta has to offer."

"I don't listen to defeatist talk of that sort. Let's go to the movies, for the love of Mike."

Before leaving our table, I carefully pocketed the receipted bill. It would prove to our fellow-prisoners, in the event of recapture, that we had indeed lunched at Firpo's; otherwise it would be useless to try to convince them. Actually, we always lunched there for the three and a half days we spent in Calcutta.

We also went to the pictures three times, to the afternoon performances in the full light of day. We felt we were safely stowed away for a couple of hours, even though we were surrounded by soldiers. And as soon as the lights went out and the whole auditorium was hushed in suspense, the tension that kept us strung up everywhere else was released. We surrendered only too willingly to the film story and forgot our own precarious situation. It was a sudden shock when it came back.

A news film showed us a few pictures of the Manipur front and left us in no doubt of the difficulties of the terrain – not a sign of life anywhere to be seen, nothing but steep hills and impenetrable jungle. Other pictures showed the British counter-attacks, making it clear that the Japanese had been halted and in places thrown back. This was confirmed by the communiqués we read in the papers, which spoke of the hardening of the front. Our hope of finding the front in a fluid state was extinguished.

Although the cinema was a comparatively safe resort, we sat on dynamite even there. Before the performance began, while the lights were on, we found we were sitting in front of a chubby young major with a large red moustache, who began in a loud voice and with a rather pompous manner to question the men in his row. He wanted to know where each man came from, what his regiment was and who were his officers. How enviably pat, how free of care their answers! "I come from Dehra Dun, major. Dehra Dun. Yes, Dehra Dun, I tell you," raced through my head over and over again. The lights went out just in time.

On another occasion – it was at the end of our first visit to the pictures – we very nearly gave ourselves away. We got up and started to go out without observing that "God Save the King" was being played and that the whole audience was standing to attention. With consternation we found that we alone had left our seats and instantly froze where we stood.

We were never so acutely conscious as in Calcutta of the strangely equivocal morality of our enterprise. There is nothing improper about escaping in itself, nothing that transgresses the moral dictates of mankind; on the contrary, it is considered an honourable proceeding and is even sanctioned by the law of nations. But the fact of being pursued by the military authorities and treated as an outlaw makes it seem a crime.

And from being chased as a criminal, the fugitive involuntarily takes on some of a criminal's characteristics and habits. He contracts a gnawing conscience and uneasy look. He is drawn to the same places that criminals usually visit immediately after the crime. He takes a roguish joy in deception and feels the fascination of the forbidden.

A bazaar in India is much more than a picturesque, or fairy-tale, shopping-centre. It is a stage on which private life is seen without walls. The street here does not separate mutually exclusive houses, like a sort of no-man's-land. It is itself the scene on which people are brought together in a common life. What goes on elsewhere between four walls takes place in the open. It is really because the doors shut in no secrets that the house can be taken into the street; for the same reason the Indians have no home life. The inside of their houses is always indescribably wretched – no chairs, no tables, no beds – just bare walls and a roof. Everything is sacrificed to the street, which makes what compensation it can.

The streets got narrower as we went along. The heat was more closely compressed between the walls; it gathered in the courtyards, and was ambushed in every corner. Glaring stripes of light alternated with black bars of shadow. Goods were piled up outside the shops – big-bellied, shining copper vessels, aluminium saucepans, oil lamps, chains, locks; mountains of fruit, oranges, papayas, bananas; trays of sweetmeats amid pyramids of cakes; batteries of soft-drink bottles filled with poisonous green, boiled-sweet-pink and canary-yellow liquids. The dealers squatted in the background, many of them stripped to the waist, with the marks of caste or sect clearly to be seen on their foreheads, teeth stained red with betel-juice. Our way was blocked by a cow. A cow in the middle of the town. That was nothing unusual for India, where a cow, to the Hindus a sacred animal, may hold up the traffic if it likes. We passed money-changers and gold-merchants. We saw them in the dim light within, busy with scales and bundles of notes and heaps of coins. Their thin fingers moved the balls of the abacus. Indian divinities in cheap and gaudily-coloured reproductions hung on the walls. Krishna, in blue, playing the flute, was popular. When we came to the soft goods it looked as if the whole stock had simply been dragged into the street. Bales of cloth in cascades, children's dresses fluttering overhead, piles of gay muslins for saris built up to form the corner-posts of the display. And now – uniforms, not one shop, but several. Complete officers' uniforms were for sale. We paused in doubt. Should we or should we not? A smart cap perhaps. I tried one on. Have only laughed. "Better not. We should look too conspicuous in correct uniform."

There was a cook-shop at a corner. One of those strongly spiced Indian dishes was being cooked in iron pans with an oil of penetrating odour. The two cooks, naked except for loin-cloths, sat cross-legged on a bench behind the fire. Their fat, shining bellies, shaven heads on which only a topknot remained, and their wide nostrils gave them the air of child-devouring monsters. Their topknots had a religious significance; at the moment of death their god would tweak them by it out of reach of the claws of the demons. Coolies besieged the counter and paid a few annas for a meal, which was given them wrapped up in large leaves. They squatted down on the ground and ate it at once in their fingers. Beggars and the dogs fell on what was left.

We had decided on a stroll through the bazaar, because we wanted to leave nothing untried in our search for someone who might help us to penetrate the English lines, or to by-pass them by means of a sailing-boat which would take us along the coast to the Japanese. We knew how vain the hope was: only sheer chance could put such a card into our hands. It was very unlikely that we should obtain any assistance, even in the form of useful information. This might have been available if the Indian population had taken any interest in the war; but to the Indian it is his private affairs that matter: to the peasant the weather and the prices, to the townsman his profits. They mattered a great deal more than the war in the Pacific, which hardly touched him. Even the operations in Burma were to him a very remote affair, which did not concern his own country.

We might, of course, have expected that the Indians would have made use of the difficulties the war had brought upon Great Britain to throw off the British yoke. But so far as any hopes of a mass insurrection went, this expectation had no foundation. One important reason for this was the sagacity of British rule, which took its stand on a minimum of encroachment and an elastic retreat upon the last (and certainly decisive) five per cent of power. But the real reason was religious. People who believe that the world of sense is mere illusion can only regard it with indifference; and when the doctrine of the transmigration of souls teaches that being born again into a higher stage of existence is quite independent of the material circumstances in which the present life is lived, there is no inducement to take arms against one's earthly lot. This explains how the Indian submits to the tyranny of caste, patiently puts up with foreign rule, and suffers with mute resignation what in Western lands would long since have led to revolt.

There were indeed organized groups which pursued an anti-British policy, such as the Congress Party under Gandhi, and the Forward Block of Bose, but the English had broken the back of both by arrests running into tens of thousands. The CID with its network of spies took good care that the slightest anti-British manifestation was known to the Government at once. It is not surprising then that we could hope for nothing from the Indian population. Any who were hostile to England kept it dark. We found the same at the YMCA, where we spent the evenings in the hope that among all the students who came in for a cold meal there might be one to answer our purpose. There was in fact one who, judging from his reckless air and the white Gandhi cap he wore, might have taken a risk. We approached him cautiously and hinted that we were deserters from the British Army. But, like the dentist, he took us for police spies and would not respond.

It was this setback that led us to try our luck in the bazaar. But after we had threaded the labyrinth of narrow streets for some time, keeping an eye out for any likely person, Have gave up.

"We shall never find our man here."

"Let's at least go as far as the dyers. I know from my own business that they have ramifications far out into the country, and they might know something about Chittagong."

On we went through the throng. Porters with loads balanced on their heads walked slowly along, taking the weight by using their knees as springs. Cyclists flitted in and out among the crowd. Coolies were harnessed to carts laden with heavy bales of cloth. A mob of naked children were having a bath at a hydrant. A loud-speaker burst full blast from a restaurant, and close to it a man was sound asleep – but there were sleepers lying about everywhere. At night in the hot season everyone who can sleeps in the street. They lie in front of the houses enveloped in white sheets like corpses laid out in a plague-stricken city, as you might actually take it to be. A palmist in a huge turban forced himself upon us. We tried in vain to shake him off. He insisted on a demonstration of his skill.

"Sahib," he said to me, considering me with a crafty eye. "I know all about you. Too much thinking and no success."

"Go to the devil," I told him.

"Here, how long shall we be in India?" Have asked, putting the fatal question.

"Let me see your hand, Sahib. Not long; certainly not much longer."

Fraud. Every Tommy longs to be home again. What else should he have said?

We had decided to leave Calcutta next morning. After long discussion, we had made up our minds to give up all thought of Assam and the northern front, in favour of trying to get through in the southern region, which Have had the advantage of knowing already. What little we could gather about Assam and Manipur was enough to be a deterrent. We still had three hundred rupees in hand, not to mention a further hundred as an iron ration and a gold sovereign which Have had hidden in the heel of a shoe. Our financial situation therefore was not unsatisfactory.

The prospect of the journey greatly depressed us. It was the last stretch of railway before the front and would be thoroughly unpleasant. Although we woke every morning with the conviction that we should be dropped upon in our sitting-room, we did enjoy relative security and were at least in a civilized place. But now the jungle was ahead of us, and privation, and danger in the raw.

I felt so strongly that evil days lay ahead – which for one reason or another we were unlikely to survive – that I suggested making good use of our last night in Calcutta. Have agreed. He too felt like being a little rash, but he was strongly opposed to going out with Muriel, because he was certain it would get us into trouble. But when I suggested that we could make a date with her at her flat, he agreed that I might ring her up; I was to back out at once if she had not a flat of her own. My talk on the telephone went off surprisingly well.

It can't have been the first time that men leaving for the front had made this their excuse for a visit, because she interrupted by laughing and complimenting me on my great originality. She said that a friend of hers would be there too and would we just bring some drink along?

"It's a leap in the dark," Have whispered when we got out of the taxi at Muriel's door.

"There's time to go back."

"No; we're in for it now. Come on."

Muriel had been so frank and jolly on the telephone. We couldn't believe that she was enticing us into an ambush. And even if she became suspicious in the course of the evening, we should be off on our journey before we could be searched for.

"Hallo, defenders of the Empire," Muriel said in greeting, and then introduced us to her friend, Joan, also an Anglo-Indian. She was an exotic type with lazy, voluptuous movements and a shape that seemed to have been ripened by the tropical sun.

"So you're off to the front."

"Yes, worse luck; and Assam too," we lied.

"Poor boys. Then we must be particularly nice to you."

Muriel poured out drinks. Have started a very harmless conversation with Joan about the pleasures Calcutta had to offer troops on leave and eager for some fun; and I unobtrusively took in all the features of the small two-roomed flat. It was on the ground floor, and besides the entrance in the front had another exit through the kitchen. Also, if the worst came, there was a veranda over which we could jump into a back garden. I saw nothing suspicious. The greatest danger was Muriel's intelligence. She was all there, and the least oversight on our part would arouse her suspicions.

Anyway, it was silly to indulge in secret broodings over one's safety on an occasion like this. My anxiety was exaggerated. Surely I might forget the nightmare of dread once in a while. Who was likely to track us down, here in the seclusion of a flat? The idea that danger was always lurking was quite out of place here. Far better throw myself into the real object of our visit and keep pace with Have, who was getting off with Muriel already.

"I warn you, Muriel, Harry's a faithless brute. You'll do better with me."

"You look after Joan and don't worry about us."

But I was not much struck with Joan. She had real spider fingers, and also—

Then the bell rang.

"It must be some friends looking in," Muriel said, jumping up. We heard men's voices in the hall, and Muriel saying a few words in an undertone after welcoming them. A moment later two young officers entered the room. They were both lieutenants and their uniforms were freshly pressed. Not bad fellows at all, but the sort who know what they want. They nodded to us in a friendly enough way, tossed their caps on the table and asked for a drink. Muriel, who obviously knew them well, went on to explain the reason of our being there.

"Oh, really – you're off to the front tomorrow?" the elder of the two said.

"We are."

"Which unit?"

It was entirely our own fault that this fatal question, the most fatal that could be put to us, burst suddenly upon us. It served us right. We should have long enough to rue it in solitary confinement. But then Have did something quite surprising. Without attempting to put up any lie about our regimental entanglements and so sealing our fate, he counter-attacked vigorously and without warning.

"I shall be delighted to give you the fullest information on that point, but not here and not now. It would not amuse me, to tell you the truth. In my opinion, this room has too many people in it, and I think something ought to be done about it. Don't you?"

"Who the devil are you to talk like that?"

"Never mind who I am. This is my party, and I don't intend to have it interfered with."

We stood up, and so did the other two. We faced them in a cold fury which banished all our fears. There was a moment of giddy suspense. Have had pushed the matter to extremes, but at least he had got it on to purely personal ground. We were determined to force our way out, if necessary, and as the other two had no arms prospects were good. I glanced at Muriel, who might have acted as arbitrator, but she showed no wish to intervene. A ghost might have been walking through the room; it was suddenly so still. Then one of the officers said in a very cool and collected voice:

"This is not the place for settling the matter. We shall do that better outside."

"Very good. We'll join you."

They took their caps from the table and went out first.

Muriel shut the door after them and implored us to stay.

"Don't be so absurd. You don't surely want to fight like silly boys? Be sensible and stay here. Please stay!"

But we had had too bad a shock. No song the Sirens ever sang would have kept us a moment longer in that room.

"Quick, before they sheer off," Have shouted, and we vaulted the veranda railing.

Chapter Five

LUCK IN BENGAL

"Not a leaf falls, and not a blow strikes a man, but it is already written in an open book." This teaching of Islam, which declares that the least occurrence was predestined from eternity by God's unalterable decree, is a source of comfort and composure and strength, we told ourselves, when we left Calcutta in the Chittagong express, sharing a compartment with several Indian Mussulmans. The Oriental owes his unshakable faith in Providence and his equanimity as regards the future to his belief in Kismet. *Inshallah* – as God wills. But the faces of the two Hindus also in our carriage, bore the same look of passive obedience to God's will, since whatever occurs to a Hindu in his earthly existence is part of a causal chain, the first links of which go back to the origins of life and which continues through the remotest reincarnations. We should therefore have sinned against the spirit of our company and introduced concealed heresy amongst true believers if we had felt undue anxiety over what might be coming to us. Come what might, our fate had long since been decided. Let Heaven lead; we would follow and obey.

It would also have been foolhardy to trust to our own powers in the face of the difficulties we had to encounter. The train went as far as Goalanda Ghat, not far from the junction of the Ganges and the Brahmaputra. There we had to change into a river-steamer and proceed downstream southwards to Chandpur, where it connects with the railway-line of which the terminus is Chittagong. If all went well we should arrive in twenty-eight hours. But how could all go well? There had been no personal check in the station at Calcutta, but that could only mean that it would follow later on, since the British would scarcely take on trust anyone who was travelling to the front line. Sooner or later we should come upon a close-meshed filter, through which we should in all probability be unable to pass.

The only possibility of our getting through lay in the indefiniteness of our appearance. At first glance, in spite of the missing badges, we could not fail to be taken for soldiers. But at a pinch we might equally well pass for civilians, because Europeans, owing to the heat and dirt, often travelled in khaki on the Indian railways. We could not, however, pass ourselves off as British civilians; all Englishmen of our age would have been in the army. So we had decided, in case of an MP check, to say we were Swiss businessmen on a business journey to Chittagong. Certainly it was a very transparent, emergency camouflage, but it offered just a glimmer of hope of getting past the MPs, who were not officially concerned with civilians.

Indians were not only our fellow-passengers this time either. There was an English soldier in the bunk over our heads when we took our seats. He had roused himself meanwhile and come down to us from on high with his topi pulled well down over his freckled face, intent on plunging into a conversation about his binge of the night before, from which he was clearly still suffering. He was too much taken up with his own sufferings to pay us the least attention, as long as we made good listeners. His teeth were long and yellow and his thirst still unquenched; and he drank neat gin from his water-bottle in long draughts. We could only approve: if he kept it up he would soon cease to be any danger to us. He recited a few dirty rhymes and released us from further worry on his account.

We passed over brown, parched earth with a hard, cracked surface, from which the heat of the glaring sun seemed to rebound. The yellowish smoke the train emitted enveloped it as though in a shroud. A fine dust percolated through the cracks of the window-frames, trickled in little rivers down our newspapers and gritted between our teeth. Here and there in the desert landscape appeared tree-islands of exuberant vegetation, which were in strange and even symbolic contrast to the waste all round. Life in India confronts nothingness; it is excess surrounded by barrenness; monsoon followed by drought that scorches everything.

We reached Goalanda Ghat at about eleven. Several military trains full of troops stood in the sidings. We saw our first hospital train with wounded. The lines came right down to the water's edge. It was the typical riverside terminus. You saw the steamers and boats from the train, heard the steamers hooting, smelt a different air and looked across to see if you could see the other side.

After helping the long-toothed Tommy out of the train, we left him to his fate and joined the crowd moving along the platform to the gangways on the river bank. There were two paddle-boats, one with her bow pointing south. She must be ours. The crowd parted before reaching the bank, and at this point we were surprised to see an American transport officer, who put a brief question to each soldier as he came along. What did he want to know? Have was a pace ahead of me, and in a moment his turn came. I heard him asked whether he was an American. He answered "Yes" without hesitation. Then stay here, he was told. Hell, what would that mean? We had to go on with the steamer to Chandpur.

"And what about you? Are you American?" I was asked.

"No."

"English?"

"No."

"What are you, then?" But he did not wait for an answer.

"OK. Carry on."

He made a mark in his notebook and tackled the next man. It was as if I had looked down the muzzle of a gun, and the trigger after all hadn't been pulled. I had made sure he would ask what my nationality was, and as I was already in such a daze that I scarcely knew how to speak or what to say next, I had resigned myself to the worst. In fact, I had thrown in the sponge and was only saved by good luck from my own incompetence.

I was so shattered by this experience that I was not fully conscious until I got on board that Have was not with me. He was still standing down there beside the American. As soon as all the men had been dealt with, Have started talking to him with great earnestness and obviously with success, because after a few words he was allowed on board and joined me on the upper deck. The only explanation we could come to was that the Americans must have been holding a section of the line in the north, and therefore all GIs were to go upstream to Assam; it must therefore have been the officer's job to see that they got on to the right boat. But there must have been some Yank contingent in the south as well; otherwise, Have, who maintained that his job was there, would never have got through.

But now another crisis: the American RTO was on his rounds, and he made straight for Have out of all the other men among whom we were standing. It seemed obvious that Have had aroused suspicions which the officer was now going to verify. But no. He only made a joke and wished him luck. Nice fellow, we thought, immensely relieved. Words exchanged with officers, as long as they were pleasant words, had the great advantage of putting one on the right footing with the other soldiers present: our authenticity was guaranteed and suspicion strangled at birth. A great many soldiers had now seen us with the American officer;

and there were so many of them that, to judge from the first and second class, the boat might have been a troopship.

The ten hours' trip to Chandpur was one continuous nightmare. We were wedged in by soldiers against a refrigerator near the saloon. A rail separated us from the deck occupied by Indian passengers. Every word we said to each other was overheard. The mere fact of our all being squeezed together so tightly was a topic of conversation, and conversation was the last thing we desired. It would be bound to lead straight to the state of things at the front and probably to our being shown up. That prospect was not exactly new to us, but being exposed to it hour after hour at high tension ended by being demoralizing. Our spirits sank and our thoughts were never free from unpleasant forebodings. We wondered how to release ourselves even for a moment or two from the clasp of the foe.

By climbing on to the refrigerator you could see over the river; the flat, treeless banks made it seem wider than it was. The Ganges there is a mile or two across. Little waves crimped the milky water and a light breeze was blowing. Distant puffs of smoke rose from the horizon. Sometimes we met other paddle-boats working their way up against the stream.

We wondered whether there were any military police on board our boat.

After making a vigorous sortie we reached the natives' deck. We might have been on an emigrant ship and looking on at the migration of a tribe in search of a new home. Entire families from babies at the breast and small children to aged grandparents camped beside their wretched traps. Any who could find room slept on the planks of the deck. The rest squatted in groups and chattered. Some coolie women sat apart, enveloped in bleached blue saris. If a European looked at one of them, she immediately covered her face angrily, leaving nothing to be seen except her nose-decoration and the metal rings on her dry, spread toes. Indian soldiers, who had taken off their boots, strode about among these family groups, and some Gurkhas were standing by themselves away from all those "natives". An old man with a beard dyed red with henna was selling sweetened tea and milk. We might have had a meal in the saloon, but as it was served at a long table and officers from the first-class sat down with the rest, we decided to do without. It would not go off as well here as at Firpo's. We stuck therefore to the tea and milk and the last two rotting bananas old red-beard had for sale.

Having concluded our tour and seen no MPs, we forced our way back through the crowd to the refrigerator. We should have to stick it out there until we reached Chandpur; if we tried to drive another wedge through the pack we should be unpopular.

The plunging of the paddles was hammering on our weary brains, when we were suddenly hailed by a man who was sitting on a rail above the rest.

"Hallo, you two blokes there—"

God in heaven, what next?

"Have a look-see. There may be a few bottles of beer in the fridge."

Marked relief was visible on our faces. I opened the door. He had had the right idea.

"About a dozen," I reported.

General uproar. "Hand 'em over. Share 'em out. Pass 'em along. Quick."

It was an embarrassing demand. We might easily get into trouble with an officer if we simply handed the bottles over as loot. But if we refused we should be branded as mugs. We were rescued from our predicament by an Indian boy, who set up a howl. The beer was for the officers. The door was shut upon the bottles.

"Hear that? For the officers. And what about us? Always the same bloody story!"

The officers now bore the brunt of all recriminations, and we were forgotten.

As soon as it was dusk we got rid of our pay-books. A lot of good they had done us – we hadn't once shown them; they had been nothing but a curse, and if they were found on us anywhere near the front, the British might turn very nasty. And yet what miracles we had hoped of them. Their worthlessness was now quite clear, and Zoja and Simone were condemned to drown. We squeezed our way to the taffrail and threw them overboard.

Lights shone out on the shore – we should soon be at Chandpur.

Commands rang out. Bells clanged in the engine-room. The paddles churned the water in reverse. Lines were thrown out to the quay and the steamer was made fast. Coolies came running on board by narrow planks to offer their services as porters. And in the darkness amidst the dingy throng on the quay – wasn't that a glimpse of suspicious red? Right in front there, near the gangway and over there too? Wrong. They were only red turbans. No; now they came into a better light, they weren't turbans. That glimpse of red among all those heads was another red, the unmistakable carmine of the MP. Yes, there they were, the Red Caps forming a nice orderly cordon all along the quay. One of them shouted an order across to us. The soldiers took it up, "All members of the Forces stay on board for a check-up." So now for the screening. It was good night. We'd had it.

Our first reaction was a sort of paralysis. We went pale, felt that famous weak feeling in the pit of the stomach, and were incapable of forming a thought. Next, horrid visions of solitary confinement flashed across our minds, and until we could arrest them it was impossible to consider how to avert disaster. But what was to be done? Unless we were to wait for the snake to strike, like a couple of hypnotized rabbits, there were only two possibilities. We could either hide on the ship or leave it immediately. Better leave it. But how? Should we bluff our way through as Swiss? In that case we should have to pass the MP at the head of the gangway with every eye upon us, and besides— But there was no time to think. We had to do something, and quickly. I searched Have's face. We were beyond speech. He had had the same idea as myself. He hailed an Indian youth, whom we loaded with our military haversacks, topis and water-bottles, so as to have as few military trappings about us as possible, and then we made straight for the lower deck and the gangway. The soldiers were thoroughly annoyed at our pig-headed and perverse behaviour. There were shouts from every side to tell us that we had to stay on board, all in perfect good faith; we belonged to their crowd and had to obey orders the same as they had. We forged ahead, undeterred by the indignant clamour, but our boy could not get through and had to stay behind.

And now for the decisive moment.

With all eyes on us, we advanced upon the MP, who was standing there in the light of the arc-lamp. We tried to push past him as though he could not possibly be of interest to us.

"Stop!" he called out, and barred the way. "Didn't you hear me say you were not to leave the boat? Back you go."

"But have civilians to stay on board too?" Have asked with an air of utter indifference.

"What d'you mean? You're Forces, aren't you?"

"Us? We're not soldiers."

"Not soldiers?" he repeated doubtfully.

"Look at our tickets, then," Have said, seized by a sudden inspiration. He produced our ordinary railway tickets. The MP examined them and seemed to be shaken for a moment; he looked us up and down and back at the tickets, and before we knew what had happened the magic words "Pass along" rang in our ears.

The incredible had happened. We had been screened. The odds had been a thousand to one. And yet we had got through. We blessed our stars now that we had never worn any badges of rank. If we had, the change from soldiers to civilians would never have worked. And if we had bought correct uniform in Calcutta we should have been lost.

"Where the devil's that fellow got to with our traps?" I heard Have say at my elbow.

"He's there at the top of the steps to the upper deck. Can't you see him, wedged in between those soldiers?"

"Yes; I see him now. I must go and fetch him."

"Are you crazy?"

But he was off, up the gangway, past the MP, on to the boy, who he took in tow, back past the MP to join me again with our gear, in the best of form. It was a stunt after his own heart; the charm of the situation was too great, and he could not resist going back. Have could indulge himself in such by-play. He was without fear or nerves, and had an unfailing instinct for the narrow margin between what is possible and what is not. I never knew him rattled, and even in the most desperate situations he had a disarming smile on his face as if to say, "Leave it all to me." After the event it always seemed as though he had taken his measures in advance; and when I was at my wits' end, as was often enough the case, I simply left it to him. He would find the way out – and he never failed.

It was only a minute or two's walk from the river bank to the train. The platform was in darkness, and we waited a long time for the train to come in. And still no soldiers came from the boat. We looked for an empty second-class compartment, pushed up the bunks and made ourselves small. But we had chosen badly. More than once members of the station-guard used our compartment as a passageway to the platform beyond. But it was so dark they never saw us. After a time one of the railway staff came along. I got down after he had gone and found he had locked us in, and also chalked up the carriage for officers only. So we climbed out of the window and went to another compartment. We were soon asleep, and when we woke in the morning we were close to Chittagong.

Chittagong is situated on the Bay of Bengal and is the terminus of the South Bengal Railway. It is about 160 miles from the Burmese frontier, and we had to cover those miles before we could strike the Japanese line. The whole borderland between Burma and India, tens of thousands of square miles of mountainous jungle, was open until the war, and formed a refuge for savage tribes, head-hunters, such as the Nagas, among them.

In those days one travelled from Chittagong to Burma by steamer through Cox's Bazaar to Akyab. Now, of course, the steamers had stopped running. The war forced the Allies to build roads and so link those untrodden wilds to the civilized world. We had now come roughly 1,500 miles from the camp and had taken two weeks about it. But henceforth our progress would be slower; we should have to rely on our feet and make use of sampans whenever possible. The whole coastal strip is a maze of waterways which carry most of the indigenous traffic.

Apparently the British had turned Chittagong into a military base; that was the impression it made. There were many African soldiers, huge fellows of unwieldy bulk. The thought of falling into the hands of these monsters in the jungle made us shudder. Our aim was to reach the bazaar, because Have, whose second visit it was, thought he remembered seeing at the far end a landing-stage for sampans, which might ferry us across the wide river on which Chittagong stands. I was astonished to see so little bomb-damage in a place of such military importance. The Japanese air-menace did not seem to have got very far.

We had to wade through mud to reach the sampans, as it was ebb-tide. We made our bargain with one of the boatmen and pushed off. The sun was murderous and the water coiled like molten metal. The boatman plied his oar indolently – we made headway very slowly across the wide river. The whole waterfront of Chittagong could now be seen. On the left towards the open sea, tall wireless-masts rose from among white, one-storied official buildings, next came bungalows sheltered by trees, and then the native town. Barrage balloons hung motionless above.

The sampan entered a backwater which led by twists and turns into the interior. The mouth of it was thickly overgrown with prickly scrub. A few strokes of the oar hid us completely from sight. We let the Indian carry on and then got out at a village, our first object being to get our bearings and reconnoitre the country. We went to a booth where cups of tea were for sale and learned that we were only a mile or two from a road running south. We decided to proceed parallel to this road, but only by night. For the rest of the day we resolved to lie doggo. It was easier said than done. Villages and cultivated ground left no room for cover of any kind. In our search we ranged the country in all directions, with the eyes of the natives on us all the time. At last we came to a few aloes beside a pond and lay down to rest. But our rest did not last long. We heard someone approaching our retreat. It was a wizened old man who, without seeing us, crouched down close beside us to relieve himself. A loud "Hi!" caused him to jump up in a fright, and after staring at us with a gaping, toothless mouth, he limped off as fast as he could go to tell the dreadful story to everyone he met. Soon other Indians approached and eyed the two extraordinary Englishmen from a respectful distance. So we thought it best to be off, and followed a path which led us at last to the bank of a stream, on which many boats were passing to and fro. We hailed one of the boatmen and told him to row in a southerly direction as far as he could go.

The sun was no higher now than the palm-tops; the heat was mitigated. The smooth surface of the water was on the level of the rice-fields and patches of green. Indolently stretched at full length, we glided in our magic gondola over the turquoise blue of the canal. Cows were being driven home along the paths; the smoke of the evening fires curled up from the village; a distant temple-bell pealed. What joy to get out here and let time pass! We forgot all our troubles.

As daylight faded the waterway passed between extensive marshlands. There was a long white building against the dark background of the jungle some distance off. We asked what it was. A police station – the place we were going to, he supposed. This piece of news startled us out of our dreams. But he said he could take us only a short way further; there the canal came to an end. Another boat had just reached the end in front of us and an Indian stepped on to the bank. He proceeded to address us, taking us for the pilots of a machine which had crashed. He told us to go to the police station. They would ring up the airfield and give us all possible assistance. He was going there himself, he said. We did not at all care for this officious gentleman. We pretended we were coming along and then made off, leaving the police station on one side, and going as fast as we could in case the Indian put the sleuths on our trail.

Meanwhile, night had fallen.

We walked on southward by field-paths and roads, and as we had moved about openly by day we thought it wiser now to conceal our tracks as far as possible; and so if any Indians approached we hid behind a bush or in a ditch. We heard them a long way off because the Indian peasant at night, like a child in a wood, talks as loud as he can, or sings to himself if he is alone, to keep evil spirits at bay. It was nervous work going through the villages, where the dogs always barked. We hurried noiselessly along the streets and tried to get by unheard and unobserved. It was a help that the night was as dark as pitch.

At about midnight the road suddenly came to an end at the edge of a broad waterway. We soon had to give up the search for a boat to take us across, as there were huts on all sides and the dogs started barking. We turned back, hoping to strike another road, but found ourselves in a village, where a marriage feast was taking place, one of those occasions when Indians mortgage house and home and all they possess in order to raise money for the celebrations. We looked through a bamboo hedge and saw an open space, where the elder peasants were sitting round a fire and the younger standing together in groups, talking excitedly after drinking too much. We could not find the way out of the village immediately and wandered about between the enclosed gardens. Some of the wedding-guests on their way home must have seen us as we stole along; suddenly a full-throated shout of "Thief! Thief!" burst out close behind us. It was taken up on all sides, and before we knew what was happening the village was in full cry. We shot off as though the first cry had been the starting-pistol for a track-race and gained the open. They were after us, one with an electric torch; but its beam did not reach us. We increased our lead and soon outdistanced the field. When we were at a respectful distance we lay down in a rice-field for a short sleep and left the village to rampage after us in vain.

We had to be on our feet again before the sky was grey, before the Moslem recited his first prayer, in case the peasants might come upon us asleep in the open field. Day follows instantly upon the night in tropical latitudes, and as soon as it is light it is not long before it is hot; so we made use of the coolness of dawn to follow a canal which led us back to the broad waterway of the night before. Here, surrounded by bamboos which rose up like great green sheaves, we found the scattered buildings of a small waterside market. The thatched cottages of sun-baked clay were awake; girls were coming back from the well, carrying pitchers on their heads. The men, with dirty white loincloths round their lean shanks, were squatting on the hard trampled earth at their doors, winding their turbans and smoking their long pipes. A hungry ox was lowing. We met peasant women on their way to the fields, carrying heavy hoes and infants in arms; it is always the women in the East who bear the brunt of the hard labour. We came upon a temple beside a pool, where an aged banyan tree, whose rib-like roots were like the arches of a medieval Gothic church, made a wide roof of shade. The rude effigy of a bull, the symbol of divine creation, could be seen within. A priest was seeing to his laundry in the stagnant and infected water. Peasant women were setting out shallow baskets of fruit and grey rice, in which weevils seemed to be busy, on the shadeless marketplace at the water's edge, and a few men were drinking their morning cup of tea at a booth.

Our appearance caused an immediate sensation. It may have been the first time any Europeans had set foot in the place. We sat down near the men and asked for tea.

An old man, whose face was a network of minute wrinkles and who could speak a little English, spoke for the rest:

"Where do the Sahibs wish to go?"

"To Cox's Bazaar."

"From here?"

"Yes; from here. Tell me – is there a police station here?" Have asked, just to be sure.

"Not in the village. The nearest one is some miles away."

Now we should be able to carry out our plan.

"That's bad. We need help."

"What is it?"

"We must have a boat to take us to Cox's Bazaar."

"That will be difficult," the old man replied. "It takes two days from this village, and a sampan very seldom goes so far. But if the Sahibs used the military road, the Sahibs would be there with a car in a few hours."

"You are not asked to give us advice, but to provide a boat, and quickly too. We have orders from headquarters to proceed to Cox's Bazaar by sampan immediately. Summon the village elder."

"I am he," the old man replied.

"Then I order you to put a sampan and a boatman at our disposal as quickly as you can," Have said.

The old man scratched his head behind his ear to show he was plunged in thought, and muttered something about difficulties and impossibilities before he dispatched a couple of fellows to round up a boatman. It would cost much money, he said.

"Never mind that," I said. "The Army pays, and you shall have your baksheesh too," because that, of course, was what he was after.

We felt almost ashamed to lead these simple people by the nose like this. It was too easy. We could make them dance to any tune once they took us for British officers, for persons of importance too.

By degrees the village had come round us. Dark eyes by dozens regarded us – huge, precocious eyes of children; tormented yet at the same time covetous eyes of men; and from a shy distance, tender, forlorn and velvety eyes of girls. In view of the necessity of impressing the onlookers, we put on the grand airs of stage heroes; and the old man, who also wished to impress the other villagers by his intimacy with us, asked if he might examine the contents of our haversacks. We refused on the excuse that they contained important documents, maps and pistols. He had never yet handled a pistol, he confessed, and wouldn't we make an exception and let him at least look at one of ours. As we had no weapon of any kind, we gave him instead, and with much ceremony, our large electric torch to examine.

A boatman arrived and had first of all to have a long talking-to by the village elder. He was not at all eager to undertake such a long trip. When he finally agreed, Have, with the air of a field-marshal, told the old man to translate his further commands.

"Tell him that we are on an unannounced tour of inspection and that he must not on any account permit himself to mention to anybody that he has two officers on board his sampan."

This was a necessary precaution, because we had noticed how the boatmen always exchanged news when they met on the water. Naturally, having two Europeans on board would be the very first thing our man would talk about.

"For the same reason make sure that the boat is provided with an awning of palm leaves and is provisioned with bananas, eggs and cakes."

The man went off to carry out his orders.

Meanwhile, the village elder told us about the famine, which in recent months had cost several lives even in their village. He spoke of the disaster as he might have done of the weather, something that couldn't be helped and had to be accepted, and about which nothing could be done. The Indian is in the world to suffer, and hunger is only one of the many afflictions flesh is heir to. This explains why the frightful famine in Bengal, as well as in those regions it affected behind the Burma front, did nothing to loosen the British hold on the country.

The boatman arrived at last in his boat. With great pomp and a large escort, like princes up the nave of a cathedral, we proceeded to the sampan, where hands were shaken all round and leave taken. We felt nonetheless relieved when we were water-borne, because in spite of our assumed air of confidence we were secretly apprehensive of a police patrol, or the presence of a spy among the villagers, or some other unpleasant surprise.

A sampan is only a few paces long and just wide enough for two to lie side by side in the bottom. Both ends are blunt. The rower stands on a raised platform at one end and propels the boat by a stroke of his oar, which rests in a fork. He accompanies the stroke by a step forward, throwing in his weight at the same time, after which he returns on the swing to his starting-point.

Our boat was provided with an arched roof of palm leaves, which was so low that it was only just possible to sit upright. We draped the arched openings at bow and stern to conceal ourselves entirely from sight. The floorboards were covered with a thin fibre matting. This tiny space was our refuge for three nights and two days. We might have been stowaways, lying hidden in a ship's boat.

The success of our trip depended entirely on our boatman. If he kept his mouth shut, we might cover a sixty-mile stage of our journey without mishap; there was no reason to fear that boats were being searched; it was too far from the battle-zone for that. We should be discovered only if our man talked to his fellow-boatmen on the way, or if he reported us to some military post or police-station. We treated him therefore as carefully as a new-laid egg, and with all imaginable tenderness, so that even if his suspicions came to be aroused he would feel for us, and not betray us without more ado. He was a dark-skinned South Bengali in his middle forties, sturdy, and Mongolian in feature. He wore a clean black shirt and short, wide breeches and had a decent and reliable look.

On the first day we threaded a labyrinth of waterways such as traverse the land near the coast. As there was much traffic on them, we kept hidden and only took a peep through a spy-hole now and then. We could see nothing as a rule but mud-banks owing to the low level of the water. All these waterways are connected with the sea and are affected by the tides; and at low tide the water sinks almost to the bottom of the channel. There is then not enough water to float even the flat-bottomed sampans, and we often had to wait hours for the tide to turn. We suffered torments during these times of waiting, because there was usually a whole flotilla waiting with us, and we knew how strongly tempted our man must be to reveal the secret of his freight. It was dangerous enough even when he spoke to us. We talked to him in a mixture of English and Hindustani, and that alone would excite the curiosity of his fellow-boatmen. We had promised to reward him handsomely if he held his tongue, but we couldn't believe he would really do so. So at every halt we prayed that he might not betray us and never let him out of our sight. Yet all this was nothing to the heat. The water resembled boiling oil; the mud-banks formed a casket of oozing lead. Lying in a bath of sweat in our crib, we thought we should meet our end from sheer heat.

Once the sampan was in motion again we went along at a good pace; our man was untiring and rowed without a break for hours on end. With each stroke we saw his broad, brown foot slide forward on the plank and approach our heads, and from time to time we heard his long-drawn guttural "O-ay", his warning cry to avoid collisions at the canal junctions. Standing above us against the sky with his yellow head-cloth wound round his forehead, he looked as romantic as a pirate.

By the time the light failed, when the shadow of the earth rose violet-grey above the horizon, we were passing through wide and desolate flats. We tied up beside a grove of horsetail-trees; the boatman lit a fire on which to cook his rice, while we walked about to stretch our legs. Not a sound was to be heard, except the chirp of the cicadas. We slept in the boat.

Next morning we did not look out for quite a time, and when we did it was because the sound of the water slipping past the beam had altered. The even swish of water had changed to the sound of little waves lapping against the side. One look outside explained it: we were on the open sea. On our left at some distance was the sun-warmed, golden sand of the coast with a fringe of palms; on our right we saw a large island. It was Kutubdia. Dark-coloured sampans plied to and fro, and among them glided white-sailed boats. This was indeed the tropic sea, the deep blue islanded-sea, where the many bights and inlets glowed dark sapphire – an archipelago of the blessed.

A junk laden with water-melons passed close beside us. Our boatman gave a shout, and two melons were pitched over to us. Their red flesh quenched our thirst.

At noon we put in at a blue inlet on the coast of Kutubdia. High walls of scrub prevented our setting foot on shore. We had a bathe.

It was a ravishingly lovely scene, but we, harassed by our old worries, had no eyes for the charms of scenery. We were due at Cox's Bazaar that night – that was the overriding, irreducible truth, which obliterated everything else. Have had a horror of that place, near which he had been recaptured on his first escape. If only we could avoid going there! Well – there was a way of doing so, and it was actually within our power. It only meant persuading our boatman to circumnavigate Cox's Bazaar. But would he consent? Should we not by merely proposing it throw ourselves wide open to suspicion? Even now it must seem odd to him that we had not anywhere undertaken any sort of inspection, in spite of the tour we had mentioned.

We consulted our maps. It was possible to by-pass Cox's Bazaar either by going south along the coast, or else by proceeding up the Ramu River, that is inland, to the east. We discarded the idea of the sea passage because of the risk of running into British patrol-boats. But would our man agree to take us up the river? We kept putting off the painful ordeal of making the suggestion, and it was dusk before we took the plunge. To our great relief, he agreed without hesitation, though it is true his pay was raised by twenty-five rupees to seventy-five, which was unprecedented for a few days' work, and a temptation he could scarcely ask himself to resist. Or were his high earnings possibly not the real reason of his instant consent? Perhaps he only wished by lapping us in false security to prevent us getting out somewhere before Cox's Bazaar, where he would not be able to inform on us. Originally we had agreed that the first glimmer of suspicion in his mind would be revealed by a refusal to take us further; now the very opposite suddenly dawned on our minds; namely, that immediate compliance with our wishes gave grounds for drawing the gravest conclusions. We now feared that Cox's Bazaar would indeed prove fatal a second time. We searched the face of our Bengali to see if it betrayed any kind of emotion. No; his oar alone seemed to concern him. We lay down to sleep, resigned to the truth – that it was idle to attempt to rob the future of its secrets, and consoled by the doctrine that "not a blow can fall on a man which is not predestined." *Inshallah*.

It was already fiercely hot when we woke up. The sun beat down on us. The sampan was tied up and rocked on the oily water in a huddle of other boats. The hubbub of busy life and much traffic met our ears. We lay in the sampan-pool of Cox's Bazaar. Our boatman had put in during the night without our knowing, and now he was squatting with an abstracted air on shore in front of his boat. Our first thought, that he had informed the police already, was not borne out by further reflection; if he had, the police would have acted on his information without the loss of a moment. There was therefore no immediate cause for fear. We summoned him and told him to buy us some provisions, and he soon came back with what we wanted. We now felt quite safe in our hiding-place among all the other native boats, and felt no grudge against the boatman for having put in there.

Our feeling of security dwindled as we proceeded up river, and the signs that we were entering a zone of military activity increased. African soldiers with arms at the slope were posted on a bridge beneath which we had to pass. A string of petrol-tankers passed over it. More and more aeroplanes were seen, many flying low over our heads as though they were either about to land or had just taken off. It began to look a bit tricky.

It is only about six miles from Cox's Bazaar to Ramu, but we made very slow headway. The water was low, only a thin trickle between the mud-banks, and we had several times to make a halt. Moreover, our man seemed to have lost all his old zest. He leaned slackly on his oar and any excuse was good enough for a pause.

We now saw our first aerodrome; a machine roared along the runway. Others came into view on both sides of the narrow stream. There were planes under camouflage-netting among palms and bamboos, with some huts near by.

We made a long stop at a bend in the river. The boatman started cooking his rice. We watched him closely. His eyes wandered anxiously to and fro, and once we caught a strange look on his face. Aha – it was dawning on him. He knew that there was something wrong about us. We tried to guess his thoughts. If he informed on us, he might perhaps get a reward, but would lose his pay and bring all sorts of difficulties on his own head. If he did nothing, he would be sure of his handsome pay, but he would be involved in whatever we might be up to; that we were escaped German prisoners would certainly never cross his mind. But some danger he might suspect, and how he acted would depend on how great he thought the danger might be.

"Come on. Get going."

Reluctantly he took to the oar.

The sun was low by now. The planes were returning from their sorties. A fine haze hung over the water. And now the end came. He would not for any money go any further.

"I am afraid of the Gurkhas—"

"But there aren't any here."

"There are in Ramu. I know it."

So he had come down on the side of silence, and therefore on ours.

"Here," he said, pointing to the bank. "You could get out here. I shall wait for the dark."

We got our traps together, paid our trusty servant, and when it grew dusk waded ashore through the shallow water. The sampan turned about, and a few rapid strokes of the oar took it out of sight.

Chapter Six

INTO THE JUNGLE

It was black night. We could see nothing. We were panting from our hurried scramble up the bank, and the blood hammered in our temples. Once on the level ground we paused a moment, not knowing what was in front of us, and then walked gingerly on. A few steps and we dropped – lights flashed out ahead of us. We lay flat and felt the ground: it was hard and as though trodden firm. Next, a short sharp challenge, answered by someone behind us. Then silence.

Had we come on a post? We felt we were on a flat and open space with danger ambushed all round. Silently, with many pauses, we wriggled forward.

Stop! My foremost hand touched something; it was metal – a wire cable. We crept cautiously past it. I put my face close to the soil. But it wasn't soil. It was lime. I was halfway across a wide white line. This turned suspicion to certainty. We realized with horror that we were on an Allied aerodrome.

We consulted in whispers whether to go on or go back to the river. It was all one. Any moment searchlights might turn night into day and make us a target for bewildered sentries. There was no cover on that flat surface, no escape. We should be sitting ducks and surrounded by marksmen. What was needed was a night-landing.

The possibility that this might happen cut short our deliberations. The first thing was to follow the white line and hope that it would show us the quickest way across. We chanced a few short rushes, crouching low as we ran, before throwing ourselves flat to listen.

Then suddenly – like a murderer from a trap-door – a dark figure stood motionless in front of us and only a few paces away. Sweat broke out on my forehead. I jumped to the conclusion that he had seen us lying there and was surveying us, uncertain what to do. When he gave a shout in English to someone nearby, I naturally thought he was summoning reinforcements. Then he bent forward as though to see better. It needed all my strength to lie still; all I wanted to do was to stand up and surrender, merely to end the unbearable tension.

The man who had been summoned came along – but it had nothing to do with us. It was about a jeep, in which they were both going off somewhere. Once again I had seen ghosts. Fortunately, the jeep's lights were not turned in our direction when the two switched on and drove off. Much relieved, we pursued our way. What a difference between walking and crawling across an aerodrome! We were more dead than alive when we finally arrived at the farther side, where we passed what appeared to be workshops, with Indian sentries on the prowl. Our exhaustion was so great that indifference had set in – we hadn't the strength for fresh sensations. We took our last fences in a haphazard style, and with a sigh of relief left the hideous place behind us.

We next found ourselves in a marsh, where we sank to our knees, but waded on towards the vast black silhouette of the forest, blocked out against the sky. When we reached dry land we struck into the jungle and climbed a low, thickly-wooded hill, where we lay down, dirty and done-in.

We were in the heart of a patch of jungle which covered a chain of low hills and was so dense and luxuriant that we lay hidden like wild game beneath a roof of leaves almost impervious to the light of day. Lianas were looped high above our heads from branch to branch; feathery tree-ferns nestled in the forks of tall trees and themselves harboured tufts of pendulous grasses, and through a gap in the tent of greenery a palm-frond swayed in the upper air. Large ants were busy in the mouldering leaves on the ground, and lizards were darting from place to place. The wind brought the distant sound of engines from the aerodrome, and at our feet lay the marshy ground projecting like a tongue into the forest-land of which our little eminence was only a tiny outpost.

Our plan was to spend the days in hiding and to venture out only in the dark, and to keep to this plan for our future movements – age-old tactics of all night-birds who rely on the veil of darkness and sleep to cover doings which cannot bear the light of day.

We also agreed that we should never get any further if we had to find our own way through the jungle. There was bound to be some road to the front from Cox's Bazaar or Ramu, and this would be invaluable in giving us our direction. But why should it not do more? Why not make actual use of it? It would be far the quickest way to our goal. We would travel by night, taking care only to avoid the traffic, not because we had anything to fear, but because we should undoubtedly be offered a lift and be put down at some HQ or other, where we should certainly have no desire to be.

We set off at dusk, and first went to a water-hole at the edge of the marsh before plunging into the forest. We had just emerged on to a mule-track when we heard voices and saw two women talking as they came along with pitchers on their heads. They made a charming picture against the dark gold background of the west, and their saris fell in graceful folds as they stepped lightly over the ground. As soon as they saw us they broke off in terror, and ran away screaming. Not Pan himself could have given them a greater fright. Even we caught the infection, and after dashing on to the water-hole to fill our bottles stampeded back into the forest.

A narrow path led deeper and deeper into its dark recesses along the bottom of a phantasmal gorge, on the sides of which trees of gigantic size towered up. Their tops met for long stretches to form a roof far above our heads, through which we could only rarely see a star. In the under-growth rotting branches gave out a ghastly yellow phosphorescence. Now and then there was a crack; then a whistling. Behind every bush lurked some ambushed terror. Fireflies danced their spookish rounds, flaring up and dying down. The thought of being fallen upon haunted the mind continually in this black pit of darkness. Now and then a pair of green eyes glinted. Was it a tiger, perhaps a man-eater? And when was it going to spring? But probably there was no big game in this bit of forest. We had to reckon with the chance of meeting a tiger on our nightly treks, but the prospect did not greatly worry us, because tigers very rarely attack human beings; as a rule they avoid them.

We must have followed this forest track for hours before it brought us into an open clearing, where we found a lonely village. We asked one of the inhabitants where the nearest soldiers were. He could not understand us, but went to a hut in which several men, clothed only with loin-cloths, were squatting on the ground, one of whom spoke a few words of Hindustani. The glow of some embers showed a strange race of men – small, dark, flat-nosed and curly-haired. They must have been a pygmy breed, one of the primitive tribes who still live in the depths of the forest. All we could make out was that there was a road at about an hour's distance, on which there was much military traffic.

Sure enough, at about midnight, we struck a wide, unmetalled road running in a white strip through the dark jungle. This, in the heart of the wilderness, was the channel which carried the whole volume of the enemy's activity. We approached it therefore with caution, keeping a look-out on all sides as though snipers might be waiting to pick us off at sight. But after making sure, we boldly took possession and stepped out, taking cover only when a distant gleam or noise warned us of an approaching vehicle.

Once a passing car lit up a market ahead of us, and Have, who had taken on the delicate task of quartermaster, decided to buy our next day's rations there. Most villages have some little shop where cups of tea can be bought until all hours of the night. Our intention was to make our purchases late in the evening, so that we could vanish at once into the darkness. On this occasion Have returned empty-handed, which meant tight belts for the next twenty-four hours.

We held on along the road until the first signs of dawn, and then took to the jungle to find a refuge for the day. It was the moment when light first shows in the east, and in an instant we were witnesses of the glory of Buddha, the rayed fan which every morning is flashed over the earth. For the moment all was dark; nature held its breath; nothing moved, not a sound was heard. But even then the forest emerged in phantom shapes and pale, cool-shadowed masses, and on the world's edge a faint blush was swallowed in a sea of gold, barred by azure cloud, from which streamed the fan-shaped glory of the sun, with an escort of delicate feathery pink clouds. A few moments later the forest was bathed in the full light of day.

We found that it was simply impossible to sleep by day. Dog-tired after our night-march, we could not even close our eyes; we listened to every sound, took the rustle of a snake for stalking footsteps, imagined ourselves watched by unseen eyes, and behaved, in short, like victims of persecution mania. As we had come upon a patch where the foliage was thin, we had to roast in the sun, and could hardly wait for it to go down. But no sooner had it set than we felt the utmost reluctance to abandon the relative security of our hiding-place. Now at last sleep might come to us, and it was all we could do not to lie on where we were. Every night it cost us a frightful moral effort to break camp.

We were on the road again by dark, and at first it was not too good; we had only gone a short way when some English soldiers passed so close that we almost brushed against them. They could tell from our shape that we were not Indians, and were so much taken aback by the encounter that they abruptly stopped talking. This was only a warning of what we had to expect, so we made off as fast as we could and took to the jungle for the time. But even there it was not much better; we suddenly heard a buzzing and humming close beside us in the forest, as if an electric motor was running. The forest seemed to be bewitched. We quickly discovered that we had come upon a sort of van, in which machinery of some kind was installed.

We returned to the road, feeling very uneasy. It soon led through an open space where the forest had been cleared on either side. Lights shone out at the farther end; but before we came to these signs of habitation, tents appeared on both sides of the road, with lorries parked among them, and there were also some huts. We were in the middle of an Army camp. Motor transport approached from the village and the headlights threw a faint illumination on the road we marched along. There was no cover; but then we saw that on each side of the road there were coffin-like excavations, from which the soil had been taken to build up the road. We quickly dropped into one of these, resolved to remain there until the camp calmed down. But if we had really been in the grave and a clay-cold hand had touched us, we could not have been more horrified than we were when an Indian soldier crossed by the small partition left between our grave and the next. He only had to look down to see us showing up against the light-coloured earth. With our hair on end and pulses racing, we took to our heels through a gap between the tents and crept away from the camp. We got away unobserved and recovered our breath in a plantation of sugar-canes.

We made a wide circle round the camp and got back on to the road, which went straight on across a wide, open expanse. The night was clear and the sky so brilliant with the flash and twinkle of stars that it might have been a firework display; the numerous shooting stars trailed fire behind them like comets; and as each flashed across the sky we wished the wish that our adventure might have a happy ending. The cool breath of night gave wings to our feet, but we should have got along even faster if we had not had to drop into those wretched graves each time some motor-vehicle passed. We were all over scratches and dirt.

We were in the heart of the vegetable kingdom, surrounded by growing things. There were tall trees soaring up smooth and straight to overtop the level of the forest; lianas coiled around their cement-grey trunks and fell in hanging baskets of green. Then there were the trees of medium height and thick-leafed foliage, which with bamboos and an occasional palm were the real substance of the forest. Then came a tangle of black-branched, twisted scrub, and a riot of parasitic growths which might have been brought together as an exhibition of priceless orchids. Close to the ground were large twayblades on thin, slender stalks.

We fancied we had this dumb and noiseless company to ourselves, but soon learned our mistake. The sun had scarcely risen when we heard a crackling sound in the undergrowth, followed by the ringing strokes of an axe. We were close to some men felling trees and they felled their way slowly towards us. Before long we saw the crowns of tall trees crash through the branches. We had to move, and spent the whole day in a continual and nerve-racking migration from one resting-place to another. Every time we lay down in a bower of ferns and broad, shady leaves we were hunted out. However hard we tried to get away, it was no use; the tree-fellers had made a complete ring round us. So we had to lie close and suffer the pangs of the hunted even during our hours of rest. Sleep was out of the question.

Evening found us once more on the military road, which now traversed dense forest. The sky was obscured by cloud, and the road, of which we could see nothing at all, pitch-black. The night, fraught with secrecy and menace, seemed to promise no good. We hurried noiselessly through the dark on rubber soles. All round, the silence of death. With shattering suddenness – it went through us like a knife – something sprang from the undergrowth at our side and shouted, "Stop!" The ambush was so utterly unexpected that in the first shock we involuntarily walked on without noticeably quickening our pace. Then we heard the click of a safety-catch being released, but it was too dark to see anything against the black wall of the forest. A second challenge followed. Then a third. But we did not stop even now. We instinctively kept going, I can't explain why, and retreated into the darkness. No shot was fired.

"I say," I whispered to Have when we were round the next bend, "are you tired of life?"

"Not yet."

"Nor am I. So next time we'd better stop when we're told."

"You're right. We were being too casual. By the way, that was an Indian, I fancy."

"Then we'll tell the next one to get out of our way."

"What do they want a sentry here for?"

"Another camp, perhaps."

I was right.

The jungle on the right-hand was alive with troops. Fires could be seen blazing through the grid of branches, and we heard horses snorting and stamping.

We had gone a few paces further when once more a figure leapt at us out of the dark, and with a tremendous bound and a shout of "Halt!" planted his bayonet within an inch of my stomach.

"We are Sahibs, you idiot," I said, and to prove it shone my torch on Have and myself.

He muttered confused excuses and at once let us pass.

"You see, there's that way too," I said as we walked on, much consoled. "Getting past sentries is only a trick."

Our existence was one of destitution and abandonment; the very life we lived was upside down. We had exchanged night for day, and we wandered about in the wild, utterly unequipped to meet its many dangers, unarmed and unprovisioned. Uncertainty, or rather flat ignorance, had become our native element. We never found anything to go by, no fixed quantity or measure on which to base any calculations. It was very seldom we had any accurate idea of where we were, and even when we did identify some locality, its position in relation to our final goal was merely guesswork, if only because this, unfortunately, was itself as yet unknown. Our enterprise was now in its fourth week, and how long it would go on, whether it would succeed at all, where the next step would lead us, what the next second would bring forth, were always uncertain. The only certainty was that we had always to be ready for the unexpected; perhaps for the final blow; at any rate, for the unknown. We had undergone such a revolution that the surprising thing was a matter of course, whereas the usual was the surprise. Anything normal put us on our guard: the unexpected was quite in order.

Our notion of time was also distorted. Time had become spasmodic, hectic, and went by fits and starts. Sudden entries of the unforeseen cut into that ordered succession of minutes and hours by which life as a rule is lived. Events were packed into breath-taking moments, between which there were long tormenting pauses, empty stretches of time. We waited tensely for the lightning-like irruption, and then the tension and the haunting dread were renewed.

Any moment might drain our last resources. And this meant that reason had to give way to instinct; we relied on hitherto unsuspected reactions and reflexes. If we had stopped to deliberate, the first predicament would have been our last. This was no doubt the reason for the extraordinary unanimity with which we faced accidents we had had no chance of discussing beforehand. In such cases instinct takes over.

These continual onsets of the unforeseen would have proved too much for us if nature had not come to our help by an unloading apparatus of its own. By this means the experience of a moment before was removed into the past, and so lost its crippling after-effect. We had not gone twenty steps from the sentries on the road before they were out of our heads and forgotten. And, secondly, we grew less sensitive to danger; as our circumstances grew more dangerous, they seemed to us less formidable, and the strongest excitement lost its stimulus when it was repeated. The first army vehicle was an event; the next was scarcely noticed. We took the necessary action automatically. If we had had to cross a second aerodrome, it would have been almost a matter of routine.

Our new camping-place gave us a view in all directions. As far as the eye could see, forest and jungle extended in wave after wave in the flickering air, and on the right, imagined rather than seen, there was the remote blue streak of the Bay of Bengal. The cultivated patches were mere gaps in the jungle, soon to be overrun and greedily swallowed up if they could not defend themselves. Far to the south a range of mountains floated in the blue haze.

It was the hottest hour of the day. The country lay prostrate, hypnotized by excess of light; the sun, its merciless enemy, blazed down with fury. The air quivered, the leaves were turned each one into green, mock looking-glasses, every exposed surface was surfeited with light. The eyes ached from the glare. To breathe was difficult. All movement was abolished. A brooding oppression seemed to fill the very air itself. All nature was in a lethargy.

We were thirsty. Our supply of water for the day was restricted at most to two water-bottles. It had better have been two buckets. We were therefore compelled to ration it, and every hour we took an agreed number of sips. If the other was not looking, one quickly took a few extra. The result was that by midday we had not a drop left and were tortured by thirst. We yearned for the next village, where we could renew our supplies, not only of water, but of food, which for some days had consisted chiefly of fruit.

The military road had given us many unpleasant surprises, and we should have been glad now to leave it; but there was no other way of getting through the country, and so we continued to make use of it by night.

The first pale light of dawn had shown us a horrifying sight. The outlines of a full-scale military establishment were gradually revealed.

We, poor wretches, were in an acute angle formed by two roads; one was our military road, on which we looked down from a distance of only a few yards. The other passed behind us and gave a perfect view of our hiding-place, because the bushes on that side were low and scattered. But as if that were not enough, the military road debouched on to a wide, open space, on which supplies of all sorts were dumped; and beyond were sheds on the bank of a canal. A placard could be seen with the words "Transport Centre" painted on it. So there we were, in a supply and reinforcement centre. Even that was not all; there was an ack-ack battery on a steep hill on the far side of the open square. Sikhs, who manned it, were clearly visible behind a wall of sandbags. Just above us, too, there was a post, which was manned.

The whole place gradually came to life. Coolies were first on the scene, carrying coal and stacking it in the open; they worked all day. Next we heard the beat of marching feet, and a battalion of Gurkhas in battle order marched to the waterside, where a paddle-boat, which had arrived meantime, took them on board. Troops who had previously dis-embarked from it were now marching along the road in the opposite direction. They were so close to us we could have counted the hairs on their heads. Later British and Indian soldiers, attached, presumably, to the Transport Centre, were to be seen. From then onwards there was never a moment's peace. It was particularly nasty whenever a car drove past on the road at our rear. If anyone had glanced in our direction, it would have been all up.

So this was the hornets' nest in which we had planted ourselves the night before – after we had marched along the military road and found abundant indications that we were once more approaching a camp, and one that must extend a long way. What with crossing open spaces, creeping past sentries and wearisome circumventions, we only arrived at the quay, where the road abruptly ended, shortly before sunrise, and we could neither cross the water nor venture to explore along the nearer bank in case daylight might surprise us in the open. So we had to retreat, and with speed, because it would soon be day. We hurriedly climbed a hill and found a place to hide among the bushes – the very hiding-place in which we now were.

It was out of the question to stand up, or even to sit up, throughout the entire day. There we had to lie as still as mice without a change of position, while the sun beat down as though it meant to roast us alive. We still had as a last resort a tin of Australian ham, and we opened it to appease our almost cannibal hunger. It was good ham, but so salty that it could hardly be got down without plenty of water, of which we had not one single drop. All the same, we had to eat the lot, once the tin was opened, whatever the effect on our thirst, because it would not have kept in the heat, and also for fear of dogs.

Our thoughts reflected the state we were in.

We thought, for example, that if we were caught the British would instantly try us as spies, as had happened to Have and his former partner merely because they had been captured at Cox's Bazaar, the whole of which had been declared a military zone. They had been cross-examined with the utmost severity for six days on end in the Red Fort of Delhi before they were able to establish their innocence. And what wouldn't the British say now if they caught us red-handed just behind the line in the very heart of their support and supply system! Painful as these reflections were, they had their good side. They made us doubly cautious and forced us to stake all on getting through.

Time seemed to stand still, as it always does in critical situations, and we counted the minutes until we could leap up like two springs which had long been compressed. Our plan was to advance upon the canal, as soon as darkness fell, to see whether it might not be possible to get along the bank. Should it not prove possible, we should have to return through the whole Centre and then by-pass it.

All days come to an end, and so did even this one.

We then left our cover and crept down the slope, where there were concealed strong-points in all directions. When we finally reached the quay we found marshy ground on both sides of it, and so had to face the alarming retreat.

It was not easy to find our way back through the Centre in the darkness, and we made rapid progress only when a mob of drunken Tommies staggered past us and we were inspired to fall in behind them. When crossing a lighted space we had to stagger too, to show that we were drunken stragglers. The way those fellows talked was beyond description. One of them wished to take the life of some cook or other and heaped him with expressions which were not just the limit, but well beyond it. Our Bacchanalian escort did not take us far. A halt was made for a song, in which we did not see fit to join.

When we were once more outside the place, we decided to go back to the nearest village, Gundum Bazaar, and there buy a good stock of provisions; after which, instead of starting on our outflanking march, we would find a hide-out and spend the rest of the night there. We had, in fact, changed our plan and wanted to husband our strength for the next day, which was to see the execution of a great exploit.

Breakfast next morning was a strange combination; it consisted of sweetened lemon-juice and a tin of butter. We had come on both at Gundum Bazaar, and it was a pound tin of butter, which we consumed without any accompaniment, just as it was. We followed up the repast by shaving in the rest of the lemon-juice, putting on our reserve shirts, and thoroughly cleaning our shoes with bunches of grass. After which we rose from the jungle in the guise of two smartly turned out Englishmen and awaited a favourable moment for stepping briskly out on to the road.

We had spent two nights in the vain attempt to emerge from the camp, and it seemed equally impossible to outflank its vast extent of strong-points, depots and fortified positions. We had therefore to adopt the extremely rash plan of walking straight through to the quay in broad daylight and mingling with any troops who might be embarking by water for the front. It was a risky but speedy way of reaching Burma. Now that it came to carrying out this plan, we did not at all like the look of it. But that was no help; zero-hour had come and off we had to go.

We got on to the road unobserved, at a point where one or two bends still parted us from its junction with the other one. At first nothing happened. We kept walking on, even though rather numbly, until we came to the last bend, after which we should have a clear view along the military road. But no sooner had we rounded it than we wished the earth would swallow us up. At the road junction stood – an MP.

He saw us at once. There was no turning back. We were about eighty yards from him. Have was walking behind me, and I remarked in an undertone that the fellow would open his eyes even wider if he knew that we were German internees. But I only got a growl of reproval in reply. As we walked on I experienced the now familiar sensation of walking to meet my fate. With suspended breath, an inner vacancy, and legs of lead I propelled myself forward like a condemned man to the place of execution. Twenty steps to go. Fifteen. Then at the last moment the reprieve. A lorry came down the military road and took the MP's attention off just at the critical moment. He held it up and asked the Indian driver for his pass. Making use of this diversion, we slipped by when his back was turned.

Once more chance was trumps, and in defiance of all rational expectation we had cheated certain disaster. Gundum Bazaar now ranked with Lucknow and Chandpur. In each place we had had incredible luck, without making any contribution of our own. The intervention from outside had come just when our need was greatest. It was tempting to believe that we had got into what is known as "a run of luck". But we were in a situation where even luck is little consolation. It might get us up one rock-face, but at once we saw the next one tower above us, and trembled and shivered and swore and saw no end to our troubles.

So it was now. We had next to run the gauntlet of the whole Transport Centre, which was in full activity. Motor vehicles of every sort and size drove to and fro; parties of Indian soldiers advanced to meet us; British soldiers were to be seen on every side. Two privates, stripped to the waist, strolled past without paying us the slightest atten-tion; but later there was one who followed us with a searching look. Once a major came along on the other side of the road, and for sheer terror we dared not raise our eyes. Lucky thing, I thought, that saluting isn't taken too seriously near the front line. By now we had reached the middle of the camp. There was a sentry-box there, and in it a British as well as an Indian MP; they were talking and scarcely noticed us. Next we passed a canteen where tea was issued free. We had our water-bottles filled and bought cigarettes. Finally, we got to the quay in good order. But, far and wide, no troops awaiting transport, no paddle-boat, not even a sampan, were to be seen. We thought we would wait a bit, and meanwhile discovered that on the right-hand side of the quay there were a few planks – unobserved by us in the night – leading over ditches to the narrow dyke on the edge of the water. Waiting about became uncomfortable after a time, but we stuck it out until the approach of two officers forced us to beat a hasty retreat. Now the dyke came in handy. We crossed it with the embarrassing feeling of being observed from the rear, and at last found a few bushes behind which we could take cover. Once there, we decided that as we had now found a way out of the camp we would abandon our original plan and not embark with reinforcements for the front, but make our way there unaided and alone.

For two hours we lay on the mud in the mid-day heat; and then at last a sampan came gliding by with a few naked fellows on board. We hailed it and were put across. On the other side the profoundest peace reigned. Military activity was confined to a few points and to strategic roads.

By our estimate it was still a good thirty miles to the front; or to Maungdaw, which was over the frontier of Burma and the goal we strove to reach. The famous road to But Hidaung, often mentioned in the communiqués, because it was so fiercely contested, ran from there. Our dream was to cross this road; Japanese troops were bound to be close to it. We had not the vaguest notion of what was going on in any other part of the front.

We had now tumbled on a perfectly simple method of avoiding British military stations. We first enquired of the natives where the nearest one was to be found and pretended to be making for it. Then at the last moment we would turn aside. There was the further advantage that the natives could not then doubt our military vocation. We now learned that there was nothing to fear in the direction in which we were heading.

Towards evening we came on another vast and forbidding expanse of jungle. Wild and unkempt, the taller trees flaunted their creeper-hung tops above the dark mass of the forest and against the sulphurous light of the sky.

It was night when we reached a village.

The black huts seemed to crouch among the trees and bushes, and only a few of the doors showed a flickering light from their hearths. We wanted to know how we were to get to Nihla, the next place of any size on our route, and entered one of the huts to make enquiries. As we called out our Salaam we heard the clatter of ankle-rings – a sign that the women had hurriedly withdrawn to the back of the dwelling. An Indian, whose forehead had red and white caste-marks on it, whose face was gloomy, fanatical and dark-skinned, shot with a leaden pallor, informed us curtly that the path to Nihla was impassable by night. We had apparently interrupted him in a ritual ceremony; he turned away at once to some sacrificial vessels he had set out and dipped the tips of his fingers in a bowl, in which flowers from a temple-pond were floating. As we had no choice, we set off to follow the path in spite of his warning. We had to pass through the middle of the village on our way out, and found there too the symptoms of some mysterious disorder. Figures, some female, flitted past, a hoarse murmur of voices was audible, as well as the dull but flagellant rhythm of music on one note, accompanied by the clapping of hands. Then a song burst forth, which, now loud, now soft, rose occasionally to an ecstatic yell, intended apparently to drown the urgent cries uttered by another single voice. The place was sinister. It had a bad atmosphere, as though its inhabitants had retreated into the wilderness to practise dreary, hideous rites.

The trials of our pitch-black path soon began. Almost immediately we had a long, foot-wide bamboo bridge to cross without a hand-rail. It switched so wickedly that it made you dizzy, and in the middle threw you into the spasmodic twitchings of a dervish. After that we had still to walk the tight-rope of narrow dyke-tops, off which we continually slid into tepid mud. Suddenly behind me I heard a throttled outcry and a watery gurgling. I turned round. Have had gone. In his place I saw a ghostly light rising from the ground. That was where he must be. He had fallen into a hole and was up to his head in water. In his fall he had not only dropped his torch, but switched it on, and was now illumined by it from the ground. It was some time before I could haul him out and it cost us a quarrel, because I could not smother my laughter. Then we stumbled on barefoot and short-tempered along this knife-edge of clay, which was sometimes soft and greasy and sometimes as hard as glass. On our left was a stretch of water with scrub-covered banks, and on our right the black sloughs of a desolate marsh. Frequently we were arrested by a bubbling of water at our feet; that was where the dam had burst. At last we got through on to dry ground and had a rest behind a haystack. I had had enough and voted for a sleep; but as we were close to native huts Have insisted on our carrying on. I groused at this and angrily led off at a tremendous pace. Have said nothing, but kept close at my heels. And soon the laugh was on his side, when I pitched head over heels into a ditch owing to the pace I was going, and could not speak for rage. I had smashed a hole in my water-bottle, which was now useless. After this we were reconciled and resumed our journey in good humour, and, coming to a hut which showed a light, we went in, hoping to buy food; but a man was lying sick and uttered such a piercing yell at the sight of us, whom he took for the demons he may have been expecting, that we quickly ran out. Finally, we climbed up a steep hill, on the very top of which under a very large tree we made our camp for the day.

A sudden change of weather followed, bringing torrents of rain. Although in India the monsoon sets in at the earliest around the middle of June, in this region, which lies on the edge of the zone of the world's heaviest rainfall, there are heavy downpours before that. Our tree could afford us only brief protection and then let its overflow patter down on our heads. We were soon soaked to the skin and stood hour after hour in the rain, until we began to shiver in spite of the high air-temperature.

When the clouds lifted we made an exciting discovery from our hill-top. Burma, the long-desired end of our wanderings, lay on the other side of the Naaf River, which here had the width of an arm of the sea. The Naaf was the frontier. Running from north to south, it makes a narrow peninsula which has the sea on the west. Maungdaw is opposite the southern point of the peninsula, which is still in India and on which we now were.

The sight of the hills on the further shore gave us a complacent feeling. We had broken all records by getting within sight of them. No member of the camp had done as much. But we had no illusions; the most difficult stage was still ahead of us. Our problems would multiply with every step, and the outcome remained as painfully uncertain as on the day we had set out.

We got off in good time because, with our purchases to make, we did not want to get to Nihla too late at night. Our course led south along the peninsula. The Naaf was on our left, and a range of hills, densely forested, which formed the spine of the peninsula and hid the sea from view, was on our right. There on the ocean side we assumed there would be a military road, whereas here along the narrow strip bordering the river there was only a rough track.

By degrees hunger was becoming a major concern. Since we left Calcutta we had not really had a proper meal. We were not as fit as we had been; we tired quickly and were showing signs of wilting. So we were out after food like jackals, and searched all the villages for what we could find. After a long search we now rounded up a couple of eggs, which we swallowed raw on the spot. All the natives had to offer besides were mangoes, an oval fruit with a large stone and orange-coloured flesh, very juicy and delicious in spite of a flavour of turpentine. Of these there were plenty, as it was the season for them.

We lost our way before reaching Nihla. Night surprised us in a large morass which lies in front of the village. Once involved, we found it incredibly difficult to find our way out again; and if we had not swum a backwater we might never have done so. With all this it was midnight by the time we got to Nihla's bazaar, too late to find any shops open.

We had to be cautious here, because there were soldiers in the place; nevertheless, we knocked up one of the shopkeepers, who had light showing through the chinks of his shutters. He was having a party, and invited us to try his rice-wine, but we wanted nothing but solid nourishment, and asked him for biscuits and bananas.

While we were talking, a young Indian came out of the darkness at the back into the light of the shop. He listened to what we were saying in silence for a time, and then when the shopkeeper went out to fetch some things for us he addressed us in fluent English. He first introduced himself in flattering terms as the man on whose shoulders the war-effort of the whole district rested; it was he who got everything the Army wanted, and he had many friends at headquarters. We had not the least objection to make to all that; but what pleased us less was when he

101

wanted to know, without in the least disguising the suspicion in his curiosity, to whom he had the honour of speaking. He had never seen us anywhere, he added, and yet he knew every Englishman in the neighbourhood – we must surely be strangers to these parts?

"Certainly we are," I said casually, and thought of the impression our wretched state must be making – we were covered in mud and wearing gym-shoes.

"Have you billets anywhere?" he persisted.

"We came in a boat and are on the way to Gundum Bazaar," Have replied, evasively.

"I have not seen any boat come in. Odd—"

"Look here, my friend, you need not poke your nose into matters that don't concern you."

"I only wanted to be of assistance to you."

"We don't need your help. You can clear out. Off with you. Go to bed."

He drew back a step or two and then stood still.

"If you don't make yourself scarce, we'll take you off in the boat."

He grinned at that and withdrew.

We had only been able to procure a few bananas, for which we paid. We then hurried off. The Indian's behaviour was altogether too menacing. Our aim now was to reach the safety of the jungle, where we should not be the object of investigations. But to reach it we had to traverse the whole of Nihla, and had not gone many yards before we found we were followed by someone who flashed a torch in our direction. It could only be our Indian friend, but to make sure I flashed my torch towards him. It was he all right. We quickened our pace, and so did he. We stopped. He stopped too.

"Let's go up to him," I said softly to Have.

"Right."

The man retreated, and then dogged us again as soon as we walked on.

"I'll lie in wait for him and land him one on the jaw," I suggested.

"Splendid idea. We shall never get rid of him otherwise."

There was a bank down on the left of the road and a shed on the right. We stood behind the corner of the shed and waited. The Indian came on, suspecting nothing, and as he drew level I met him with a hook to the chin, which in the darkness rather missed fire. Have then hustled him across the road before he knew what had happened and pitched him down the bank on the other side.

He gave a yell as he went, and we had to take to our heels with all speed. We ran past a wire fence behind which we heard mules sneezing. We climbed over and ran between the stables and found ourselves on another road on the far side, which as we very soon discovered led to a camp on the edge of the jungle. We were now involved in a difficult night-exercise among concealed strong-points, trenches and barbed wire on the slopes of the hills, all of which we successfully negotiated, and then, owing to our spot of trouble with the Indian, carried on for a good bit farther, until at last, utterly fagged out, we lay down to sleep beside a stream.

We lived the life of the hunted, and even in this region of the blessed, where every corner seemed to open on a new paradise, we had no rest. And now the sparkling freshness of the morning suggested serene contemplation and the enjoyment of nature. There was not a cloud in the radiant blue of the sky, arched above a stretch of country, wild enough, and yet as idyllic as an enchanted garden, where small groves of palm gave place to reedy pools and then to great forest-gorges and rocky amphitheatres. Although we had had scarcely two hours' rest, we did not delay. Keeping to the fringe of the jungle, we avoided paths and all signs of habitation.

We carried on until midday, when the jungle edged us up to the bank of the Naaf. A wood-cutters' path leading through low bush, often crossed by wide streams over which large dragonflies darted, brought us after a longish march to some huts thatched with yellow sedge. We asked at one of them for water and fruit, which an old man said he would bring out to us. As we went out, meaning to wait on the path, we saw a patrol of Indian soldiers at the entrance to the village. We jumped up and took cover behind the hedge and made for the shelter of the jungle. But the old man came after us with a jar of water in his hands, and the faster we went the faster he came tottering after us. Thirst won the battle with fear, and we ran to meet him and then took to our heels. On the other side of the village there was one of those swaying bridges, made of undressed tree-trunks, which rose to the middle of the stream and then sank to the other side. Without the help of a little Indian boy, who put his bare feet behind ours to prevent us slipping back, we should never have got across.

The rest of the day and half the night were spent crossing backwaters and having hair-breadth escapes in the crossing of bridges. It began to rain, and we saw sheet lightning on the Burma side. There were distant growls of thunder. We were completely all-in and suffered horribly from hunger, having had nothing all day but a few mangoes. We looked

Chapter Seven

A RACE WITH HUNGER

Near the place where we had spent the night shivering in the rain we found a mound of stones to mark the spot where a year ago an Indian soldier – as was to be read on a wooden plaque – had been buried. Shallow trenches, hearths and empty jam-tins showed that there must have been a post here. Probably British troops had withdrawn across the Naaf at this point when the Japanese had attacked Maungdaw the year before.

Our intention was to push on that same day to Teknaaf, the last village of any size on the peninsula, and directly opposite Maungdaw; thence we should try to get across into Burma.

We followed an old forest path, on which the hills soon encroached so closely that it could scarcely squeeze along between them and the river. Just at this point, as we discovered with a stab of horror, and just as we were bursting right in on top of them, there was a strong-point manned by Indian soldiers. Fortunately, the men on guard had their backs turned; so our precipitate retreat was unobserved. But this early-morning encounter must have unnerved us very thoroughly, because we could not summon up the recklessness to walk straight past, and chose rather to climb the precipice which rose perpendicularly behind the post. It seemed easier to brave the natural rather than the military obstacle.

We began our climb of the rock-face when we were immediately above the post, but as neither of us had any experience of climbing this task was almost beyond us. By pulling ourselves, and pushing and hauling each other, and by digging in and hanging on by our finger-nails, we worked our way painfully on and reached the top in spite of sudden onsets of vertigo. But then I dislodged a large piece of rock which went crashing down accompanied by others it dislodged on its way. It arrived at the bottom with a tremendous report. We looked anxiously at the post – a man ran out on to the small platform in front of it and looked up.

There we were clinging to the face of the precipice not far from the top. In a moment the whole garrison had assembled. They gazed up at the two mountaineers, with their heads bent back.

"It would be good sport if they started shooting," I said.

"Shooting? Never. They'll take us for mad Englishmen, or any of those crazy Europeans who are always up to something Indians have long ago seen the folly of."

"Let's hope, then, they recognize us as Europeans."

"To make sure, we'll wave our topis to them."

The men waved back, looked at us for a short while longer and then went away.

Once on the ridge we were in the jungle again, which clothed the mountain here with primeval luxuriance. We followed the path along the ridge in the hope of getting a view, but trees with large, leathery leaves shut it off. We had to climb one of them before we could see through its branches over the plain of Teknaaf. A tongue of land girdled with white foam on the west and south ran out into the sea at the end of the peninsula. Far below us we saw palm-groves, villages and expanses of green, all bathed in sunshine, and a road running beside the sea. British patrol-boats were visible on the blue-green surface of the Naaf.

We began the descent, taking a short cut through the undergrowth which clothed the steep mountainside. This was our first opportunity of making a close acquaintance with bamboos. So far we had admired with aesthetic satisfaction the way their graceful canes let fall their foliage of tender green; now we fought our way through thickets of them for hour after hour. They barred our way with palisades of tall, spear-like stems, which whipped back at us with malicious ill-will and came together near the ground in order to catch our feet or even our whole bodies in their grip. If we caught hold of them, their leaves were as sharp as razor-blades. We might well have spared ourselves this experience, weak as we were from lack of food and sleep. It was a relief, therefore, when we got into a narrow gorge, the bottom of which offered fewer obstacles. A solemn gloom enclosed us; wreathing plants hung down from the precipitous sides, luxuriant ferns were rooted in the rocky crevices, and now and then a large blood-red flower gleamed out from among fleshy leaves. By degrees a trickle grew from little springs and green-reflecting pools, which, constantly nourished by tiny waterfalls and the moisture dripping from the walls, widened to a stream. Soon it took up all the floor of the gorge and we had to wade in places to follow its course. The air was steamy and relaxing.

106

When the sun was high, we found ourselves on the summit of a hill which showed that we could soon leave the jungle and emerge on to the plain. It told us also what we had to reckon with; on the edge of the forest-land at our feet large tents and huts extended in a semi-circle.

We approached with the utmost caution, making use of a sunken road, where we saw fresh imprints of soldiers' boots in the wet ground. At the very moment when we came to the last of the bushes we observed an Indian sentry on our right, standing with fixed bayonet at the entrance to a tent, staring to his front. We silently retreated and, making a small circuit, got unscathed into the open. As the pangs of hunger were now intolerable, Have went off at once to buy food in the nearest village. He was a long time away and returned empty-handed, and in very bad humour, to our hiding-place. Our disappointment was so keen that, merely to still our ravenous hunger, we were on the verge of committing the sheer folly of entering Teknaaf, which was occupied by troops, in the full light of day. The sight of all the tents and huts restored us to reason; we remained in hiding and endured our pangs.

To add to our troubles, loud reports started up in the shrubby border of the jungle in which we were lying. Indian soldiers were engaged in an exercise. We saw them advancing in open order between the bushes, and a stout corporal, whose black moustache was waxed in the English style, came within five yards of us. We lay like corpses, resigned to Fate, which would strike if it chose. But the horror passed and soon after it grew dark.

Lights shone out along the edge of the jungle. We had to beware. They were from strong-points. But, exercising great caution, we crept to the wide road and crossed the camp to the outskirts of Teknaaf. We then stalked the market, fearful lest any dimly-seen passers-by might be a night-patrol. We were thankful to find a shop among the very first huts, and here we bought bananas, biscuits and cups of tea. We were very noticeable from the first moment in the lighted shop, which was already patronized by one or two old men; but we had to stick it out at any cost, to get information about traffic across the river. We had set all our hopes on Teknaaf, expecting to be able to cross the river from there and land behind either the British or the Japanese lines. Lately we had indulged the hope that part of the Burmese bank of the river might be in Japanese hands. We questioned the company very cautiously and were told that all sampans had been requisitioned, or at least were strictly controlled. But if we wanted to cross to Maungdaw, we could take a steamer from the landing-stage: they ran several times a day – not very cheering news. If private river-traffic had been cut out, how were we ever to get across?

The steamers were only for military use. To board one so close to the front would be madness.

As we left the village in search of a hiding-place, Have expressed his first doubt of the practicability of our plan of crossing by boat. I agreed with him, but set my hopes on the next day, when, cost what it might, we would do our utmost to pull it off. But I too had the secret fear that we had landed ourselves in a blind-alley.

We had to be on our feet by first cock-crow because our bivouac was in a danger-zone and gave us very poor cover. There was a British HQ dangerously near on the outskirts of Teknaaf, and at our back were tents and huts. We heard reveille at that moment. We had made up our minds to explore the farthest tip of the peninsula and to make a thorough search for a boat on the way. There was also another possibility to consider; our map showed a small island, named Shapuri, lying off the peninsula to the south, which we believed to be occupied by the Japanese.

The country was most unfavourable to our plan. The inhabited places almost touched one another; there was cover only in the neighbourhood of the dwellings, and there was every likelihood of running into the Army in one form or another all the way. We therefore advanced very gingerly, and did not trust the footpaths until we had elicited from the natives what places were in military occupation.

We asked more than once about the possibility of finding a sampan, but the replies were always completely discouraging; and as any talk of the kind was desperately risky and entirely contrary to all our rules, we abandoned further enquiry.

We next went to the bank of the Naaf, scouting very carefully as we went, to see if we could set eyes on a boat which we might make free with for a crossing by night. We walked along the dyke, but did not see a sampan anywhere. They had vanished from the scene. We had a view over the water to the opposite bank. A pale blue range of mountains beyond the level plain ran parallel to the course of the river, and on its bank just opposite us was Maungdaw. We estimated the width of the estuary to be between two and three miles.

"Do you know what?" I said. "If all else failed, we might swim it."

"Only as the last resort, and then only at night. It looks a hell of a long way."

"I'll try it now to see how strong the current is."

The experiment was no joke from the start. The water was shallow, but it swirled between trees with spiked leaves and even getting through this obstacle was almost beyond my strength. When at last I was able to swim, I soon felt sure that the attempt to reach the other shore would be too much for us. It wasn't so much the current as that we no longer had the energy of the early days. We might have done it if we had been fit, but in our present condition we should have drowned within a mile at farthest. Have saw the hopelessness of it at once, and besides, it would cost us all our possessions. But what alternative was there? There was still Shapuri, although for that too a boat would be needed. So we set off for the far end of the peninsula in very poor spirits.

In the afternoon we got into country that was neither sea nor land. Flat stretches of grey mud, shining like metal in the sun, formed an ambiguous region which it would be impossible to cross. Somewhere in that no-man's-land India came to an end.

Shapuri was visible on the horizon as a fringe of palm-trees, which owing to an optical illusion seemed to hover above the glimmering surface of the sea like a mirage. We made these observations from the edge of a large expanse of parched grassland, the last spot of what could be called terra firma. It was absolutely impossible to advance another step.

It had already struck us as we came along that there were no defences of any kind in the country opposite Shapuri, and this hardly bore out our earlier belief that the island was held by the Japanese. Nevertheless, we wanted to be sure; so we went back to some lonely cultivated plots we had passed near the coast. We found a native squatting at his door.

"It is hot today."

"Yes, Sahib, it is very hot."

"How low the sea is: you might think you could walk out to Shapuri."

"No, no; that is impossible. There is much water between."

"Have you been over there?"

"Earlier. Not lately."

'Of course, now there is war, and so only soldiers can go." This was a shot in the dark.

"It is true. Only Gurkhas may go there."

So our fears were only too true. Shapuri, our one hope, was eliminated. This man also told us that the whole bank of the Naaf opposite us was in British occupation, and that it would be useless to look for a sampan or a sailing boat.

A clammy feeling came over us – the suspicion that there was no way out and no prospect of one. We had spent all day in circumstances of extreme danger, making desperate researches into the possibility of reaching Burma – and all in vain. At every turn we were confronted by an invisible wall, without being able even to form an idea of any way of getting over it. If we could even have imagined that by waiting patiently we might achieve our aim, then we should have waited until the devil shed his tail. Unfortunately it wasn't a question of a favourable opportunity, but of a sheer impossibility.

As we walked on, a lorry drew up not far away, and soldiers jumped out and scattered. We naturally thought it was us they were after; a patrol had been dispatched to round up those two suspicious-looking individuals. We took cover among the bushes in alarm. It was a great relief when the supposed search-party assembled again, climbed in and drove off. We could make no guess why they had come. For some time the view we had from our hiding-place of the mountains beyond the further shore so fascinated us that we stayed where we were. The promised land was so close and so enticing. Must we really give up hope after coming so far? Now we heard distant gunfire. The British batteries had opened up again after a longish interval.

"We must get across at any price," Have said.

"Yes; we must."

"It would be intolerable to fall at the last fence. Compared with the distance we've come, this last bit is laughable."

"But hard. And you know why?"

"Well – ?"

"Because it makes the whole difference between success and failure. It makes no difference, from the point of view of success, having come so far as this if we don't get across."

"I should kick myself until the day I die if we didn't do our damnedest – and I mean our damnedest – to make it now. The time has come to risk everything. We shan't get any farther without."

"Right. Then let us swim across tonight."

"No; we've rejected that already."

We discussed other extreme measures, none of which were any good. At last Have said:

"I'm for trying the steamer from Teknaaf landing-stage."

"Then we may as well save ourselves the trouble and surrender to the British right away," I replied. "As soon as we show our noses on the quay, we're finished."

"It's a risk, but I don't see what else."

"Well, I do. We must give up Maungdaw and go back. We must try it overland by But Hidaung, which is right in the battle-zone."

"What – you want to go the whole way back along the peninsula?"

"I do. Once it's obvious we can't get across, it's better to make a safe retreat to better ground than risk all on a fool-hardly stunt which could ruin our chances for good."

Have thought it over, and I could see it was only the effect of fatigue and privation which induced him to accept my argument. He made little further comment.

"Agreed. We'll do that, but we will still look out for a sampan on the way. We might try to build a raft in the jungle."

"If we see any chance whatever of getting across we'll take it, of course."

"Right, then. We'll turn tail."

We resolved to pay another visit to Teknaaf after dark to buy food. We had traipsed about all day with fiery pangs in our innards, and want of food day after day was beginning to tell on us.

Meanwhile, the onset of evening was depicted in clouds which glowed like distant purple mountains.

Teknaaf's little bazaar was deserted and dark. The stalls had long been closed, and there was a streak of light to be seen under only one of the doors. We knocked and were admitted, and began hurriedly bargaining with the owner in the dim light of an oil-lamp for some earth-nuts and a stick of sugar.

We had just concluded the bargain when an Indian in a white robe with heavily pomaded hair, a sharp, beaked nose and oily movements, came in at the door. After an obsequious greeting, he went on at once to offer his services. If we thought of buying provisions it would be better to return in the morning, when the bazaar would be fully stocked. He would be at our service to take us along the stalls. We could find no better guide, he added with complacence, throwing in as an irresistible recommendation:

"You see, I am the detective officer of Teknaaf."

The very man we had been waiting for.

"What a pleasant surprise to make your acquaintance. However, I fear we cannot avail ourselves of your kind services, as we are returning to Maungdaw early in the morning."

"Then I wish you all the best, gentlemen. One cannot wish soldiers good luck often enough. Good night, gentlemen."

He vanished with all speed into the darkness.

111

Harried to death and stunned by the day's reverses, we dropped among some bushes not far from the village.

We passed a wretched night. It rained without stopping, and we searched the undergrowth far and wide for a dry spot. Have, who, owing to his latent malaria, was sensitive to changes of temperature, had an attack of the shivers.

It was an unavoidable necessity to pay another visit to the bazaar at Teknaaf before starting on the first stage of our retreat, because we had practically drawn a blank the night before, and we should have no means of provisioning ourselves on our march through the jungle. Have pulled himself together at nine to face the unpleasant errand; and I spent the time until he came back in a torment of anxiety. We had agreed that if he were captured, he should return with his captors to where I was hiding, so that we should share the same fate. Besides, it would be pointless to carry on alone. More than an hour went by before he got back, and then only with the news that the bazaar wouldn't open until twelve. I could not expect him to go a second time, and said I would go myself. He warned me that there was a constant coming and going of orderlies between the market-stalls and the HQ in Teknaaf. He had met one just as he was going to cross a bridge; the man waited to let him pass, but looked hard at him, as much as to say, "You're someone I've never met before." Have said he had returned his look with interest, and the man had thought better of addressing him.

So off I had to set a little before midday. I could not avoid the company of an English NCO who was walking with an Indian, but I managed to turn off very soon and reached the market without further accident. There was an open space in the middle, where a number of roofed stalls had been erected for the sale of country produce. Inhabitants from all the villages nearby fairly seethed round them. First I tried to get an overall view of the scene and observed a crowd of British soldiers at a lemonade counter. I gave that spot a wide berth. I kept my eyes open anxiously for other dangers as well as for eatables. I was lucky to secure a dozen eggs and as many bananas, and had just set my heart on a crock of yogurt, when I suddenly caught sight of an MP, with slouch hat and revolver, in another of the crowded lanes between the stalls. He was just opposite me, parted only by a double row of stalls. He was buying poultry with the aid of an Indian interpreter, no other than the detective officer, as I saw to my consternation. He too recognized me at once, and was visibly astonished to find me still there.

However, he gave me an oily smile and then said something to the MP. The MP looked hard at me, as I'm sure I had gone white to the lips; and immediately afterwards the spy left the MP, no doubt to worm his way along to me through the crowd. I had some small start of him, and no intention of awaiting his arrival. Just before the lemonade stall, I squeezed into a side-alley and reached the outskirts of the village. There I waited; I could not give up the yogurt. The mere thought of its sharp, invigorating flavour would have spurred me to any act of heroism. So after a pause I returned to the attack. The policeman was no longer to be seen. The crock was still there; and I returned full of pride to my trusty companion.

Soon after this our retreat began. As we did not like to venture too near the camp, we had to make a detour and were often held up by water. Twice we had to swim through stagnant, putrid swamp, carrying our belongings on our heads with great difficulty. Just behind a village we turned off into the jungle. A native came out of one of the huts and followed us at a distance. The climb into the mountains was hard going. First we ran into an Indian patrol, and in giving it the slip we lost our way and got entangled in thorns and scrub. Besides this, the Indian seemed to be on our tracks; he looked up at us for a long time from below, and later we caught sight of him in the jungle. Not that he had the slightest chance of following us through the thickets we had got into. We poured with sweat as we struggled up the mountain-side, where everything strove skyward in close ranks of straight stems, and the ground was cushioned with smooth leaves which made us slip back half a step for every one we took.

Suddenly Have let out a choked cry of horror.

"Oh God, I've broken an egg in my pocket."

We had divided them between us to lessen the danger of breakage. This was our first loss. Have with many contortions tried to coax the casualty out of the breast-pocket of his shirt. But it defied him and started oozing through the fabric of his shirt. It was lucky I did not laugh, because the same thing happened to me soon after. My hip-pocket began to feel suspiciously moist. My salvage operations were more thorough than Have's. I took off my shorts and carefully decanted the contents of my pocket into our cup. When a third smash occurred we decided to avoid further sacrifices by devouring the remainder there and then, although it was flatly contrary to marching orders.

We never succeeded in finding the stream in the gorge we had followed in our descent, and this failure cost us hours of vain and fatiguing scrambles. It was nearly dark by the time we got out on to the ridge, and found a good camping-place in a high, secluded clearing, grown over with elephant-grass. Dense jungle was all around us. Huge single trees with black trunks soared up majestically above it, and far below the Naaf flowed darkly. In one spot the grass had been cut for hay; we burrowed into the heap in case there might be a shower, and after midnight it did, in fact, rain hard.

The layer of dry grass was far from being impervious, and soon formed a chilly, sodden blanket over our shivering limbs. I too began shivering for the first time and could not stop. I lay beside Have, who was in an even worse state, with my teeth chattering, and cursed myself and our escape and the unsurpassable folly of mankind for our ever having got into such a situation. I should never have believed that continuous rain could be so demoralizing. I would have thrown up the whole business for a dry shirt and a cup of hot tea.

"Don't make such a racket, in heaven's name," Have called out to me while I was struggling to pull down some coils of liana from the trees.

"I'm being as quiet as I can, but however careful you are, it can't be done without noise."

"If it takes all that racket, we must give up the whole idea."

And that was the end of the raft, never from the first a very promising or practicable notion.

It was after coming down from the clearing where we had slept that we thought of trying to construct one. The spot was not far from the outpost manned by Indians, above which we had made our first climb. We had to choose that spot because there was suitable timber there, cut and stacked by woodcutters, and we were not likely to find it anywhere else. Our plan was to fasten the logs together with bands of fibre and lianas, but it was not possible to do it without making a noise; it would be equally impossible to get the raft to the water's edge unobserved. Besides all this, we did not know how large the raft ought to be or how to steer it or propel it along. In view of all these difficulties, we dropped the idea.

As we followed the path back to Nihla, along which we had come only a few days before, we were weighed down by the depression caused by abandoning a plan on which all our hopes had been set. It made our situation look completely hopeless, and we felt deflated and disheartened. Even after reaching But Hidaung we should have several days' marching to face, and our strength was ebbing rapidly. The life of

114

improvisation we lived made great demands on our resourcefulness, and now we were bankrupt; the good luck, so essential to our enterprise, had also given out.

We came to a backwater over which there was no bridge, and at the same moment a broad, solid sampan was passing with a load of logs. We hailed it and asked the Indians to put us across. There were three of them in the boat, two men and a boy of about twelve years old. They agreed to ferry us over for a small payment. The boy, who was spokesman, had all his wits about him and was far superior to the men in intelligence. Have suggested casually that I might sound them about taking us across to Maungdaw. I agreed to try it on, useless though I thought it, and as soon as we landed I took the boy aside while the men waited in the boat.

"We should like to make a fine deal with you," I began. "Do you see all this money?"

"Give it to me," he cried greedily, grabbing at the notes. I did not pull my hand back, but let him touch them. His covetousness seemed to have taken the bait.

"You can have more than that if you like. You only need to take us over there," and I looked across the Naaf to the opposite bank.

"Over to Maungdaw?" he asked.

"Yes, to Maungdaw."

"That can't be done."

"Why not?"

Instead of answering, he crossed his hands at the wrist, meaning that the British would handcuff him. Imprisonment was the penalty for any black-market ferrying.

"You would not do it even for much money?"

"No; I am frightened. It is too dangerous."

"Pity—"

I said no more. It was useless. The usual disappointment.

We had only been walking on for a few minutes when we heard the patter of bare feet behind us. It was the boy.

"Well? What's up?"

"I have spoken with my brothers. They will take you across."

We could not believe our ears. The chance we had looked for and longed for and given up hope of had arrived. We had to believe it, unbelievable though it was. Could they take us now, I asked.

"No; first we must unload the wood at the quay. Then we will come back. We shall be back in two hours or so."

We agreed on the price, which was probably more than a month's wages of one of these boatmen, and said we would wait where we were until he came to fetch us. He ran back to the boat.

The fact that they were going first to Teknaaf seemed to us suspicious. Perhaps they might change their minds on the way and bring some soldiers back to surprise us. This was not a possibility to dismiss out of hand, so we did not stay where we were, but hid ourselves on the bank of the river, whence we should be able to see the sampan approaching from a distance and discover in good time whether they had soldiers on board. In that case we should have time to make ourselves scarce.

We kept a look-out for more than two hours, getting more and more anxious as the time passed. It seemed altogether too unlikely that the Indians would dare to make the crossing in daylight, considering all the traffic there was on the river. They would be liable in the circumstances to a severer penalty than we should be. Presumably they were not coming back at all; it was half-past three, and not a sign of them.

It was an oppressive day of tropical heat. A sunless glow suffused the blanket of cloud. The Naaf resembled a mass of molten pitch oozing slowly to the sea. Far off towards Shapuri a black trail of smoke hung in the heavy air, unable to rise above the surface of the sea. A British assault-craft was chugging along.

Wasn't that a sampan coming from behind the hill? It looked like it, broad in the beam too – it must be our fellows. It was, and alone, only the three of them on board. We could safely return to the rendezvous.

When we were in the boat and drawing slowly away from the Indian shore, I thought of the last three days, how we had driven ourselves so hard and worried ourselves nearly out of our minds in the desperate attempt to get off the peninsula. I thought of the way our spirits had ebbed from day to day, until at last we nearly gave up hope altogether, and how the turn had come. I thought of the distance we had travelled from Dehra Dun, and of the amazing luck it had needed to bring us all that way, and even now I could not help attributing this last success to a special providence. I remembered what an instinctive repugnance I felt when I first set foot on Indian soil, and how ever since, though always in vain, I had longed to shake its dust from my feet. But India held me fast, as though it was so decreed. And now I surveyed with astonishment a chain of events in which free will and predestination had joined to rid me, as I hoped, of that land for ever. Was I mistaken in seeing a predestined and providential meaning in the course of events? To see in the Indian boy and his simple brothers who were now rowing us across the Naaf the instruments of Fate, destined to take us to our goal, appeared to me perfectly natural. I learned that the powers of Fate were effective in proportion as one took one's fate in one's hand.

"The mantle of God floats past us and we grasp it by the hem."

"Did you make that up?"

"No; I read it somewhere."

We were now in mid-stream and saw an English patrol-boat coming towards us. There was also a boat coming from the direction of Nihla which was bound to pass quite close to us. If our sampan had not been so flat we should have lain down on the bottom, but, as it was, we should have exposed ourselves at full length to hostile observation. The patrol-boat was coming rapidly nearer. It threw the water from its bows as it bore down upon us. We crouched down in misery, but could not refrain from peering out under the rim of our helmets. An Indian in uniform was steering; others sat near him, and two British privates sat dangling their legs over the side. With one accord they all turned their heads in our direction, and I thought I could read the look of surprise on their faces when they saw two white men in the sampan. I was sure for a split second that the engine would stop and the boat fetch up in a wide sweep alongside us. Then the two criminals would be taken on board. But no. Nothing of the kind happened. It held on its course with undiminished speed. We rocked violently in its wake. Probably its job was to keep a sharp look-out for Japanese, so that the sight of two British soldiers, who were heading for the front, and so could not be deserting, did not arouse any particular interest.

We had not the least desire to put in at Maungdaw, and could not imagine that the boatmen would wish to do so either; on that matter their views would surely coincide with our own. Also they would have a long row to Maungdaw, whereas to put us off among the rice-fields opposite would shorten their labour considerably. They agreed to this without any persuasion.

So it was that, on the thirty-first day since our escape, we stepped on to the soil of Burma, feeling as proud as if we had conquered it.

In front of us there was a strip of flat country stretching along the river bank to a depth of about six miles, and beyond it the foothills of the Mayu Mountains rose steeply; somewhere there ran the front line. There were villages among the rice-fields, bamboo thickets and backwaters,

117

and at the foot of the hills we thought we could distinguish a good-sized camp. Enquiries confirmed our suspicion. A canal of the size of a decent river led off on our right in the direction of the camp, and as marsh headed us off on the left we were compelled to make straight for the camp along the bank of the canal. We passed through a village to which inhabitants from the front line had been evacuated by the British, but we could not get any definite information about the actual position of the line.

We were walking on over large, flat fields as dusk fell. A wind got up and it began to rain. Suddenly there was a flash in front of us, followed immediately by a report. This was repeated a second time, and then a third. A battery of heavies was firing only five or six hundred yards in front of us, concealed by a few trees.

It quickly got dark. We debated whether to go farther. We tried to turn off, but found we were in a trap and could not get out without a boat; and in our search for shelter we drew nearer and nearer to the gun-positions. We could see the outline of a small hut within earshot of the battery, and heard voices. No doubt this was an outpost, and we must have been heard, because a man came out and shouted a warning in Hindustani. We silently retreated.

It was impossible to find shelter anywhere. The ground was bare and flat as a table-cloth. We wandered round in pouring rain, soaked to the skin. Finally we crouched below the bank of the canal, despondent and yet excited. We were awake all night, listening at regular intervals to the firing of the battery. If we listened carefully we could hear a second distant detonation after each report.

"Hear that? It's the shell bursting over the target."

"Yes; so it is," Have said.

"We ought to listen how long the interval is."

"Are you thinking of a mathematical calculation?"

"Any objection? It wouldn't do any harm to know roughly the distance to the front. We only need to know how long the burst takes to reach our ears."

"Well, off you go."

The result of our experiments gave a distance of at least ten miles.

The rain came down without a pause, and a chill breath crept along the ground. We felt it so at least, although in fact it must have been warm. Have, poor fellow, suffered the worse. He shuddered from head to foot. Even his lips fluttered. The ground we sat on turned to mud and every now and then we took off our shirts and wrung the water out of them.

Soaked and sodden, body and soul, we waited for morning. When at last it came I was shocked at the sight of Have's sallow and sunken face.

A brilliant day followed. Ushas, the sacred, life-giving sun, rose in glory. The Mayu Mountains soared into crystal air; the plain overflowed with light. We poor fugitives shared in the invigoration and were in good heart and fettle again.

Our first task was to press forward to the mountains and exchange the open country for the protection of the jungle. Next we should need to get our bearings and find our way over the mountains. We could not simply plunge blindly into the primeval forest. Crossing the river or canal was the first thing; we were still caught in its noose. Luck came to our help. We found a small boat and rowed across. But even so we were forced by the waterside thickets and marshes to take the road to the camp, which we were so eager to avoid.

On the way we passed some native huts and asked for a drink of milk. The man went to milk his cow, and while we waited we were surprised by an Indian soldier, who came round the corner from the yard. He was a Gurkha corporal. He stopped at a respectful distance, saying nothing at first, but watching us closely. Meanwhile, the peasant returned with the milk, which we drank with covert glances at our silent spectator. Suddenly he stepped up to us, saluted smartly and stood to attention, his forefinger on the seam of his trousers, and said that the Sahibs were on the wrong road: the road to Maungdaw ran higher up along the edge of the jungle. We thanked and dismissed him.

We had to pass within less than a hundred yards of the camp owing to a tongue of marshy land. There were some troops on parade, but as they were paying more attention to what their officer said than to us, we got past unnoticed.

We came to a road behind the camp which led south to the foot of the mountains. We went on at the double so as to be hidden in the jungle as soon as possible. The road was barred some distance ahead by a pole with a noticeboard on it. We tried to read the notice as we advanced, but our attention was taken off by the sound of a car approaching rapidly. We looked round expecting trouble, and saw a jeep, in which there were several officers, coming towards us. At that moment we reached the pole and hurriedly climbed over it. The jeep would actually have reached it before we could – a predicament which surprisingly did not arise, because it turned off into the open field a few yards before reaching the obstruction and joined another road higher up.

"We nearly copped it that time!"

"Prepare for worse than that," Have warned me.

And it was true. To the dangers of recapture, being tried as spies, or dying of starvation, we now, so near the front, added the risk of being shot out of hand.

The mountains were craggy and densely overgrown. We crossed trodden-out paths and came on soldiers' boots, jam-tins and cartridge-cases all over the place; and later on trenches and strong-points. But they had been abandoned. Obviously all the peaks, heights and ridges had been connected in a large defensive system, now no longer occupied. Shelters and dugouts had been constructed at important and salient points and connected by paths. It looked as if it might be a second line to fall back on, and was kept up and patrolled; fresh footmarks forced us to this conclusion. We therefore advanced with special caution. It might have been one o'clock in the afternoon when we reached the top of the highest hill and sat down for a rest in the gun position at the top. Looking back, we saw the plain and its villages, then the Naaf and India beyond. In front of us the ground fell away steeply; there was a rough track running along at the bottom, and on the far side, like an impregnable bulwark, rose the first massive range of the Mayu Mountains. The fighting was somewhere in there.

"This is the place for a last consultation," I said. "Look at all that impenetrable mountain and jungle. That's only a foretaste."

"It will be a matter of life or death."

"Sure thing. Once in there we shall have burnt our boats."

"How many ridges behind that one?"

"Plenty. We shall see how many when we reach the top."

"And how do we avoid being shot out of hand? I don't want to die in the jungle without one round of applause."

"If we only keep on slap east, we can't miss the way. We can't fail to find the Japs."

But as our compass did not function any more, keeping direction was not such a simple matter.

"And we can't reckon on any sort of food supply. Do you know we've two mangoes left?"

"Do I know? As if I thought of anything else!"

"We can't go on without a stock of food," Have said. "We shall first have to go back to those villages down there and collect all the grub we can possibly find."

"Then we shan't start before early tomorrow?"

"No; and there's this advantage – we can have a good sleep first, here in this shelter where the rain can't get at us."

"By the way – have you any idea of the range of a tommy-gun?"

"No. Why?"

"Well, listen—"

It did not occur to me until later that it cost us no particular effort of decision to take the last fatal step. Whether it was the circumstances themselves that drove us forward, whether we blindly followed our star, or whether it was through thoughtlessness, we seemed to take it in our stride.

There were several villages between us and Maungdaw, and we made for the nearest. Even before we got there we thought it odd to see no cattle and no one in the fields. We soon discovered the reason; the place was mostly in ruins and completely deserted. The village was dead, no sign of life anywhere. We went on to the next one. The same ghostly stillness. There were even signs of fighting round the houses. There was now only one more village; the next place after that was Maungdaw. We went on, as we did not like to leave any chance untried; but the last of the three was the worst. It was nearly all burned to the ground. We vied with each other in curses. We were almost out of our minds with hunger and thought only of how to appease it, and there was our last hope gone.

"I don't mind going to Maungdaw and raiding the quarter-master's stores. I'll damned well get hold of something," Have swore in a fury. "We can't start over the mountains in this state."

"Then we'll go to Maungdaw. Come on."

It was lucky for us that a strip of marsh barred the way. We should otherwise almost certainly have been captured in our search for food, since Maungdaw was nothing but a military depot.

Full of rage, we beat a retreat.

"Mangoes," we both shouted at once as we caught sight of some mango trees in the next village, with fruit still hanging on the branches. There were not many and they were high up, but we knocked down all we could reach, ate some and saved the rest, about twenty, for next day's journey. Then we felt the earth tremble slightly and next moment the thud of hoofs drew rapidly nearer. We only just had time to duck down behind a slope in the ground when a British officer and his mounted servant galloped past. The two shot by in wild career and then the hoof-beats died away in the distance.

We struggled back through the desolate country to our dugout, preoccupied by thoughts of the days ahead – they would mean either success or the end – when ping – a bullet whistled past our heads.

"That's for us!" Have cried in horror.

Another shot followed instantly.

"Some swine is drawing a bead on us!"

We lay still and waited until it was dark.

Chapter Eight

BAKAGONNA

The cubby-hole we spent the night in proved an excellent doss-house and gave us a good night for once. I was awakened by a violent tug at my shoulder. Have, who had got up first, had horror written all over his face.

"The whole hill's surrounded."

I rushed out into the observation-trench, which ran all round the dugout.

"How the devil have they got on to us up here already?"

"Anyway, we must get clear at once."

When a moment later we were in the thickets below we heard an order passed along the line in front of us. Our hearts thumped furiously as the men assembled and in single file climbed the hill we had just come down.

We had long since given up trying to explain such occurrences.

We set off at a run over some stretches of grass and when we were crossing the rough track through the jungle at the bottom we caught sight of a signboard on which was painted: BAKAGONNA GAP. Odd-sounding, exotic sort of name, Bakagonna, I thought, as we slackened our speed, and as I repeated the word to myself it took on a romantic, mysterious quality, both dangerous and enticing. So that was the name they had given this gap in the mountains in what, for us, was the decisive sector; and now we had this valley of tangled thickets between us and the first ridge of the mountains. There were dry beds of loose stones and boulders winding along here and there; and we used one of these to get us over the last of the level ground. On we staggered, bodies bent forward, feet slipping back. Our haversacks got heavier as we went. Yet physical exhaustion was only one aspect of our state; it had in it a mixture of strange exultation, as if the exhaustion were in itself a stimulus of our whole beings. It acted on our nerves and spurred us on. We were coming into the straight, when the last spurt demanded a supreme exertion.

Before starting the climb we threw all superfluous gear into the under-growth, strapped our lightened haversacks to our backs like packs, and

123

pressed on into the forest. The branches closed behind us. We had crossed our Rubicon.

There was not a gap in the tangle; it rose from the ground, trunk by trunk, and stem by stem, each one crowding upon and striving to overtop the other, and tied and netted together with the snaky arms of creepers into a closely woven web. As though it were not a fine enough mesh, aerial roots and liana-nooses were let down from high above. Leaves laid themselves out in vast terraces, fantastic umbels descended in cascades, and creepers united in stout, tightly wound spiral columns. Vegetation teemed in the steamy twilight; great fronds broken under their own weight, ropes which had neither end nor beginning, plants with fat, sticky leaves, or with hairy or scaly stems, or stems that opened out like fans, and some with large, luxuriant flowers, exuding a strange and deathly scent – it is not any sane and measured growth that urges this turgid vegetation, these gigantic ferns and myriad parasites. It is a rank and morbid luxuriance, a spendthrift and suicidal pullulation. The powers of generation and destruction work together in the teeming fertility of these forest gorges; birth and decay are only dung for more birth and more decay.

We had to force a way through by throwing the whole weight of our bodies against this vegetable congestion; and we had to keep close together; if we were parted only a few paces, we lost sight of each other altogether. Then one felt the terror of perishing alone in this treacherous and murderous jungle.

The ascent became steeper; we pulled ourselves up by the hanging ropes. We should never have made it if the matted verdure had not now changed into a forest of bamboos. Here we found tracks running in all directions. We were afraid at first they might be of human origin, but soon saw from the droppings we came upon that they had been made by elephants.

We were on the top of the first ridge at about midday, after several hours' climbing; and, eager to know what view we should now have, we parted the bamboo stems and peered through. We saw nothing but the steaming wilderness, nothing but the fermenting brew of mountain forests. And yet in the far haze behind blue knife-edges there was a streak of silver – the Mayu River. There at the very least we should find the Japanese; we knew from the communiqués that it was in their hands. We thought it an infinite distance still. Far down below us we made out a road along which tiny vehicles were crawling, and in a hole to our right there was a camp. Immediately behind this road, which was no other than the road from Maungdaw to ButHidaung, rose the next jungle-covered ascent.

It was clear what we had to do. We had to cross the road, climb our second ridge, then the one behind, and so on until we solved the riddle. We knew as little as ever where the front line ran. All was hidden by the jungle.

There was a path along the ridge on which we now stood, and we followed it in our search for a good place to start our descent.

"Look out. Telephone wire," I warned Have, who was behind me. I had a hunch that danger was very near. And an instant later, as I was rounding some shrubs, my heart gave a bound. Only a few yards from me a squad of Gurkhas were crouching on the ground. There was no time to see whether they faced and had seen me, or whether their backs were turned. I only saw their shapes against a light background and dropped back. We turned and fled down the slope.

We decided during a breather, sitting on the roots of an ancient tree, to take off our khaki shirts and not to wear them again. The English might make short work of us if they caught us near the front in uniform even remotely resembling their own. We put on blue polo shirts we had bought in Calcutta.

It began to cloud over. The air was sultry. The rat-tat of machine-gun fire could be heard in the distance.

We found the jungle treacherous as we scrambled down. Where everything rots and decays so fast, it is hard to tell by the look of a stem or rope of creeper if it is mouldering, or else loose in root or joint. Often we were let down by appearances and took a toss. Once Have might have broken his neck. We had to cross a rock-face with a perpendicular drop of over sixty feet, and were making our way along the slope when a bamboo, to which Have had entrusted his whole weight, broke off level with the ground. He began sliding and just caught hold of some creepers on the edge of the precipice.

We were lucky. The stretch of road we had seen from above might have been made for our purpose. It was shut in by two sharp bends close together, and so was not overlooked from far in either direction. Still we had to wait for several strings of laden mules to pass; then we glided across like shadows.

We had lived so long in the jungle, and our senses had become so sharp by contact with nature, that we saw and heard as only the savage can. We were aware of the least suggestion of danger and could find our way through any labyrinth.

We had scarcely plunged into the forest again to begin the next ascent when our antennae warned us that we were in serious danger. Against our will we had to take cover in the densest thicket and wait and listen. But after a while these pauses during which we stood motionless and nothing happened became unendurable, and we yielded to the obsession of getting on at any cost. In one of these forward rushes we suddenly heard voices, and a second later saw through the foliage the flat steel helmets of Indian soldiers, who were scanning the slope from a strong-point bristling with automatic weapons. We retreated hastily and tried to make our way up by another stream-bed. There too an outpost barred the way. We risked more and more daring attempts under the double pressure of having to get out of a trap as well as of having to get on. It was all in vain. Telephone wires warned us in good time before we ran into one of these concealed listening-posts, but there were so many and at such close intervals that there was no getting through. We could have got through unseen, but never unheard, owing to the rustle of leaves and branches. Once we wormed our way close to a post and then at the last moment thought better of it and crawled back.

Then it began to rain.

It looked like being a tropical downpour. The first heavy drops were falling. Soon they were pattering on the leaves and, as the deluge increased and the very sky burst, the sound rose to such a pitch that any noise we might make would be completely drowned. In this way we passed through this formidable line of outposts.

We struggled on up the slope without a pause and without looking round, starting when shots sang over our heads. Shreds of cloud drifted through the dripping bamboos on the top. It was dark, the day was drawing to an end; but on we plunged and down the other side. On and on. There were other ridges ahead; we were still far from our goal. We kept on down rocky clefts and crags until our legs were numb, and we were tripped by roots and creepers and could stagger no farther. We stopped in a pitch-dark gorge under an overhanging rock and leaned, dead-tired, against the stone.

We were knee-deep in water, famished and done-in, and there we had to stand all the weary hours till morning. It was impossible to lie down in the flooded torrent-bed; and our only shelter was the over-arching rock. But water came out of every crack and dropped from hanging curtains of moss. The torrent surged round our legs. The forest groaned and creaked; there were suspicious crackling noises; lights shone; we fancied we heard shrill cries, and the whole gorge seemed haunted. Our

126

nerves were on edge. Every now and then bursts of machine-gun fire rose above the sounds of the forest; they seemed to be quite near.

Where on earth were we – on English or Japanese ground, or perhaps in no-man's-land? Probably still on the English side; we could not have passed through the Japanese line without knowing it. But we could not be sure.

Next we heard the dull rush of shells passing overhead, as though on heavy wings.

"Tomorrow will decide," Have declared abruptly. He spoke as one who knew.

"I am not so sure," I replied. I was afraid we should still spend many a day wandering about the country. We said no more.

The rain went on without a break and promised a dreary day.

We were devoured by impatience and resumed our wild career at the first hint of dawn. All the hill-tops were veiled in low cloud, and in the early mist we could see only a yard or so ahead. We had to aim for the next and third range, and felt our way towards it almost blindfold. We avoided all clefts and gorges which furrowed the hillside and provided perfect cover for outposts. It would have been a simple matter to get shot out of hand as we bent back a branch or came round a rock. In jungle warfare no chances are taken, and the man who shoots first wins.

All the same, it was not this ever-present and by now familiar danger that worried us so much as the way we began to walk in circles at the bottom of the vaporous cauldron. We observed with increasing anxiety that the sun, which occasionally showed as a blotch of red vapour through layers of cloud, was now in front and now behind us. It was an immense relief when the sky cleared and revealed the mountainside we were looking for; but it rose straight up in one tremendous wall of rock to a height that made us dizzy, and we saw at once that it was an obstacle we could not possibly overcome. In one place only there was a steep and narrow path, but as it was the only way up, it must obviously be kept under close observation by one side or the other. It would be madness to make use of it. So we explored along the foot of the cliff in both directions, searching for some other possibility we might perhaps have overlooked. But we found none, and so took our lives in our hands and decided to climb it by the only path available.

There was every chance of being sent rapidly to another world, and we examined the ground anxiously at every step for signs of land-mines or booby-traps. It was the very place for such contraptions. The path, as steep and narrow in places as a ladder, was cut through walls of prickly scrub, and never gave room for more than one.

But in our experience the expected never happened. And so it was this time. When we reached the top, which we approached only after careful scrutiny, we found that it was not being kept under observation, although according to all the rules of war such a commanding position should never have been left unaccounted for.

However, on closer inspection of the summit we discovered excavations and galleries dug out in the sides of a depression. The reddish-yellow soil showed up through the leaves. When we went to have a closer look we stood still in amazement. It was a deserted post – but this time a Japanese one. It was plain at once from the letters on the ammunition-boxes, the labels on the tins, the worn-out rubber shoes and, if further proof were needed, from a white flag on which was the rising sun of Nippon. There were also large shell-cases lying about, bashed-in sun-helmets – not of English pattern – cane-work baskets, and, here and there, grains of rice, which were beginning to sprout. Our first indubitable contact with the Japanese! It was strangely moving to see these significant objects and this outlandish lettering; here in the wilderness thousands of miles from home, the Japanese had left this proof of their presence and given us fresh energy to seek them out.

If we had only known where we were – but we were no clearer about that than before. And what an extraordinary thing about that flag! How could the Japanese have left it lying there? And why had not the British taken possession of the trophy when they drove the Japanese off the hill? And where did the line run now? Perhaps there wasn't one at all in that sense? Probably not. There was just a continual sniping and scouting about in the depths of the jungle, without either side knowing precisely the position of the other.

Nevertheless, we stuck to our original plan of making straight for the Mayu River, and therefore plunged without delay down the next descent. While we were scouting our way down a slope we heard voices, and at the bottom amidst the network of leaves we saw soldiers, or, to be exact, their closely-shorn heads. They were Gurkhas. This put a stop to our descent in that direction. But in order to turn aside we had literally to tunnel our way through the dense undergrowth, abandoning all the small clefts which led straight down and eased and shortened our descent considerably.

We had to make frequent pauses to husband our rapidly ebbing strength, which in fact was now exhausted; we had come to the end of our physical resources. Our feet were swollen from standing all night in running water and they hurt at every step; we had to cling to bamboo-stems for support; and wherever the descent was steep enough we let the force of gravity take us down. I doubt whether either of us left alone could have summoned up the energy to carry on; the determination not to let the other see him wilt was to each of us an invaluable stimulant. We now had, all told, two mangoes by way of food; but as they were green and smelt of gherkins it wasn't worthwhile eating them.

Meanwhile, we were not quite unmolested. The hillside we were on came under artillery fire. Shells passed just over our heads; shell-splinters tore through the trees and ripped yard-long slices from their trunks; a hail of stones clattered down to earth; birds rose up and flew away in alarm. Our retreat from this unkindly spot boiled down to this:

Whether we liked it or not, we had to follow a gully for a short distance until it joined a narrow gorge, and at the point of junction the way was barred by a tremendous boulder. We were in the act of scaling it when we heard running feet, loud words of command and the click of safety-catches. The order to fire was about to be given immediately behind this rock. We dropped as though felled, and wormed our way back to safety. The fear of being picked off by a well-armed enemy the moment they showed over the edge of the rock forced the other fellows to keep their heads down, and gave us the necessary time for our retreat.

The shock, the mortal terror which for a moment suspended every vital faculty, found its release in a wild rush from the spot. We barged on as though we were actually being fired at, and took the first way up the hill we could find. And as we didn't know what we were doing, we lost each other. We went through a terrible half-hour in the conviction that we should never find each other again in this endless sea of greenery; and then suddenly by a miracle Have was there before my eyes. Incapable of going another step, we flung ourselves down where we stood, although the sun was still high, and fell into a dreamless sleep.

It was our last moment of utter repose before the end came.

An hour might have passed when we started up, awakened suddenly by a wild screeching and screaming. A large monkey, with its legs splayed out across the branches of a tall tree, was showing its teeth at us and uttering these soul-shattering yells. But our attention was soon distracted when I saw a large black bladder-like lump behind Have's ear. He tried to brush it away, but it stuck there and looked like a black grape. They were leeches – filthy great full-fed leeches. We leapt up in horror and I found

129

that I had them too. Most of them were not on our heads, but on our ankles, where they had dug themselves in through our stockings and blown themselves out to the size of hazel-nuts while we slept. They had to be handled with care before they could be removed. This would have been enough, but on close inspection we found the whole ground beset by armies of even bloodthirstier beasts, marching to the attack through the rotting vegetation. Given a little time, say one night, they would suck their victims to death. Many a soldier met his end thus in the jungle.

This was the final blow; panic had got us. We could not stay a moment longer in that valley where death lurked in the minutest objects. It was get out or perish miserably. We climbed over rocks and charged down slopes with reckless folly. Anything to find a way out of that valley! We came finally to a narrow gorge where the water was confined as though in a bath. We either waded or swam and had just climbed out and rounded a rock, when I was faced at single-combat distance by three figures. Have uttered a stifled "That's torn it!" as three rifles slowly covered us.

Chapter Nine

ALLIES

It had been like a blow between the eyes to be taken prisoner immediately on the outbreak of war. I was in Bombay at the time, and all attempts to get out of India had failed. I was faced at last with the dreary certainty of spending the war behind barbed wire; but I was quite incapable of forming any idea of the wretchedness of the fate that awaited me, and so it was not until the gates of the prison-camp had closed behind me that the full weight of the blow came home to me.

I felt ashamed and insulted and duped, and I told myself that it was my own fault; I should not have let myself be caged up right away; I should have had more prudence than to walk into the trap like a booby. My urge to get free was therefore due at first to the burning desire to wipe out an otherwise inexpugnible disgrace. Then as I settled down in new surroundings, and my heated feelings gave way to a cooler survey, a sense of duty was added to the more personal motive of wounded vanity; a prisoner is expected to do all in his power to regain his liberty. But as in my case there did not seem to be the slightest likelihood of success, and as it would be mere ostentation to make a hopeless attempt merely in order to say afterwards that I had tried, I did not see my way to acting on my principles. Later I got into "bad company", the company of those who meant to get out, and who found inaction and boredom and life at second-hand stale and unprofitable. They all suffered from having nothing to do, nothing to dare, nothing to pit their strength against in the life behind the wire. I tried to help them in their plans of escape, to perform various useful services as an accomplice and, so by degrees, I became infected by their enthusiasm and at last one of themselves.

But the true motive of escape lies deeper than the love of adventure or the need to be up and doing. It lies in that unceasing dissatisfaction with a wasted life, the gnawing ache which consumes the prisoner who is cut off from all means of self-development, and from sources of life which must come from outside if his personality is not to starve.

131

So there are really many motives – ambition, duty, the sense of mouldering away behind bars – even when, as was the case with us, a prisoner is treated decently enough.

We did not go into our motives among ourselves, but it was really the recovery of the right to live that was our unconfessed aim. And now, in the heart of the Mayu Mountain jungle, our escape had come to its dramatic climax, and might indeed have found its tragic ending.

But it ended differently.

For a moment we stood rooted to the ground. The others too did not move a muscle, and for a heartbeat we faced one another – we with raised hands and they with finger on the trigger.

Then one of the three signed to the others not to shoot and beckoned us forward; but the rifles were still levelled. We slowly paced the last few and final yards of our long journey. My first suspicion was that they were Gurkhas, but now as we advanced I observed that, although they were short and stocky, they wore unfamiliar uniform and caps. Could they be Japanese? Or not? Japanese could not have Soviet stars on their caps as these fellows had. So after all they must be the Chinese auxiliaries of the Allied Powers, and so— But the stars were yellow, and so they might be Japanese after all. Now we should surely find out, now that we had got right up to them.

"*Watakuschi tatschi wa doitsu jin desu* (We are Germans)," Have said, in the only Japanese words he knew. He had learnt them by heart in camp.

The corporal, as we afterwards knew his rank to be, let out a long-drawn incredulous "*Doitsu?!*" To be addressed in his own language by two representatives of his country's distant European ally in these remote forests, where he would least have expected to see them, seemed to have winded him. His small slit-eyes gleamed at us distrustfully. But as a precaution he searched for weapons, while we continued to hold our hands up, and then he turned out the contents of our haversacks. They contained nothing but shirts and medicines. When I looked at those yellow-skinned, under-sized soldiers at closer quarters, saw the tears and patches in their grey-green uniforms, failed at first to recognize their badges of rank, and noticed how rusty their rifle-barrels were, fresh doubts assailed me.

"You Nippon soldiers?" I said, hoping to reassure myself. "Nippon, Nippon," they growled in harsh, angry undertones.

So they must be Japanese troops. But were they regulars? Distrust grew and we could feel it on their side too. To diminish it as far as we could, I tried to convey in pantomime, while Have was being searched, that we had been prisoners of the English in India, and had escaped to join our allies. But I was not sure they understood. Have, who counted on speedier explanations before a higher court, insisted on being taken to the nearest officer in command. When the corporal could be made to understand, he ordered his two men to take us between them and lead on. To our astonishment, we went back, if not on our tracks, at least in the same direction as that we had come from.

"English over there," we warned urgently.

"No, no. All Nippon," the corporal assured us with a wide sweep of his arm. And then light dawned; we had in fact come upon these Japanese some considerable distance behind their forward posts. If the first encounter had taken place in the front line – which by some miracle we had got through unobserved – we should inevitably have been shot at sight.

No more doubts were now possible: we had reached our goal. Japanese soldiers surrounded us as soon as we got to company HQ hidden in the jungle; others kept on stepping noiselessly out of the undergrowth to stare at us inquisitively, but with instinctive reserve. Many were naked except for loin-cloths, but fully armed, and their yellow skin made a strange contrast with the black gun-metal. They wore rubber shoes with divided big toes, which gave their feet an amphibious look. They discussed us in guttural voices that struck on our ears in short, hard pellets of sound. We could not attempt to guess what they thought or what they said. We waited for an officer to appear, counting on a fine scene of acknowledgement and recognition.

There was a smell of fish and rice-leftovers.

We had walked to the support-line HQ in a state of utter bewilderment; our emotion was so strong that we hardly took in our surroundings. We had been saved by a miracle when we were within an inch of death. We should have had every reason to raise a whoop of joy at our first sight of Japanese soldiers – but it was impossible. There had to be an interval before our overtaxed nerves and lowered vitality could rise to the literal fact of our success. By the time we reached the post, it came upon us with an overwhelming rush of joy.

We had done it, we had got through! The air we breathed was free. We had surpassed even the most daring calculations and seen a sheer impossibility come true. We thanked Providence for many escapes and were glad too that we had played an active part in the unfolding of our destiny.

In spite of the strange-eyed creatures who formed a circle round us,

133

we rushed at each other laughing, jabbering, clapping each other on the back. Then as we had privately resolved on, we tore the labels with our English names out of the inside of our haversacks, and threw them into the undergrowth.

"John Edward Harding and Harry F. Lloyd are dead!" Have cried out.

"And 55826 and 1775 are struck off the roster!"

We were rid of them at last.

"Oi you!" a Japanese sergeant said peremptorily, holding out the two labels, which he had had retrieved. What was the meaning of that, he demanded in a harsh, third-degree tone of voice. Then he asked for further details about us – no hint in all of this of a reception with flags flying. He repeated our answers down the entrance of a dugout, out of which a voice made hollow replies. So that was the officer down there; but though we kept our eyes skinned we did not get a glimpse of him. As the exchanges between the two went on for some time, we sat down on the ground.

"What's the date today?" Have asked.

"The first of June."

"On the first of June, 1944, at two o'clock in the afternoon on the thirty-fourth day of our escape, after a journey of over 1,500 miles, we made contact with the Japanese, being the first to succeed in getting out of India."

"I can't properly grasp it even now," I said.

"You'll have to get used to it all the same."

We had been too strung up to think of looking at each other for the last few days. Now that we were beginning to come to ourselves, we mutually considered our appearance. Have's hair fell in strands over his eyes and covered his neck like a mane; and it was full of bark, leaves, and bits of wood. A yellow stubble disfigured his hollow cheeks, and the leeches had left dried trickles of blood behind his ears; his body was emaciated and his clothes hung on him as if he had been a clothes-horse. His shins were barked and raw.

"By God, you're no ornament."

"Don't run away with the notion that you are."

He was right. We were a match.

One more day would have seen the end of us; we were only just in time.

It was easy to see that the Japanese could not make us out. We did not fit into any category. We heard the words "*Americanu*" and "English" as often as "*Doitsu*". Our worn-out and dishevelled state, the blue shirts we had on instead of uniform, and our childish demonstration of joy had utterly bewildered them. Then one of them came up to us abruptly. He was slighter than the others, whose stocky frames looked remarkably strong; he had his hair close-cropped like theirs, but he wore dark-rimmed spectacles with lenses of the size of saucers. A man of education; probably a doctor. We could not understand him at first, and tried him with English. Then we tumbled to it that the language he was murdering was German. It took a long time before we could get over answering in English when addressed in German.

Our interview with the invisible OC was rapidly drawing to an end. The sergeant gave our corporal an order, and he and his two men buckled their belts and led us away. At that moment there rose to the surface of the dugout a face as round as the full moon, which gave us one look and then submerged.

Our little party left the forest for the plain; we were being taken to the rear. The paths were under water for long stretches, and we had to wade wearily through it. Whenever we met soldiers coming along on their own, the sight of us caused fresh astonishment. And each one uttered a loud grunt that sounded primitive and rather amazing. They were all young and had an air of trained ferocity. Picked troops, obviously. To our eyes one looked just like another, and their short legs and turned-in feet, planted heel first, gave them a waddling gait, exaggerated by the carrying of heavy packs. Their rifles were like great beams on their shoulders. It was apparently the fashion at the front to wear patched and much-mended uniform.

It was only natural to have painted the scene of our reception by our country's allies in brilliant colours; and the worse it went with us in the meantime, the higher rose the triumphal arches in our imagination, and the louder the acclaim of the Army of Japan. That was how we saw it, and we believed that the moment we crossed the lines our troubles would be over. Our disappointment at the way things were going up to now was therefore comprehensible, however little justified. Soldiers who faced danger themselves year in and year out would naturally see nothing remarkable in others exposing themselves to it for a short time; but just a hint of appreciation would have been welcome all the same. They had not shown us a spark of human sympathy, nothing but curiosity and, what was worse, distrust, bottomless distrust which was not only aggravating but more and more disquieting.

Yet their behaviour was understandable. It was a military necessity to treat us with caution until it was clear beyond doubt who we were. We had, in fact, to be treated as spies until we proved our innocence. And we might have known that they would seize the opportunity of indulging their national passion for spy-hunting. Our situation was all the more difficult because the Japanese, even if they had been well disposed, would not have been able to distinguish us from Anglo-Saxons – and so, as we waded along the flooded paths with our escort, it became more and more obvious that we were in a very unpleasant situation. How were we to prove that we were Germans and escaped prisoners? We had only exchanged the uncertainty whether we should ever reach our goal for the perhaps more fatal uncertainty whether our account would ever be believed. I remembered now how the British camp commandant had always warned us against attempting to escape to the Japanese, by saying that even if the attempt were successful it would lead to a miserable end, since we should either be shot in front of their lines for an enemy or behind them for a spy. I tried to read the minds of our escort, but their expressionless faces were an insoluble enigma. Have suddenly remarked at a peculiarly godforsaken spot in the midst of the jungle:

"I say, I'm not too happy about what orders they may have been given."

"You mean they've been told to make dead meat of us? I don't think so. They're far too inquisitive for that. They'll want to worm it all out of us first."

I was trying to comfort myself as much as Have.

It was some relief when we emerged on to an open stretch of grass. But the deadly fatigue, which had been held up by the onset of unforeseen experiences, assailed us afresh as soon as we fell out for a rest in a forsaken farmyard. While our escort set to work to cook their rice, we lay gasping on the ground, fighting against one of those attacks of vomiting which often follow running all out in a race, or running yourself to a standstill. We could not eat a single grain of the rice which was offered us; and when the order to start again was given, Have, whose face was like wax, could scarcely get on to his feet. His heart raced so fast that he felt he had to have a moment's rest. But the corporal insisted on setting off. There was still far to go. Where to, we asked? Next HQ. How far? They would not say.

We supported each other as well as we could and staggered on, yapped at by our guards if we wavered. When it got dark the corporal made a halt, and ordered his men to bind us. When we saw them produce a cord we attempted to protest in view of our sorry plight; Have was obviously suffering from heart-cramps. It was useless; we were roped together with our hands tied behind our backs. But after a time they relented so far as to loosen the cord, and then at least we didn't stumble over each other. Meanwhile, the forest around us came to life. Beasts of burden were driven out of the cover where they had spent the hours of daylight, and continued their journey to the front; a fatigue party emerged from a side-path carrying ammunition-boxes: detachments of soldiers marched past at a quick step, and once we saw stretchers with wounded men. We had reached another sector of the front. There was heavy artillery as well as machine-gun fire.

It was late before we turned into an empty hut for the night. After being set free we lay down, each with a guard on each side of him. What with over-exhaustion, jangled nerves and incessant mosquito-bites, we were unable to sleep.

". . . And after that, what did you do after that?" The words rang through our heads time after time all through our interrogation next day. The two Japanese Intelligence Officers sat on the ground opposite us, with their legs folded under them, and let themselves go in an undisguised orgy of curiosity. They had a roll of paper in front of them, which they hastily covered with long columns in their mysterious characters. A coloured sketch-map of our route was carefully drawn out, and each day's journey entered upon it, also where we spent each night and the date. In case their pleasure might be interrupted for one unnecessary second, they kept up their "Yes; and after that?" even while making their entries.

The bamboo hut where the wearisome examination took place was at the HQ to which our escort took us early in the morning. It was so well hidden in the jungle that we did not see it until the last moment. It would have been impossible for a reconnaissance plane to see the slightest sign of the huts from the air.

After handing us over, our escort of three had vanished almost as suddenly as they had come into view the day before. Although they were utterly alien in their attitude to us and mysterious also in themselves, we felt an unaccountable intimacy with them all the same. It was them we had to thank for being alive. At the critical moment when our lives were in the balance, it was owing to them that the needle quivered in the right direction. We would gladly have said some friendly word, but they had gone, and their departure seemed to emphasize the impersonality of the whole procedure.

The examination had begun immediately. After giving personal details, we had to describe our escape. We had agreed beforehand that,

137

in the event of being recaptured by the British, we would suppress having all seven bluffed our way out, and say instead that we two had climbed over the wire by ourselves at night; and now we involuntarily stuck to this agreed story. It was not in accordance with the truth, but once said we decided to stick to it; they would never have believed the real facts in any case. Apart from this variation, we gave an accurate account of our escape, forbearing only to mention the gold hidden in the heel of Have's shoe, which was not in fact ever discovered.

Our interrogators, who spoke wretched English, were a perfect professional blend of boundless curiosity and poker faces. Their impassive features never betrayed the faintest indication even of having heard what was said to them; we might have been addressing space. Also we now came up against the difficulty of making our escape sound credible. We were always coming to places in the narrative which sounded so improbable and fantastic, and also, from the Japanese point of view, so very open to suspicion, that we began to feel alarmed lest our two Intelligence Officers, whose duty it was to be distrustful, might not believe a word of the whole story. They did not show their incredulity by the slightest sign – that would have been quite out of keeping with their professional technique – but from the points they went back to in their cross-examination – for example, our encounters with English military police – we were forced to conclude that they doubted the truth of our account. It went very much against us that these officers compared Japanese procedure and measures with those we described. This made them seem impossible, as indeed they would have been in any other setting but that of India. Unless one took into consideration the position of white men in India, the psychology of the British, their laxity in the matter of saluting and uniform – in short, the whole background of our escape – it could only be dismissed as a concoction. We therefore laid great stress on these aspects of the case – only to find that, even after this, there was still an irreducible remainder which seemed to them incredible. This remainder, in default of a better explanation, we put down to luck – which certainly had stuck to us with amazing persistence all the way. Finally, they asked what our further intentions were, and we replied that we wished to return to Germany by the quickest means and to be treated in all matters according to the terms of the alliance between our two countries.

We were assigned a neighbouring hut for the night and were soon visited by a major, who put his head in and out again and departed.

So there we were – as uncertain as ever how our case stood. And we had the impression that the Japanese had not come to any conclusion themselves. And even we found it hard to understand, although we had lived through it ourselves. At one moment it all seemed to have happened quite naturally, one thing leading to another in the most obvious way; at another we were tempted to explain it by the intervention of a higher power, as though we had been guided through the labyrinth of danger by holding a magic thread. There was also a great temptation, now that we had come through, to attribute our success to having always done the right thing without fail. Superficially that was true enough: if we had ever made the slightest mistake we should have been finished. But was it not rather the truth that, after the event, everything was seen in the perspective of success and was given credit for being right, whether in fact it had been right or wrong?

So far we had only had rice and biscuits, and as we longed for a proper meal I made a demonstration to our neighbours. We had to be patient, was the reply; as soon as we reached the next HQ our wishes would be met. On the strength of this highly promising announcement we lay down to sleep.

It was a sultry monsoon night, and we tossed restlessly on our beds. Suddenly we heard voices and saw several people at the door of our hut in the flicker of a lantern.

"We have an urgent announcement to make."

It was the major, for whom one of the Intelligence Officers acted as interpreter. Soldiers with fixed bayonets could be seen in the background. We leapt up in great alarm.

"We have just had orders from Army HQ by telephone—"

There could be no further doubt. We were to be taken out and shot. We stared at their yellow faces which the flickering light distorted. The major was in his underclothes – he had been hauled out of bed owing to the urgency of the case.

"Our orders are to put guards in your hut for the night."

We received the news with undisguised relief. If that was all, they might as well put as many guards over us as they pleased, it would not worry us in the least.

When the major had gone, Have said, "We've many a tussle ahead of us yet."

"That's so. We're through, and yet not through."

We went further and further to the rear. On the day after our examination a lieutenant and three men took over our escort to the next higher command. We made a night-journey by motor-boat down the Mayu in moonlight between groves of palms. Next day we had to march. We went by paths at the jungle's edge and took cover whenever enemy aircraft were overhead. The Japanese could march indefatigably, but they fell out for five minutes in every thirty, just as we were getting into our stride. They would never ask anyone the way, and much preferred going wrong to making enquiries. Asking for information appeared to be considered highly undignified. The lieutenant's behaviour to us was correct; and as he understood a little English, we were able to pick up a few words of Japanese. His men were fishers and rice-cultivators, true children of nature, who were never at a loss in scrounging food and finding good billets.

We never came to a road and never – in sharp contrast to the British side – saw any motor transport. The small detachments of soldiers we met were always on foot, and I remarked to Have, when we made a halt to cook the inevitable rice, that we had left the realm of beefsteak and steel for that of rice and bamboo. Rice was in every billycan, in every knapsack and in every store; the day began with rice, went on with rice and ended with rice. There were Japanese in every Burmese village whose job it was to see that deliveries of rice by the native cultivators did not fall off. As long as they had their rice, they would face any toils and any hardship, and as it was a product of the soil and carried with his kit by every soldier, Japanese troops were more mobile and less dependent on supply-depots than their adversaries. Some of them told us that they had once lived for three months exclusively on rice cooked in brackish water, far from any line of communication. We ourselves were not among the worshippers of that pallid grain. Its monopoly of the menu depressed us; and we suffered many unpleasant consequences from the radical change of diet. We were unable to recover from the privations we had endured; however much we ate of it, the pangs of hunger soon returned. Any recovery of strength was out of the question. We called it "death by inches".

We had been impressed, on our journey across India, by the lavish war-equipment of the Allies; what struck us now was that the Japanese were almost without modern armament of any kind. We never, near the front, saw a single car, or tank, or any Japanese aircraft. Nor could the equipment of the individual soldiers compare with that of their opponents. Anything captured from the British was in great demand – automatic weapons, knapsacks, boots or socks. It was a godsend when enemy supplies were dropped by mistake within the Japanese lines, as

140

happened fairly often, we gathered. Owing to the scarcity of metal, they made great use of bamboo. Harnesses, implements of all kinds and water-pipes, were all made of bamboo. With very few cuts of a knife our escort made us chopsticks and spoons. Thus the new world we had come to seemed to us to live under the sign of rice and bamboo.

The mere fact of being prisoners prompted fresh thoughts of escape. We had not, of course, the slightest intention of trying it on again, but as every movement we made was closely watched, we were unable to resist giving the idea a secret and cursory examination. We agreed that it would be hopeless for any European to attempt it; he would be too obvious, and anyway would have nothing to eat.

We were occupied with these unpatriotic reflections when we saw some soldiers coming along who were clearly not Japanese. "Look. There are some Indians," Have said. "They must belong to the Indian Freedom army." He was right, and as they passed us, tall Sikhs and Punjabis, we saw INA, for Indian National Army, on the shoulder-straps of their old British uniforms. They did not speak to us and no doubt took us for British prisoners of war. We were glad to see Indian soldiers, once members of the Indian Army which had provided our guards, fighting now on our side, even though for their own ends. We decided to speak to them at the first opportunity.

Every evening the hunt for billets was repeated. The villages were crowded with soldiers. We used to drag on from village to village until our escort at last found quarters. On this occasion, it was clear at a glance why this particular Burmese dwelling had been left for us. The occupant, an old man, lay with his back turned to a dying fire, groaning as though his last hour had come. There was a large festering sore on his back that would never heal, and his body was so closely tattooed that it looked as if it had been damascened. We settled ourselves down outside the house, which was built on wooden piles, and when it was dark joined the Japanese soldiers under a large mosquito-net. The officer gave every one of us a tablet of quinine before we turned in. Malaria was very prevalent, and now that Japan had conquered Java and taken over its monopoly of quinine, they had ample supplies. They had been very short of it before, and so we were supposed to accept the gift on each occasion with indications of boundless admiration for the dispensers of it. The prevalence of malaria, in spite of the large supply of quinine, must have been shocking; we were constantly encountering fever-stricken men dragging themselves along at the rear of the column.

Next morning our escort, instead of asking anybody, searched the jungle hour after hour for the HQ we were bound for, and which was close at hand. We found it at last after stumbling on a sentry who was guarding the entrance.

So far we had been treated only with more or less concealed distrust. Here at regimental HQ we encountered undisguised hostility.

We were taken into the camp by the lieutenant to be handed over to another officer, but before we had reached his quarters we were roughly pulled back by the sentry on guard and pushed down on to a bench in the shelter that served as guardroom. After a time a captain came in, trailing a jingling Samurai sword, and addressed us in the following words, to which we listened standing:

"Please", pause, "wait", a longer pause, "five", another pausing, during which he closed his eyes, "minutes". He then drew in his chin sharply, turned round and marched out with ponderous tread.

We sat down again and began at once to deliberate on the order in which we should express our desires at the forthcoming interview. First roast fowl, coffee, cigarettes, the barber, then new clothing, and finally departure from Rangoon by air. When half an hour passed and no one came, we decided that the captain had intended rather to counsel patience than to count minutes. We continued therefore to wait without loss of confidence, and meanwhile took a closer look at our surroundings. The hut in which we were, was on the top of a slope descending steeply to a stream, on the other side of which rose a thickly wooded hill; it was this that gave cover to the camp itself. A tree-trunk bridged the stream; for reasons of concealment a proper bridge had not been built. Opposite the guardroom there was a dilapidated bamboo hut, and not far from it a second smaller one; it was locked and, to judge from the groans we heard at intervals, there was someone shut up in it.

Over an hour had now elapsed, but still nothing happened, although officers frequently passed, to whom the sentry presented arms with an ear-splitting clatter. But not one of them deigned to give us a look. Why did no one come to fetch us? Had we misunderstood? Should we ask the sentry sitting there to ask the captain? Better not. The sentries were rough brutes, and we should only be told off. So we settled down once more to wait in patience, and we waited another hour and then one more. Midday came, and we were brought a plate of watery rice-soup. We now discovered who was shut up in the neighbouring hut. The door was opened and a dish of rice put in. We were astonished to find that there were two Indian soldiers shut up in that windowless hovel, prisoners tied together by a rope round both their waists. They were lying on dirty

142

straw, unshaved and completely cowed; one of them was shuddering from fever. They were a lamentable sight, and we did not find it a cheering one. Who could say what might be in store for us too?

Before we finished our rice one of the soldiers told us to go and wash our dishes in the stream. He followed us with fixed bayonet and showed us the exact spot. There, and nowhere else. All these harshly barked orders were designed to put the fear of God into us. Then we went back to our penitents' bench and waited all afternoon. We had quite forgotten our list of requests by now. Once the sentry on duty made us the condescending offer of his cigarette-end, holding it out behind him without looking round or saying a word. We did not stir. He turned round and threw it at us with a curse. Where was the officer? we asked him. He grinned contemptuously and turned his back.

The five minutes we had been asked to wait became five days. During that time nobody came near us except our guards, each of whom did his best to make our lives as unpleasant as he could. The dilapidated and unwalled bamboo hut opposite the guardroom was allotted us, and here we lay day and night on an unboarded floor made of branches, not daring to move, and escorted, when we had to take a short walk, by a soldier with drawn sword. Our guards took a childish pleasure in ordering us about. The first ordered us to lay our blankets one on the other; the next said they must be spread out, a third insisted on their being hung up. Our resentment grew; we began to hate these unmannerly brutes and would have thoroughly enjoyed giving them a hiding. At night they came along every hour to pull up our mosquito-net and make sure we were still there. The Indian prisoners were treated in the same way. After making sure of us, the guard went along to them and shouted, "Indian – number?" "One" came through the door in a shudder, followed by "Two" in a tearful voice. So it went on all through the night.

What, we wondered, did this shoddy treatment and deliberate neglect mean? We racked our brains to account for it. One reason might be that the Japanese, who never surrendered, despised all prisoners and did not consider them worthy to live. But as they made an exception of civilians prisoners and we had been internees, this could not be the explanation. Their behaviour pointed rather to a belief that we were spies. Our first examination had left us with the impression that our story was not believed; no doubt a report to that effect had been received at regimental HQ. Why therefore should they, in default of proof to the contrary, believe merely in our own assertion that we were not enemy agents? But why give us no opportunity to clear ourselves? We could not, it was true, produce corroboration of our story on the spot; but if we persisted in our assertion that the nearest German Command or Embassy would be able to obtain proof of all we said, surely this would convince the Japanese of our good faith. We went through every aspect of the case, so that we should be able to dispel all doubts, and meet every imputation; and in the course of this review we came on a theory we might find it difficult to disprove.

"Now suppose," Have said, "that the Japs took this to be the situation behind our escape. Two German prisoners escape from Dehra Dun and are recaptured, but are not returned to the same camp – instead, they are put in solitary confinement for the duration. Concurrently, the English send two German-speaking agents in Burma, with all the proofs of identity and the life-stories of the recaptured prisoners. These two agents would be able to authenticate their escape and worm themselves into the confidence of the Japanese."

"If they carry suspicion to those lengths, it will be no good being brought before a German commanding officer. Even a confirmation of our escape by the Protecting Power would be useless."

"Well, there you are. But how are we to get out of it?"

"We must name some person in the Far East who knows us personally."

"That might do it. Do you know anybody who meets the case?"

"I must think."

So we went on all day long. It seemed more difficult to get past our Japanese allies than all the British in India.

We knew little of what went on at HQ. Like everything else in the Japanese Army, it was wrapped in impenetrable secrecy. We could see nothing, and hear only a little, of what occurred. We heard reveille and the other calls during the day, and whenever enemy aircraft were seen there was a shout of "*Schikoki! Schikoki!*" from an invisible observation-post; whereupon all movement ceased. Sounds of battle were invariably heard in the late afternoon from over the stream, produced by the sword-play of spirited warriors falling upon each other in the style of Old Japan, and accompanied by an indescribable roaring from the pit of the stomach, which was supposed to inhibit all movement on the part of an enemy in hand-to-hand combat, and also to arouse the primitive instincts of the champion himself. The day ended with a hymn which drifted away over the darkening jungle in a dreary minor key.

The fifth day came to an end, but just as we were falling asleep we

144

started up at the sound of a loud, menacing voice shouting, "You Germans better get out."

We were told by an interpreter that we were to report immediately to the Commanding Officer at HQ. We dressed at once and followed him.

The stage for this great occasion was already set on a dry bed of pebbles down by the stream. A large packing-case served as table, and ammunition-boxes, on which several officers were already sitting, as seats. At one long side of the table were two unoccupied stools – for the two accused apparently – and on the opposite side a chair with a high back. This was not yet occupied. Soldiers with fixed bayonets formed a cordon on all four sides.

The immensity of the surrounding jungle could be felt. The moon rose in dimmed splendour above the gorge – a court-martial by night, we thought, as we glumly sat down on the stools. The interpreter sat on my right and now told us how to behave. As soon as the CO appeared, we were to stand up and bow low until he had sat down. Good Lord, was it the Emperor in person who was coming? Have asked what was the rank of the commanding officer, in order that he might address him correctly. The interpreter hesitated a moment and then said it was lieutenant-colonel. What could be the meaning of all this pomp, we wondered anxiously, while the company sat round us in stony silence. They might indeed have been carved in stone – and yet they gave us the feeling that at any instant they might leap to their feet and hew us down in a flash, and resume their seats again as though nothing had happened and sit in the same stony silence as before. But they were certainly impressive in their olive-green uniforms and long boots, devilish hard and masculine.

A command rang out and everyone sprang to his feet. Someone was crossing the tree-trunk which spanned the stream. The guard presented arms. We made a far too tiny bow and then hastily inspected the new arrival. He was of medium height, slight, slit-eyed, scant-moustached. Ears like traps which had been set. He promised no good. He wore a tropical shirt instead of uniform and no badge of rank.

The hearing began with innocent questions about our personal background, family, education, occupation; interest was shown in our residence abroad. Our interlocutor greeted our answers, as they were interpreted for him, with a prolonged sniff, which expressed incredulity, boredom and contempt. Then he asked whether we spoke French. Have said no, although he understood it. I was going to say yes and addressed the interpreter as follows, "Please say to the lieutenant-colonel" – it was the first time either of us had brought in his rank. I did not get any further. The colonel darted at the interpreter like an adder, reprimanded him with the utmost severity and dismissed him into the outer darkness. One of the officers immediately took his place. We did not know what was said in this outburst of rage, but its meaning was clear. The unfortunate interpreter had been guilty of treason in that he had told two possible spies what was the rank of a Japanese commanding officer. And now the colonel turned his wrath upon us. Did we imagine he was such a fool as to believe our ridiculous story of an escape? It was all invention and lies. We could not possibly have got through first the English, and then the Japanese lines without help. He said this to me in French. Then Have interrupted with a contradiction.

"What's this?" the Jap hissed. "You say one moment you don't know French and now you speak it fluently. And you both look like Englishmen, you had English names on your labels, and when you were addressed for the first time in German you replied in English. And now I am to believe you are Germans!"

There was a pause, and in the silence it became very clear to us how utterly we were in their power. We felt how forsaken, how cut off we were. If we met our end here, no one would ever know.

The CO beckoned his officers. They all drew closer up to us and the fun began. One asked:

"Who gave you your instructions?"

"What instructions?"

"The instructions to come to us."

"No one gave us them. We came of our own accord."

"Tell us at once who are behind you. To confess will make it better for you."

"We repeat that we are escaped German prisoners, who came to Burma with no other aim than to get to Germany as quickly as possible."

Another pause followed. They gazed at us impassively. They seemed bent on our destruction.

"The commanding officer says that you are to go back to India."

"Back to India? But we have just come from there," Have burst out as though it were a jest.

It crossed my mind in a flash that the order to return was our death-sentence; once on the other side of the line again, they could shoot us with a clear conscience.

"We must resist that for all we're worth," I told Have. And now we got down to our defence with the courage of despair. What had we done, we asked, to deserve this treatment? Was it only because we were unable to prove our identity? Did that mean we were spies? We could not believe that Japanese escaped prisoners would meet with such treatment at German hands. We had come to the Japanese front confident of a friendly welcome, instead of which we were treated more harshly than if we had been the worst of enemies. There was no saying whether all this made the slightest impression. They merely growled in deep bass tones without the least change of expression.

"If you took us to any German authorities we could very soon prove we were Germans."

"Do you know anyone at the German Embassy in Tokyo?"

"No."

"Exactly."

The colonel at this point sent a man for our haversacks. Meanwhile coffee was brought by an orderly. We felt we were in no state for drinking coffee and left our cups untouched.

"Prenez votre café," the colonel ordered in a fury.

The soldier now returned with the haversacks, which were emptied out on the packing-case table. The first articles to be inspected were our blue polo-shirts. They were carefully examined. Unfortunately they were marked "Made in Burma". This was a fresh ground for suspicion. Burma? So we had been in Burma before?

Next. What else was there? Another shirt was inspected. It had the label of a shop for sports-equipment in Hamburg, in spite of our strict undertaking to include nothing which could point to our German origin; but now Have's oversight told in our favour. The same with the German atebrin tablets we had with us. For a moment there was a feeling that things were easing up. But then they were off on the Burma clue, pestered us with a lot more questions, and tried us with Burmese. We defended ourselves hotly and left nothing we could think of unsaid. If our liquidation was already decreed, they might as well know what we thought of them.

Suddenly the colonel said, "Je comprends," gave a curt order to one of his staff, got up and walked away.

We were led off under armed guard.

Chapter Ten

THROUGH BURMA

India was behind us for good. We had escaped from its burning soil, dusty wastes, human sickness, and numerical nightmare of a population; we had turned our backs on Karma and the need for reincarnation. The country we travelled through now abounded in life and colour. Burma had cast off the Indian thirst for redemption; it did not flee from this world or turn a weary look on earthly joys. Its people lived happily in a timeless world of sunshine. But although the land of pagodas had its rubies and its orchids, it had not India's great soul.

The sun was out again after a cloudburst. The pools of water on the paths dried up at once. The air was like a bath of steam, and a film of vaporous moisture coated our flabby skins. Our path twined through dense undergrowth, out of which grew tall trees, making a second wood above the first. Now and then natives appeared with silent, catlike tread and vanished as silently. They were Arakanese. Their bodies were cast in the mould of antique sculpture; their very dark, soft skin and gentle unenvying eyes had the animal beauty of South Sea islanders.

We still did not know what decision had been come to about us. The colonel had apparently ordered that we should be sent southwards under strict arrest, but beyond that nothing was known. For the time we continued our journey on foot, and with us came "One" and "Two", the two Indian prisoners. Our caravan must indeed have been an unusual sight. First a Japanese soldier plodding along; behind him the two dispirited and enfeebled Indian prisoners, smelling of long confinement in the dark; then another Japanese soldier, who like most of his compatriots walked without lifting his feet; next Have and I came chattering along, looking with our waving manes like two lost conductors in search of an orchestra; over our shoulders on a bamboo pole we carried a heavy sack of rice. The rear was brought up by another Japanese soldier. The Indians ought to have carried their own stock of rice but, as one of them was suffering severely from fever, we had to carry it for them whether we

148

liked it or not. Two white men, two Sahibs, carrying a sack through Burma! Under armed guard like convicts! This would have been incredible only a short time ago; now it was an incontestable reality, and more – a symbol. The white man, stripped of his prerogative of overlord, was degraded to the low estate of coolie.

The dominion of the white man had been abolished, but his departure did not bring freedom any nearer; Burma only acquired new masters when the Japanese entered on the heels of the British. And lest there might be any doubt about it, they had themselves addressed as "Master" by the Burmese. But the frequent use of this term by the native population was not enough, and it was often used by the Japanese soldiers instead of the first person: "Master wants this" or "Master is coming at once". We found it amusing that the Japanese, who pretended to come as deliverers, should use this term, in English too, with its imperialistic associations. From any point of view it was a crass blunder in psychology, and all the more so because the British had never laid any stress on such forms of address. It was easy to see what sort of figure the Japanese cut as the masters of Burma. We had observed at once that they were far superior to the lazy Burmese in energy and capability, but we now observed how badly they came out of a comparison with the British. Although they were related to the Burmese as fellow-Asiatics and had the immense advantage of the battle-cry, "Death to Western imperialism", which might have swept all before it, yet if the Burmese had had the choice they would have chosen the British, in spite of all the anti-British indoctrination. We saw many proofs of this; and it seems that subject races are more influenced, when choosing between two masters, by their immediate convenience than by considerations of relationship, or distant prospects and higher ideals. The British doubtless were the more comfortable masters, particularly as they did not go in for interference on a large scale. The Japanese sinned gravely in this way, poking their noses into everything, bossing every little village, trusting nobody, taking every decision, however trivial, into their own hands and leaving no one in peace for a moment. When the Burmese came into contact with the British, it was with people who kept their lordly distance; but they saw the tawdry Japanese at close range and had no illusions. And of course the Japanese, after the conquest of Burma, had the war to carry on against the Allies, and had no time to make any advantages of the "co-prosperity sphere" available to the Burmese. On the contrary, the Japanese were compelled to live off the land, which was thereby impoverished; and so stark reality contrasted strangely with lofty ideals. They

149

came as liberators, and settled in as "masters"; instead of having anything to give, they took all they could, and the result, for the Burmese, was general disillusionment.

And the upshot was, as we told each other with the sack of rice on the pole between us, that whatever mistakes the Japanese made, and whether they remained in Burma or were driven out, things would never be the same again. The white man had lost his undisputed dominion for good and all.

"Are you aware that we are the walking symbols of a new age?"

"Stow it and swop shoulders. That's more to the point."

The path came out into the open, and we were met by some Buddhist monks, in yellow robes, with shorn heads and each carrying a small copper alms-bowl. Their faces were utterly empty; they had reached the last stage of self-annihilation, snapped the link with mortality and united their entity to nonentity.

Oxen up to their bellies in water drew the plough over the rice-fields; white cranes, with beaks retracted, trod the narrow dykes. We were approaching a village. There were light-coloured dwellings under tall trees, some of them built on posts high above the ground. We halted in the market-place in the middle of the village, an open space bathed in the warm-toned shadows cast by the trees. Our guards, after putting a wide distance between us and the Indians, set about cooking. Some villagers came along in their slow and sleepy way, and gazed at us in silence. Their brown faces had prominent cheek-bones, wide mouths, and lifeless, obliquely-set eyes. Some had athletic bodies with well-developed muscles. They wore the lunghi, which resembles a skirt and is always pink, wound round their waists. But there was an old man who wore only a short cloth, and his thighs were so closely tattooed that he looked as if he were wearing old-fashioned, lace-edged drawers. The men wear a silk cloth, also pink, the favourite colour, round their heads. There were some women too; their faces were powdered white and they had long black cigars in their mouths. There was also a girl, shy and slender as a deer, wearing a jacket over her young breasts and a raspberry-pink lunghi, and an orchid in her fine, black, silken hair.

A river-trip seemed to lie ahead of us; our Japanese started bargaining with one of the village boatmen, and in Burmese too. The parties kept up a guttural chant by turns on the vowels o and u ; and when they had come to an agreement we broke camp and walked through the village to the landing-stage. The inhabitants reclined outside their dwellings, smoking or sleeping. They say in Burma that a sleeper must never be roughly or suddenly awakened, because his soul is outside his body in the form of a beautiful butterfly – and woe to the sleeper who is aroused before his soul has time to return to him.

The water was deep and sluggish. Our sampan clove the oily fluid without causing a ripple or a sound. It was bordered by marshland, from which rose hundreds of thousands of tall palms. Backwaters branched off in all directions and promptly lost their way in the mazy green. The shadows lengthened. What was our destination? Was it Akyab, in whose latitude we must now be? Or was it again some Army HQ? I tried hard to get an answer out of one of our guards. He thought long and hard, but got nothing out. He then astonished me by continuing the conversation in German, not in order to tell me where we were bound for, but to say that he had been a student in the philosophical faculty of the Imperial University of Tokyo. Had I, he asked, read Martin Heidegger? He had had his work, *Existence and Time*, to read in the course of his studies. If his intention was to impress me, he had achieved his object. I was rendered speechless. When I had recovered, I observed that even for a German the work was difficult to digest, and what could a Japanese who was not even at home in simple everyday German make of a sentence beginning: "The wherein of the self-referring understanding as the whereon of the letting-itself-be-met of the existent . . ." Difficult it was, he admitted, but nevertheless he had held doggedly on to the last page. A very significant and illuminating conversation.

It was dark by the time we landed; after that we did an hour's march, which brought us to some huts, and here we were handed over to a Japanese sergeant. There were also some Indians present, who took charge of "One" and "Two". Our guards, including the existentialist philosopher in uniform, turned round and vanished into the night.

The place in which we now found ourselves was in a wilderness of stagnant marshes cut off on every side. We did not know what its name was; perhaps it had no name. Some bamboo huts were concealed beneath enormous trees and accommodated a few Japanese, and nearby, likewise concealed by trees, there was a camp of small huts occupied by Indians. Here recently captured Indian prisoners were converted into fighters for freedom. We could only approach the converts with great caution, because fraternization of this kind was not desired by the Japanese. As we were now on what might have been a leper island, surrounded by wide stretches of water on all sides, we were left unguarded. We were merely confined within a certain area beyond which we were not allowed

151

to go. We shared the hut of the Indian who cooked for the Japanese. Nothing at all happened, and all we could do was to lie about doing nothing. After much pressure the sergeant informed us that his orders were to keep us until he received further orders. He could not say when these might arrive, and warned us, when we showed an eagerness for more precise information, against demonstrations of impatience. We at once, on the strength of this inconclusive reply, made enquiries of the Indians, hoping to learn something about the prospects of being sent on to Rangoon, four hundred miles away. Prospects, we were told, were bad. We should be wise to allow for a wait of several weeks or, even better, months. One INA officer, for example, had been waiting for six weeks, and did not consider the prospect any more promising than on the first day. It was also a peculiarly difficult journey: first there were eight days by boat on inland waterways, then there were the Arakan Mountains, one of the last spurs of the Himalayas, to cross, then the crossing of the Irrawaddy River, and finally a railway journey. We might think ourselves lucky, in fact, if we ever got away at all.

Information of this vague and ambiguous kind was the very thing to cause us deeper anxiety than we cared to admit. Our fate was as obscure as ever. We had not had the least success in rebutting the charge of being spies; we had merely not been sent back to India. Possibly we might be left to rot. From the Japanese standpoint that was by far the easiest solution. "Succumbed to their privations", or words to that effect, would meet the case. If that was their object, the place was well-chosen. The stretches of stagnant water provided an admirable breeding-place for the *Anopheles* mosquito, and there were innumerable rats as well. We could hardly keep them at bay. They had the free run of the hut by night, gnawing everything with poisoned teeth, making havoc of all they could, and running over us with shrill squeaks. There were other agents of destruction – wasps with long bodies, scorpions, vipers, spiders, white, yellow and red.

But worse than vermin was the hunger we had to endure. We had two meals a day, a plate of "death by inches" at ten in the morning and at five in the evening. And that was all. The Japanese, certainly, got no more, and seemed to survive on it all right. For us it was quite inadequate, and we were afraid that our last reserves of strength would be slowly sapped.

Have had an attack of malaria on the third day of our sojourn, and the day after he had dysentery as well.

I did all I could to find extra food, and implored the Indians, who were famished themselves, to give us some of their chapatti, flat bread made of flour and water, baked over the fire on a flat tin. I was caught in the act by one of the Japanese soldiers and driven off. But at night a Punjabi brought us two pieces and disappeared as suddenly as he came, cursing under his breath at the Japanese. What he brought us was not worth mentioning, and so I had to scout about for other supplies.

Hunger was now so acute that I would have stopped at nothing to satisfy it. If it had been merely a physical privation, I might have borne it; but the insufferable part of it was that hunger acquired the over-whelming force of a primitive instinct, and subdued and degraded the mind into thinking of nothing else but food. One took no interest in anything else, dreamed of it at night, and was a human being no longer. When we woke our whole attention was engrossed by the cook, sepa-rated from us by a fibre screen. We listened to what he was doing at the fire, sniffed the air to catch any smell of cooking; and any kitchen sound threw us into hallucinations. When the time came for a meal, our hopes were already set on the one after, because each was bankrupt before it started; we never caught up on our famished condition. So there was nothing for it but stealing. I found a box of brown cane-sugar among the meagre kitchen-stores, and on the supposition that the cook pinched our rations, a supposition which is never wide of the mark in the east, I took as much as I thought we were properly entitled to. The cook apparently noticed what I was up to, because after a few raids the box was no longer there.

Have looked like the fresco of Death in the cathedral at Basle. He was pursued by bad luck. As soon as he had got over his attack of malaria and while still suffering from dysentery, he got blood-poisoning. The need for a doctor became urgent when his leg swelled up to a dangerous size. We were given permission to go to the next village, where there was a clinic, and one day we dragged ourselves along there. Two doctors and an orderly were at work in a hut, which was completely hidden in papaya trees. Their patients were mostly Burmese victims of Allied air-raids. They submitted to treatment like dumb and frightened animals. The doctors lanced Have's leg, which gave him great relief; they were also very friendly, and a great consolation.

They gave us a drink of milk, and some coffee and sugar to take back with us. Like most Japanese doctors, they spoke a little German. We asked them to give us lessons in Japanese. They agreed willingly, and in return we had to give them auditions in the singing of German songs, which they rendered with great spontaneity and boyish enthusiasm.

Their selection was the *Heidenröslein*, the *Lindenbaum*, and the *Lorelei* – the three German songs every educated Japanese knows from childhood. They put us in an awkward fix by asking us to recite all the verses. We tried to get out of it by improvisation, but our ruse was discovered on their next visit, as by that time the authentic text had come back to them. We visited the clinic whenever we could. These visits were the only ray of light in our dreary existence.

In spite of their indolence, the Burmese have a fiery temperament, and are capable of flying into a frenzy without warning. We were witnesses of this one day when we were dozing on our beds, thinking with despair of our hopeless state, with no responsible officer anywhere near to appeal to, and the risk of the British raiding Akyab, or landing from the air, in which case we might again be taken prisoner, when our thoughts were interrupted by a sudden wild uproar. We looked out and saw two soldiers going for each other like madmen with stout bamboo staves. We retreated hurriedly to the back of the hut, for fear that if they caught sight of us they might turn on us instead. "Burmese soldiers," the cook said. "They often get into a fury all of a sudden. It's best to leave them alone and let them calm down." This was the first time we had heard of a Burmese army; it was not, the cook informed us, employed in front line operations. We had taken the two combatants for Japanese because they wore the same uniform, with the exception of the two black Burmese braids on their caps.

It was the monsoon. The downpours increased in violence and duration, until they reached a pitch which was almost exhilarating as a demonstration of nature's unnatural excess. The whole scene was wrapped in a fantastic deep-sea twilight; all vegetation rolled helplessly like jelly-fish in the surging masses of water. Outlines dissolved and everything was seen as though through dripping window-panes, and then it suddenly ceased and the scene was transformed. The sun shone; there was a hothouse air; the plants raised themselves up again, all their milliards of cells set to work like fury and their roots reached out greedily in the saturated soil.

We were at the end of the second week of tormenting uncertainty in our outpost of desolation, but nothing whatever had happened to suggest any change. We felt ourselves getting weaker and more starved, especially as Have, cured of his vomiting, had the appetite of a convalescent. There was nothing left to steal, and so I now got in touch with a Burmese in a neighbouring village, in the hope of exchanging our last Indian rupees for some polished rice. He said that if we had gold to spend he could procure us something good, something special. So I told him to bring what he had that evening, because we still had – besides the gold sovereign which we did not want to touch – a little gold in the form of a dental stopping which Have had sewn into the seam of his trousers.

The man came as agreed, bringing the rice. We consumed it on the spot. We then asked what else he had to offer. He called out a name in a low voice and a girl came in out of the darkness.

"Well, what has she brought?"

"Herself,' the man said in a whisper.

The girl did not look up, but knelt silently on the threshold. Her delicate hands were laid flat on her thighs, and she waited with the submissiveness of a sacrificial victim for our decision. She was very young, scarcely more than a child.

There was an embarrassed silence, while we reflected on our wasted bodies. Then I said:

"A chop would please me better."

"The old pander doesn't know what it's like to be starving," Have added.

Anyway, we kept our gold stopping.

Next morning an escort unexpectedly arrived and took us away.

Now we were in movement again at last, we kept going, however slowly, and with however many interruptions and alarms. Our conveyance was by Japanese assault-craft, small broad vessels of fifty tons' burden, which maintained communications along the tortuous waterways of north-west Burma. They plied only by night because of the danger of enemy aircraft. As soon as darkness fell, the boats emerged from their hiding-places, took on their passengers, and proceeded through the dark, primeval landscape, which seemed contemporary with the age when coal-beds were formed; then just before sunrise they put down their complement in the forest somewhere, usually in the neighbourhood of a native settlement. The soldiers billeted themselves in the villages and waited until it was dark. Thus we journeyed on night after night in an overcrowded boat, wedged in among the oblique-eyed, fish-odorous troops, unable to stand comfortably, let alone sit or lie down, and spending the days in one Burmese hut after another.

Our escort was unchanged during the ten days this river-voyage lasted, and was four in number, a lieutenant, a sergeant and two men. They were well-disposed and had no suspicions; they behaved as an escort purely and not as a guard in charge of dangerous criminals. The four of them made a tightly knit group, like brothers, and the lieutenant was more the eldest brother than a superior. They ate in common, slept under the same mosquito-net and consulted together, and yet maintained the proper distance between an officer and his men. The Japanese Army was built up on this patriarchal relationship and was in this respect a faithful copy of Japanese family life.

The lieutenant, whose name was Fujita, had recently passed out of the military academy in Tokyo and had arrived in Burma from Java. He was in his early twenties, neat of figure though very strong, and he had a lean, aristocratic skull, eyebrows softly marked as with charcoal, and an expression which was at the same time gentle and hard as a diamond. His manner with us was that of an elder brother, strict and considerate, and he did us a great service in introducing us to his fellow-countrymen as Germans, which made a friendly atmosphere for us everywhere, and particularly on the boats, where our arrival naturally aroused great curiosity. The soldiers stared at us as if we were fabulous monsters, marvelled at our height, asked permission to pull the hair of our legs and arms – their own being notoriously hairless – made jokes about us, laughed good-humouredly and gave us cigarettes.

There is not much to say about the sergeant; he was quiet and taciturn. His chief merit was that he was an excellent billeting officer. He always got the best hut for us, usually that of the village elder. He was also a good shot, and shot jungle-fowl for us when we asked him to. Our appetites amazed him; mine in particular he could not get over. I was in this respect an insoluble problem to the Japanese, but I must allow that the scantiness of the country's resources was against them. We were able, thank heaven, to tap new sources of supply by singing German songs to our Burmese hosts on the strict understanding that they paid us with fruit. Here Have did excellent work. The villages of Burma echoed many and many a time to his fine rendering of "*Wenn der weisse Flieder wieder blüht*," while I handed round the hat.

The difficulty we found at first in distinguishing between Japanese faces was not yet entirely overcome. It is a fact that Asiatics look more alike than the white races. They all have smooth, blue-black hair, black eyes, and that stretched look of the skin across the prominent cheekbones which takes so much from the expressiveness of their faces. We therefore found it easier to recognize the third member of our escort by his height than by his face. He had the ideal build for a swimmer – he was all stream-lined. You had only to look at him to recognize that the Japanese build is not meant for running, but is perfectly adapted to

156

swimming. We called him "Verygoodka", because he added the Japanese interrogative particle to the only English expression he knew. When he came out of the water after a swim in a pool he had the flowing movements of a pearl-diver, and the amphibian elegance of an otter. He also had an excellent voice and was fond of singing. We often stood beside him in the bows during our nightly trips and listened to him. He wanted to teach us some old Japanese songs, but it was no good. We were unable to produce the half- and quarter-tones correctly.

Lieutenant Fujita, the sergeant and Verygoodka were the core of the party; the fourth was an outsider from another regiment and had only been attached for the river-trip. He was a complete oddity. He was so short that he did not come up to our chests, as round as a barrel and exceptionally strong. The muscles stood out on his child's arms. His legs, though two in number, resembled those of the caterpillar. His face was as round as a frying-pan and his tiny eyes and ears, bridgeless nose and lips which protruded like the tip of an elephant's trunk were completely lost in the wide expanse. His cap found no resting-place on his balloon-like head. He was good-natured and shared all he had with us. But he was also brutal and a man to beware of.

Fujita told us that he was an excellent jungle-fighter and had often distinguished himself in raids with his tommy-gun. After five years of continuous fighting, he was now going home on long leave to his village near Osaka, where his parents were rice-farmers. He gave us such glowing accounts of the pleasures of Tokyo that we nicknamed him "Yoshiwara Master", and he never heard us say it without an upward glint of his moon-face. As an old soldier he was up to all the tricks of the trade; he avoided all superfluous movement and could sleep in any place or position; but the moment he was roused he was at his post. He could always whip up some addition to every meal, usually the raw fish he was so fond of. He always knew when to push himself forward and when to keep in the background, and had the knack of doing business with the people of the country. As soon as we arrived at a village, the women came in from the country with fruit, small cakes of rice, cheroots and other produce which they carried on their heads in flat baskets, and offered for sale to the soldiers. Yoshiwara Master used to bargain on and on until the women became confused and alarmed by his haggling and cursing, and then when they at last gave in he had usually got twice what he had paid for.

In this he was an exception, because as a rule the Japanese treated the Burmese very well. They paid for everything they had, left the girls alone, waited patiently for their billets until the indolent owners were ready to move out for them, and cleaned up carefully before they left. It would have been folly, with lines of communication stretched to the utmost, if they had provoked the Burmese to revolt by bad treatment.

Yoshiwara Master suffered from malaria. He could not get rid of it, and had had it so long that he could not remember when he had had his first attack – probably years before in Canton. He was now having a bad attack again. He had shivering-fits every day. Then he lay quite still and his head glowed like a fireball. He used to put on a headpiece of mosquito-netting closely fastened in at the neck, and wrap his hands up in gauntlets as well, before turning in. After poking about for a time in this grotesquely comic diving-suit, he would lie down and snore loudly.

He was often in a high fever and feeling like death when the time came to embark, but however hard the going might be none of his companions ever helped him along. At first we thought they were being deliberately unfriendly, but when we carried his pack for him we saw from the looks they gave us that our behaviour was completely incomprehensible to them. They considered our wish to help a sign of servility or of womanish pity. But probably the deepest cause of their mute disapproval was that we were offending against a taboo. Pain, sickness, death, we soon saw, were to the Japanese way of thinking predicaments with which each man must deal for himself. A Japanese does not expect sympathy in his sufferings and is equally insensitive to the sufferings of others. Possibly the old belief that decrepitude is a ritual uncleanness still has some influence. On our journey through Burma we saw advanced cases of beri-beri dragging themselves slowly through the jungle to some distant hospital – solitary, Dantesque apparitions; and we saw others dying by the roadside on whom no one bestowed a look even of indifference.

It was now certain that we were on our way to Rangoon; our escort had at last let out the secret. But they did not know themselves what would happen to us there. We had been travelling by boat for a week and were at the last transit-station. Our next night's voyage would bring us to Taungup, whence our journey would be by road. We were lying in close proximity to the palm-tops in a hut on tall posts on the edge of a village. It was past midday, and we continued our morning sleep, which we had interrupted only for a meal. We lived in a world where drowsiness is the rule for the whole population and the very air is narcotic, and so it was only right that we should share the universal love of sleep. If we kept awake, wakefulness had nothing to bestow; and if we slept there was nothing we should miss.

A noise, rapidly rising to a roar, roused us from our stupor. British fighters had dived to tree-top level. We just had time to shin down the notched poles and take cover under the hut. The air-raid trenches were all full of water.

There was a terrific noise as the machines assailed the village. A burst came in our direction too. The bullets struck the earth with a thud. The walls of the huts, little thicker than leaves, were not the slightest protection. I felt completely helpless and could scarcely conceal my uneasiness. The Japanese showed no excitement, but the lively discussion which followed showed that they had been just as frightened as we had been.

A Burmese in his boat close by was riddled with bullets, poor devil.

The attack was over in a few seconds, and a moment later it seemed incredible that this sleep-drunken village had received such a visitation.

We waited a long time that night at the landing-stage, although many boats passed and the chugging of diesel engines could be heard in the darkness getting louder or dying away. I sat under a cassowary tree, among the sleeping foreign soldiers. A warm breath came from the jungle, still hot from the day. At midnight a fresh detachment joined us, and as soon as Verygoodka, who was awake too, caught sight of it he jumped up and awoke the others. They all got hurriedly to their feet and saluted. I asked our lieutenant the reason, and he pointed to one of the newcomers, who had a small box suspended from his neck by a white silk scarf. It was an urn containing the ashes of a soldier.

It was being conveyed to Tokyo, and there at a great ceremony, which would take place by night in the presence of the high priest of the Shinto religion, it would be deposited with hundreds of thousands more in the Yasukuni temple. Once enshrined there, we were told, the soul of the dead soldier was assured of immortality and joined the great army of the gods of war. It was therefore the ardent desire of the Japanese soldier to give his life in battle and put on immortality without delay. The soul of the dead soldier may be sure of being honoured by the living, and even Tenno Heika, the Celestial Emperor, would visit the shrine to say his prayers – the greatest honour that could fall to the lot of a Japanese.

We had to wait another day before a boat came to take us on. To our surprise, we embarked early in the afternoon – which in view of the British air-attacks did not altogether please us, but there was the advantage that for once we saw by daylight the scenes which, so far, we had known only under the romantic cloak of darkness.

Marshes and mangrove wildernesses stretched on all sides as far as the eye could see, lying, it seemed, under a primeval spell. Only here and there low hills of thick jungle rose above the flat expanse. Narrow water-lanes and backwaters threaded the maze of vegetation, making a labyrinth through which the boat could scarcely pass; its sides brushed against great arching roots and overhanging branches and bored its way through tunnels of foliage. For long distances there was no firm ground to be seen. The marsh plants grew out of the water from a network of exposed roots, so that the stems or branches only began at a considerable height above water-level. The sluggish water, out of which black roots writhed like snakes, the skeletons of trees on the watery banks, the restless flicker of the leaves, all made a scene which was at once desolate and prolific. No living thing could survive without being slowly drowned, strangled and submerged. We voyaged for hours through this savage flora, as we had for many nights already. Occasionally canoes flitted silently past, paddled by shy, bronze-skinned natives. Where could they have come from and where could they be going to in this desolation?

We came to the open sea before dark. The coast was much indented and out of the shallow surf, like dark bits of broken crockery, lay small islands in scattered groups; yet no life was to be seen. Their coasts were inaccessible. Mangroves fought off all invaders. Our boat was the only craft in sight – and the only target. We listened anxiously for the first drone of an engine and gave furtive glances round the forlorn horizon for the first glimpse of a plane; but soon it grew dark and the danger of air-attack was over.

We went inland again during the night and entered a canal. A party of stark-naked soldiers came on board at one stopping-place; they had had to wade out to us as the tide was low. They carried their clothing in bundles on their shoulders and were coated in grey, slimy mud to the thigh. As soon as they saw the soldier carrying the urn, they saluted exactly as though they had been in uniform.

We said good-bye to Fujita and his men at Taungup. We had been waiting two days in an officers' rest-house to continue our journey over the Arakan Mountains. On the night before we parted Fujita gave a dinner for us at which *sake* was drunk out of tiny porcelain cups – a touching compliment, considering that it was paid for out of his very inadequate pay. The war had sent prices soaring up in the conquered countries, sometimes by 100 per cent, but the yen was still at par in Burmese rupees, so that the Japanese soldier, whose pay in yen remained the same, was scarcely able to buy anything at all.

Fujita accompanied us to a nearby Divisional HQ to see about putting us on our next stage; and there, before we went on our way, we had a visit from a colonel who happened to be passing by. He was so old that he could hardly stand, and his batman followed him everywhere with a chair, which was pushed beneath him whenever he came to a halt. He had the head and the vacant gaze of a llama, which with his extreme age gave him the look of an ambulant relic, and made us feel quite pious and solemn. We were therefore very much surprised, when in the course of a brief interrogation through one of his staff, he asked whether we both had girls. When Have replied that in better days we had had one in every town, he had a tremendous success with the whole company, and the old gentleman joined in the laughter noiselessly, but very heartily, showing all his large teeth, every one of which was of gold. Then he got up tremulously from his chair, and with a fatherly nod to us doddered off on the arms of his two attendants to shed his light elsewhere.

Our next escort – we were passed from hand to hand like a courier's staff – consisted of a single officer, a captain who had been at the capture of Singapore. He took us over with reluctance and walked in front of us without a word to a road-crossing to wait for a lorry. For the next half-hour he stood motionless with his legs apart, his hands in front of him on the hilt of his sword, looking with an expression of utter contempt at the two detestable white men. His head was the shape of a dum-dum bullet, and his mouth was a streak set in a hard, square chin. He only once opened his mouth during this murderous inspection, and then it was to cough. Why did he stare like that? Even after we had got into the lorry he never took his eyes off us. Did he mean to extort by hypnotism the confession that we were spies, or at least that we were Englishmen? Such a look, even for one second, would have called for an explanation in other circumstances; as it was, we could only deliberately turn our backs. And at the same moment he asked us rudely whether we really were Germans. After this he ceased to stare, but did not deign to utter another word.

The Japanese Army, from our first sight of it, made a mysterious and even, in some respects, a sinister impression on us. It had some characteristics we found it hard to explain and others we feared. We would say to each other, "I shouldn't care to fight against them," or "They'd stop at nothing," or "We're up against deepest Asia now" – all of which

161

expressed our sense of something disturbing and incomprehensible. Even casual contact with individuals might arouse this feeling; we often did not know with whom we were dealing, what his instructions were, or to whom he would report.

There were occasions when a man would suddenly address us fluently in a European language after having deliberately employed an interpreter. It was almost impossible to foresee how they would behave on any given occasion; and we had to be always on our guard, because they usually reacted in the way we least expected, and there was always the risk that their primordial instincts, which lurked in readiness behind thin but impenetrable cover, might leap out. We began by thinking that if a Japanese did not look at us he was taking no notice of us; later we discovered that he was only apparently ignoring us and in reality studying us intently out of the corner of his eye. In this the captain who had been at the capture of Singapore was an exception. The love of indirect methods was the rule. Orders were conveyed by hints, annoyance by exaggerated politeness, and the wire-puller was concealed behind the man of straw.

Who was competent to deal with what, what was the next stage, and who had the responsibility – all such questions became blurred and almost unanswerable. It was quite impossible to guess where the lever was, and what were the guiding principles; all you could see were soldiers in small squads and parties – never large detachments – traversing the roadless country, and yet everything hung together in some mysterious way, as in an ant-heap where each ant seems to run aimlessly about, but in fact performs its task in a plan of which it knows nothing.

It was late in the afternoon when the lorry started, and so we were counting on a night-journey. Immediately after Taungup, we began to climb in sharp turns into the solitude of the Arakan Mountains. As it turned out, we drove for little more than an hour, and then stopped at some log-huts of Japanese occupation-troops in the forest. Without a word or a look, the captain vanished into one of them, and we were conducted by the driver to a narrow gorge which branched off at the side of the road, where in the tangle of undergrowth we found a bamboo hut occupied by soldiers. It stood on tall poles against the steep side of the hill, growing like a mushroom in the deep forest mould. While the meal of rice was being cooked inside, we sat on the veranda and watched with a feeling of awe how night descended on the jungle. It was the moment of transition, when the dusk allows objects to stand out for a last moment before darkness swallows them. The moment quickly passed; the shadows gathered beneath the trees, the last semblance of light dimmed and stole away secretly between the bamboos. Already every gap between the bushes was filled with shadows, which rapidly deepened and yawned at us like black gullets. The forest seemed now to bode nothing good; hinted danger gripped the heart from that unremitting oppression of nature, as deadly as it was indifferent. Now it was pitch-black night – in the tropics night falls quickly. In a few minutes the whole forest was swallowed up.

Before going to sleep we sat with the soldiers round an oil-lamp; they were stripped except for a loin-cloth, and they had the handkerchief which every soldier carries wound round their shaven heads. They told us that Arakan was full of beasts of prey, tigers and wild elephants. They could not have chosen a better theme; our imagination only needed this spur to keep us awake half the night, listening to all the sounds of the jungle – the rustle in the leaves, the distant screams of monkeys, the raucous croak of frogs, the heavy crash of a mighty tree – the cooking, singing, gurgling – the stampede of pursuit – the cries of love – and of death.

Next morning we continued our journey in good time along a road which was nothing but twists and turns. We went on without a break to the top, seeing fresh views of the forest solitudes at every turn. Except for the huts of the Japanese on the side of the road, we saw no sign of habitation; there was nothing except the undulating carpet of tree-tops, a green chaos, an uninhabitable waste. The building of this difficult section of road had been begun before the war and was hastened by the Japanese, as it was the only link with their left wing, and an urgent necessity. They spared no expense to repair damage by landslide or cloudburst. We often met long columns of Burmese coolies at work on road-mending under a Japanese foreman. The top of the pass, where there was a Japanese camp, was veiled in heavy rain-clouds; it seemed to rain without ceasing and the whole place was like a bath. After a short rest and change of vehicle, we went on our way downhill, having left the captain behind without, needless to say, any sign of parting. We now had a sergeant in charge of us. The road wound slowly down along steep and lonely gorges to the plain; it took us all day and the following night to reach the Irrawaddy at a point where there was a ferry, at early dawn. We waited prostrate in the lorry, dead beat, until the sun rose.

After a time a Japanese came from the ferry landing-stage and told our sergeant that two German generals on a tour of inspection were expected. What? Two German generals? Then our troubles were over. We should now be in a position to prove our case. What a surprising thing to run into two German generals in the middle of Burma! We sprang to life and insisted first on hearing all the man could tell us and then on his going back to the ferry-station buildings to hear more. He soon returned, and what he had to tell shattered us; it was all a mistake. We ourselves were the German generals.

Things had been going too well with us. It was time we had a setback. Nor did we have long to wait. As soon as we boarded the ferry-boat we were taken over by a fresh escort. There were four of them. They had the sinister look of hangmen; their caps were pulled down over their noses, and our practised eye instantly saw something suspicious – a cord dangled from under the flaps of their packs. They did not bind us, but only pushed us against the railing and formed a semicircle round us. But though penned in we could look at the scenery. The Irrawaddy at this point was several hundred yards across and flowed between wooded hills, from which a pagoda now and again peeped out. On its long journey from the Chinese border to the Gulf of Martaban, it passes through many strange regions, through the wild jungles of north Burma, past the district of Shaan, where dwell primitive hill-tribes, whose women stretch their necks by means of metal rings, past Bhamo and Mandalay, the ancient royal residence, through the barren landscapes of the Yenangyaun oilfields, to the town of Prome just opposite us, and then on through the plain of Pegu-Tenasserim, one of the richest rice-growing areas of the world, to the sea. Burma has so much to thank the Irrawaddy for that it is called the river of benevolence.

A lorry was waiting for us on the other side, and we were driven at great speed to a Japanese HQ. Here we were transferred to another vehicle, a sort of delivery van with seats along the sides.

"You wait," Have said in high spirits. "We'll be delivered to Rangoon in this old box. Then we'll have come to the end of the journey and have arrived at our destination."

"What you call an old box looks to me very like a Black Maria, but of course they may be taking us to Rangoon in it."

The windows were in fact barred: we used them as look-outs to see where we were going.

It was not a long journey. After going along one or two streets the vehicle stopped at a long grey wall, in which, some feet from the ground, a square hole had been knocked to form a gateway. We alighted and found ourselves at the gate of the town prison of Prome, a Burmese prison!

Our dismay can be imagined. We knew from experience that prison-doors, once they shut on you, do not easily open, and we stepped over the fatal threshold with the worst forebodings. And as soon as we were in, the iron gate clanged behind us. There was a building in the middle of the prison yard with a flight of wooden steps leading up to it. We had to go up there, and into a large room with a table at one end and, at the other, a sofa covered in dirty American cloth, on which we were told to sit. From here, while being fallen upon by the sofa-bugs, we anxiously followed the proceedings at the table, where our escort was talking to the prison governor, whose servility to the Japanese was abject. Of all the evil fates that might befall us, the worst in our opinion would be to be handed over to the Burmese. With the Japanese we had at least the benefit of a military organization in some sort of connection with the German Army, and there was the hope that some day we might get a hearing. But once at the mercy of Burmese gaolers—

When the talk was at an end, the prison governor came shuffling up to us and explained in a husky whisper and with alcoholic breath that he was instructed to take charge of us. All the best of friends – we need have no anxiety.

The Japanese then conducted us down the steps again and past a long row of cages in which Burmese were penned. They stopped at a cell.

This was going too far.

"We refuse to go in there," we protested, determined not to advance another step. "What do you mean by treating us as criminals? We insist on the German Consul in Rangoon being informed of this at once."

The Japanese lieutenant, who was not unfriendly in himself, seemed embarrassed, and uncertain whether to listen to our complaint or to order his men to put us inside by force. None of those present could translate directly from English into Japanese, so two interpreters had to share the part, one an underling of the prison governor's, a slippery reptile with a suspiciously large diamond ring on his finger, who translated from English into Burmese, and the other a boy who translated into Japanese.

By this roundabout method the lieutenant told us that we ought not to object to the lodging offered us, because British prisoners had also had to make use of it. We replied that we were German, not British, and was he not aware that the Germans and Japanese were allies? Yes, he knew that, but we had come from the British side. What else, we asked, could we have done, since we had escaped – oh escaped, had we? And how had we managed that? Whereupon the whole story had to be told him.

When we had ended our account, they still insisted that we must in spite of all be locked up, because those were the orders. Right, we replied, we would do as they wished, but on condition that our escort did not leave us. Well, if we insisted, he said, and accompanied us into the cell. The soldiers began at once to sweep it out, fetched mats, cooked rice in large quantity, and took the opportunity of a good sleep. But when evening came they thought it all rather too silly, and sent a messenger to their superior officer; he came back with orders that all of us, Germans and Japanese, might consider our friendly party in gaol at an end.

We spent the night at HQ from which we had set out in the morning. Next day we were summoned into the presence of an officer, who informed us that the order had been misunderstood and that we should not again be handed over to a Burmese prison. Before dismissing us, he told us that instructions had come through to dispatch us next day by train to Rangoon.

Either because wood-fuel had to be used owing to a shortage of coal, or because this important line was under constant threat of air-attack, the journey took eighteen hours, double the usual time. The train was constantly stopping between stations and then went on at the pace of an ox-wagon. It was full of Japanese soldiers, with a few Burmese soldiers among them. The country we passed through was a rich, alluvial plain; there were rice-fields on both sides of the line and many villages. All of them sported white pagodas like the tapered ends of ninepins, sometimes whole colonies of them looking as ornamental as if they had been turned on a lathe for the fun of the thing. The Burmese are as liberal with pagodas as people are elsewhere with altar-candles. Next we saw the gleam of a golden needle on the horizon and knew that we were not far from Rangoon; it was the tip of the Shwe Dagôn pagoda, the emblem of the capital of Burma.

We got out at a station on the outskirts and accompanied our escort into the hot and crowded streets. We took a long time to find our way, because they would not, of course, ask anybody. We ourselves were still secretly hoping that we might be taken without more ado to the German Consul, but feared that Japanese procrastination might keep us lingering. Anyway, they had apparently found the way by this time, and they stepped out with the assurance of people who know where they are going. Suddenly I let out a shout of horror.

"It's another prison they're taking us to!"

166

A long, high, grey wall was in sight, and it was for this our escort was making a bee-line with such a resolute gait.

"Impossible," Have replied. "We've just had official assurance that we shan't be put in clink again. We can only be passing by chance."

"You'll see."

A few minutes later the great doors of the Central Prison of Rangoon had closed behind us.

Chapter Eleven

IN THE HANDS OF THE KEMPETAI

Rangoon had a look of desolation. It was hard to believe that this was the place which a few years before had been forging ahead as the greatest port of Burma, a centre of world-wide trade; or that a fresh wave of enterprise and self-assertion had visited it so lately. It was in fact impossible to believe that this was Rangoon, the once flourishing capital of the country.

The war, of course, was partly responsible; but the interruption of normal business and bomb-damage – air-attacks during our time there were only sporadic – were not the true cause of such a radical change. What struck us far more was that the jungle was counter-attacking and getting the better of civilization. No resistance was being offered; the jungle was beginning to win back the town. A few more years of negligence and the works of man would relapse into the embrace of nature. Already the monsoon had combed the façades of many buildings, grass was growing in the cracks of bulging pavements, and bamboos were taking possession of every bombed site.

The forces of civilization which could have arrested the progress of nature had collapsed the moment the British left Burma early in 1942, decamping in a hurry and taking with them three hundred thousand Indians in an unprecedented stream of fugitives, unprecedented because of the trackless and uninhabited jungle through which they had to pass, before, with frightful losses, they reached the Indian frontier. Those Indians who joined the British in their precipitate flight were the most prosperous, enterprising members of the community. The Japanese when they moved in had not the means to make good the loss, and as the Burmese are villagers are heart, it is not surprising that the city came to grief.

Rightly or wrongly, therefore, we attributed the desolate state of Rangoon to the absence of the white man; and certainly there was not a

European to be seen in the streets. To anyone who had known Rangoon in the years before the war, this made a strange and melancholy impression, and we who longed to see a white face, even if it were the face of an enemy, could not help feeling disillusioned. Involuntarily we looked into each large limousine which went by, in the hope of seeing a Barra Sahib taking his ease within, but it was always a Japanese officer, stiff, stern, and stony-hearted.

It was not literally true that there were no white men in Rangoon. There were actually quite a number of them, but they were not at liberty; we saw several of them when we were handed over in the Central Prison. We had been left abruptly by our escort in the charge of Japanese warders, and while we stumped about in a rage, we caught sight through the inner gateway of some wretched creatures carrying heavy tubs on a pole; we were astonished to see that they were white men, Allied prisoners, and probably British.

We had now come to another critical turning-point. It had to be decided there and then, before passing through this second iron gateway, whether we were to share the fate of those British prisoners or not. We had one foot inside that prison; one little push and the trap would snap to behind us. It would be a grotesque and painfully difficult situation.

Could it really be the intention of the Japanese to lock us up with Allied prisoners and to treat us for the duration of the war as enemies of Japan? If so, it would be an unheard-of outrage. We resolved to get to the bottom of it without delay.

"Take us to the governor," I demanded of a passing Japanese, who appeared to belong to the prison staff.

"You wait!" he replied roughly, and left us to stand where we were.

Have saw my look of annoyance, and said:

"We shan't get any further by putting up with things."

"No; and it's odd how they've always given way when we've shown our teeth."

"It will work this time too."

There was no need to make a great scene, because as soon as we were summoned to the governor's presence and had put our case, he assured us at once that there was no intention of shutting us up with the British. He had had special instructions about us and we were to be transferred to Headquarters.

But as we could not be taken there until next day, he had to take charge of us meanwhile and had directed that we should be taken into the house opposite the prison for the night.

Now what sort of Headquarters was this, we wondered.

Close to the harbour on the river-bank at Rangoon stands the handsome building of the highest Burmese court of law, a lofty modern erection with many court-rooms, parlours and offices. During the Japanese occupation it was the Headquarters of the Kempetai, the all-powerful Japanese military police, and it was into their hands we fell in the early days of July, 1944. Naturally, when we passed the sentries, ascended the palatial flight of steps and were taken in charge by a sergeant, we had no idea with whom we had to deal; time had to pass before we knew that it was the Kempetai, and also what precisely that meant.

We were taken at once into a room, where our haversacks were fallen upon for purposes of search, quite superfluously, in our opinion, because if they had contained anything suspicious we had had ample opportunity of getting rid of it on our way. We were next informed that we were going to be held for rigorous interrogation. When we said we had already been combed and screened at numerous army HQ until we were sick of it, we were told that all previous investigations were absolutely worthless. Here and here alone could anything of worth be elicited. But they must, we objected, have received full reports about us. Yes; that was so; but it was desirable to go into the matter all over again from the beginning.

So apparently no value was placed on the findings of any earlier trial; and if the case was to be reopened from the beginning each time, it would never reach any conclusion. We wanted to bring this endless, exhausting inquisition, which had its dangers too, to an end as quickly as possible; so we demanded through the interpreter to be put into touch with the German Consul, who we hoped would be able to cut short the proceedings.

"You want to speak to the Consul in Rangoon?"

"Certainly."

"There isn't one. The nearest German official is in Siam, at Bangkok."

That was a severe blow to us; now we should have to engage in an endless slogging-match with the Japanese.

The interpreter was a young man with a glass eye, who had been at Cambridge. He took us into a large room, luxuriously furnished and beautifully panelled with rare woods, in which several Japanese, some in uniforms, sat at a table. The senior officer was a young man, who was seated in solitary grandeur at a heavily ornate writing-table of his own. With no fuss whatever, as though we were servants of the court, we were shown to two tables which would have done honour to company secretaries, while the business of the day proceeded without interruption. Persons were interviewed, many of them Burmese and some of them women, and mostly spies, as we later learnt. There was much telephoning and talk, and occasionally one of the officers in uniform would buckle on his holster and vanish for a few hours in the prosecution of some sinister errand.

So there we sat – and no one took the slightest notice of us. At least, so it seemed, although we had scarcely taken our seats before a spectacled Japanese sat down at the empty table next to me and pretended to be lost in a voluminous dossier; in reality he was fixing us with that famous oblique look which was so hard to detect. It is in the nature of things to be annoyed with the sleuth who is set on to shadow one; we expressed our dislike of ours in whispered asides which his loathsome appearance did a lot to justify.

We were simply left to sit there all day. No one had time for us, although the senior officer was unoccupied all afternoon. It was not quite the right explanation to see a deliberate humiliation in all this, or the usual softening-up process. It was not inspired by a feeling of superiority, but on the contrary by a feeling of uncertainty. We had often noticed how the average Japanese was careful to avoid being confronted with the exceptional case, how helpless he was when he had no precedent to go by. There was undeniably something of that about us, and the prosecution needed twenty-four hours or longer before it felt able to confront the problem we presented. Perhaps this in part explains their morbid distrust of foreigners, whose incalculable resourcefulness must have a disquieting and even alarming effect on the Japanese. That is why they assemble all the material they can find about the foreigner. It is to protect themselves against surprises and the unusual, to avoid the need for improvisation. Even information gained from police dossiers is not disdained if it gives them the start on the other party.

We awaited the evening with suspense, because we should know then, from the quarters allotted to us, what status we were accorded by Police Headquarters. We had meanwhile seen a number of grated cells in the inner yard, with British prisoners in them, and our old fears revived. When at last the day ended we were taken to a room on the top storey of the building where the prison staff slept, and a guard was put over us. That looked like being remanded in custody – being held as suspicious characters. We had no idea when the proceedings would open or what the result would be.

Our room was small and furnished in the Japanese style, with tatamis (Japanese mats) on the floor and no beds. Our guard took up a third of the floor-space; he had brought his kit with him and seemed to be preparing for a long stay. He was, in fact, never relieved and remained our constant companion. At night his body barred the door. He deserved all credit for his neatly slit and wide-set almond eyes and for his rather long, melon-shaped face. No one could bend from the hips in a bow of such rigid correctness – to his superiors, naturally, not to us; no one could draw his breath between his teeth in a token of politeness so smartly, with so clean a hiss. He was conscientious and dutiful; yet when off duty he invariably got drunk and paid a visit to a brothel. But his routine debauchery left no gap in the care he took of us, because he always arranged for a substitute; and this was never a good exchange, because none of his fellows was such a scrupulous stable-companion as he.

Next morning our examination began, and went on for five days. It was more searching and thorough than any we had so far been subjected to, and by the end we wondered what it was they wanted to get out of us. Some of their questions were addressed to suspected spies; others implied that we were escaped German prisoners. Many of the questions were ingenuous or silly, and many took no account of the unusualness of our situation. They wanted to know the title of the thesis I had written for my degree, which at least I was able to provide, but when it came to the names of my fellow-passengers on my last trip out of Bombay, I could not oblige. One of their tricks was to pick on one single point in one's life, and then jump without a moment's pause to the whole chain of events during several years. The most skilful liar would have had no time to make up credible answers. Finally, we were asked for references and the names of persons in the Far East whom we knew well.

After they had squeezed us until there was nothing more to be got, the deputy-chief of the Kempetai, a lieutenant-colonel with very prominent teeth and bunched lips, who powdered his neck because of eczema, summoned us to his room. He received us politely but with an icy reserve, which in an odd way went well with his quince-coloured complexion, and said what little he did say in jerks. He was careful to conceal what he had in mind, and only said that our case would be considered and that we should hear further. Decisions had to be awaited, and they might take time, much time possibly. On the other hand, they might take very little time; in cases such as ours it was hard to say. At the last words he retracted his upper lip, on which a few single spikes of stubble grew, from his slanting teeth and freed them for a glacial smile.

So we were left knowing no more than before; it was clear only that we were in the grip of the most dangerous of all Japanese institutions, one that had absolute power of life and death, and could give to our case any turn it chose. We had therefore, knowing that the Samurai sword was suspended over us, to exercise angelic patience, although we had not a grain of patience left and only wanted to enjoy at last the fruits of our escape, to move about, see people, talk in our mother-tongue, and, in short, be human beings again.

We had to attend, punctually every morning at nine, in the panelled room on the first floor and remain there until five, just as though we were required for further questioning. But as our attendance was not in fact necessary, it was no more than a form of arrest, desk-arrest it might be called – surely one of the oddest methods of restricting liberty. We were, of course, forbidden to go outside; as soon as the day's work was over we were taken straight up to our room. Our ration was the same as for the Japanese – mere starvation. Even when a fragment of sweetened meat was included, it was uneatable. And the rancid bean soup was altogether too much for any European palate. At first I admired their spartan way of life, but as soon as I had to practise this virtue myself I found it unspeakably horrible and by no means worthy of imitation.

Of all that went on around us we saw no more than a Japanese drawing shows of the landscape it is supposed to represent – a few outlines and hints of forms in a sea of mist and haze. But the little we gathered was enough to give an impression of the whole, and a very definitely unpleasant one of the dangers that threatened us. The headquarters of the Japanese military police, we soon saw, led nowhere beyond itself; no way to freedom led through it. It was a terminus, and those who arrived there stayed there or else were destroyed. We saw the rations on which prisoners starved, and were told that Japanese soldiers charged with breaches of discipline – a very rare occurrence – preferred to take their own lives rather than await sentence. Twice we saw a detachment of Kempetai men go off by lorry with spades to bury the corpses of prisoners.

We had no positive reason to apply these observations to our own situation. It was not certain that we were to be victims of the Kempetai. But it was not by any means ruled out. What assurance had we that our predicament would have a happy ending? None was to be found in those

173

rabbit-brained but influential clerical functionaries, who entered with fanatical diligence each fresh deposition in our dossier. For this was another of our surprising discoveries: the final decision in the Japanese service did not lie with the big man at the top, but with his junior clerks. And what hope was there of a fair or generous construction, or even of common human understanding, in an air so tainted by the spy-bacillus? It was a presupposition that every foreigner was a spy, at least potentially. And the Japanese fear of espionage was not without good cause. They had had some unpleasant experiences. It was British agents above all who gave the Kempetai so much trouble – usually people dropped from the air into the jungle. The official who sat opposite us at our table was dealing with the case of three Englishmen who had been dropped in East Burma and had succeeded in enlisting a small troop from the local tribes for guerrilla warfare. It took a detachment of the Kempetai weeks to put them out of action, and weeks more to capture the Englishmen, or rather their leader, as the two others were shot during the pursuit. The leader was later caught, half-dead, after a wild chase, in which elephants were employed, and was now facing a court-martial.

Englishmen were not as a rule expended on these tasks; it was usually Burmese who floated down from the sky, equipped with radio apparatus for transmitting their news. Many of them surrendered to the Japanese without delay, but there were some who were loyal to their British principals. We got to know one of them; in fact, we saw him every day, as he was one of the minor officials.

He was a young man, perhaps eighteen years old, whom the teachers of the American Mission school had taken with them in their flight to India. There he was taught Morse by the British and later dropped in Burma. The most surprising thing about him was the fact that he was alive, and had not even been punished; we found out that several Burmese with a similar record were employed by the Kempetai as clerks, translators or messengers.

One day they brought a boy of mixed Chinese and Burmese parentage into the room. His face was pale with fright and looked old, although he was only a child. He sat all day on the window-ledge, and by degrees his terror gave way to a dreadful apathy. His eyes had a fixed stare as if he were heavily drugged. That evening in our room we asked our companion about him, and he told us that his case had something to do with an agent in the service of the Tshungking-Chinese. We should have liked to know more details about him and many other matters, but we did not care to ask. The Japanese, we found, made a point of being uncommunicative; often they simply would not answer, and it was very seldom they volunteered information unasked. If we started on any subject, they never carried it a stage further. It was not only from a love of secrecy; there was also the idea that monosyllabic utterance was a sign of intelligence and good education. They called their country "the land without debate", and they thought the cleverest man was he who spoke least, not he who spoke best. It was this peculiarity of the Japanese that made conversation with them so very tiresome. But their taciturnity was not the only reason we could not discourse openly with them; we had to be cautious for our own sakes, because any question we asked might be turned against us.

The building was in a dangerous situation owing to its proximity to the harbour and the river, and every time enemy aircraft were heard we all had to troop down into the cellar. The monsoon had passed its peak, and sometimes the moon shone through a gap in the heavy rain-clouds for a few hours, casting a pale, dirty-yellow light on their edges. An air-attack might confidently be expected on such nights. The siren wailed at about midnight and we followed our guard down the dark stairs to the shelter. Here the Kempetai troops lay about among sandbags and baulks, scarcely visible in the dim light of a lamp, which gave their faces a green, corpse-like look. The peaks of their caps hid their eyes, and those hidden eyes, we felt with a shudder, were all fixed upon us. They sat as though dead and in gloomy silence, at most bracing their facial muscles when a near-miss made the foundations quiver.

These nocturnal sessions, instead of bringing us nearer by sharing a common danger, cut us off from them as nothing else ever did. They seemed utterly alien to us and enigmatic, and as we waited on and on we were overcome by the horror of being walled in and buried alive with these people to whom we did not belong and whose presence evoked a sense of the macabre.

We knew there was no extreme they would not go to; they would hurl themselves as living bombs against the enemy or charge in a desperate Banzai attack until the last man fell. They would disembowel themselves on the slightest pretext, perhaps because a rebuke in the presence of the troops had caused them to lose face, or because they had mislaid some part of their rifle – in their eyes a mortal offence because it was neglect of Imperial property.

We knew too that all those who were employed here at Headquarters down to the interpreters and hospital orderlies were bound by oath to take their own lives rather than surrender. They might speak of it, but only as a matter of course, scarcely worth mentioning. People whose exit from life meant so little to them, and who were therefore indifferent to the personal consequences of even such an extreme event as war, must have a very intimate relation to death and be, as it were, on the best of terms with it. And if at this moment we got a direct hit and these men had to give their lives for their Emperor, it would not alarm them. Death was no disaster, merely a change to a higher state.

It was this resolute composure in face of the worst that gave its peculiar stamp to the people we were among. The Army of Japan had a dedicated and cloistral quality; it dwelt under the shadow of death, and its soldiers were like monks who already lived in another world. When a soldier joined up he was promised to Death. He had put in his claim for admission to the kingdom of the gods. He cut all civilian links, and his family did not think of him with secret anxiety, but with the joyful expectation that he might never return.

To see our judges in these votaries of death, who sat as motionless as stone images in the dark cellar, was not pleasant. We felt we were at the mercy of unfathomable influences, powers beyond our ken, dark and mysterious as Asia itself. We could find nothing to rely on or to look to. There was no safety, no security anywhere to be seen. And this utter negation oppressed us all the more when we saw how entirely the Japanese war-machine was dominated by it, from mythological or religious considerations which were incomprehensible to us.

One night they brought down a casualty, one of their regiment who had been mortally wounded in the street by a flak-splinter. They surrounded him, two of them holding him under the arms, and then sang one of their fierce hymns. When he seemed to be losing consciousness they lifted him up roughly and sang louder. Probably they did this to prolong the moments during which his thoughts were consciously with his God-Emperor. If he were a true son of his people, he believed in the divinity of the Mikado, the descendant of the sun-goddess Amaterasu, and was convinced of the divine origin of his commands. Even he, a common man, might claim a share in the divine fluid which flowed from Tenno; and this share was enough to give him complete confidence in his cause. How could the cause of the gods be defeated by any earthly powers?

He departed this life accompanied by the wild and exultant singing of his comrades, and his body was covered with a strip of sacking. Now he had rejoined the universal life from which he had been momentarily detached as an actor in the temporal world. Yet his death was only an ordinary death – the Army of Nippon held out a higher form, based on the ancient practice of contemplation, the practice of the Indian Yoga. It was this that inspired the training of the Kamikaze, the suicide pilots, who were bound by oath not to return from a raid. These candidates for death had to train themselves by mental concentration for the moment when they dived on their objective, in the same way as the Yoga prepares himself for the mystic union with the divine. In both cases there is the foretaste of death.

But we white men, wedged in among these grim sons of the race of Yamato, sat on the cellar-bunks and the bombs fell – bombs dropped by white men, let be it said. We thought a good deal less of the higher and more intellectual cult of death of the Japanese than we did, with a grisly thrill of curiosity, of that more volatile side of their nature, which might, even while we looked, take a sudden turn. Their composed and colourless exteriors concealed a weakness for wild and even orgiastic outbursts, which made them see red in the heat of battle or, like the Malays, run amok.

We might now consider ourselves past-masters in the art of waiting; our existence behind the wire had been nothing but that, nothing but a marking time in time itself. Weeks had gone by here too in doing nothing but sitting time out, weeks in which we had to play the equivocal and difficult part of guest-prisoners with what equanimity we could muster. But now we thought the time had come to press the Kempetai for the long-overdue decision.

All our representations were made in vain. We were neither permitted an interview with the lieutenant-colonel, nor was any consideration given to our suggestion of communicating with representatives of Germany in Bangkok and Tokyo. Our remonstrances, too, about our insufficient diet fell on deaf ears, and this we took particularly hard, because we were showing obvious signs of malnutrition. Our hair came out in handfuls. We were becoming deaf and suffered from neuralgia. Besides undernourishment, there was the torturing anxiety lest the Japanese might adopt once and for all the notion of keeping us shut up for the rest of the war. It was not for nothing, surely, that they so assiduously prevented us getting into touch with any German official, and Have often repeated the outburst of the leading examiner, who asked whether it had never occurred to us that, instead of taking all this trouble to clear up our case, they might not as well adopt the far easier course of leaving us in suspense until the end of the war?

Our attempt to hurry matters on led only to our being ignored. We met with silence and averted eyes on all sides, as though by orders from above. There was an alteration too in our attendance during office hours. One day we were excluded on the occasion of morning prayers addressed to the Emperor, which it was not for us to attend, and put into a vacant room next door – temporarily, as we thought, but permanently, as it turned out.

Our human contacts were now restricted, apart from our room-companion, with whom we could not exchange a word owing to the language difficulty, to an Indian boy, who ran errands for the Japanese and hung about the office all day. Although he was only eleven, he was enterprising and capable; he did a little business on his own account and acted as a pimp. He could do what he liked with the Japanese; their proverbial love of children excused any mischief he got up to.

He had some strange duties to perform. One day, while we were still subjected to the sittings, we saw the senior officer get up hurriedly from his ornate chair and send the boy for the bottle of iodine; he then, with sublime disregard, let his trousers down and told the boy to paint his behind where it hurt. Although this occurred in a crowded room and an officer played the title rôle, so to speak, no one present saw anything in it – except the two of us, of course, who could not sufficiently marvel at such arcadian innocence.

When we began spending our days in isolation, this boy often kept us company and helped us pass the time with his precocious talk. One day we asked him about his family. He told us that his father had been killed in the massacre which took place after the British had left and before the Japanese had arrived. It was a massacre of the Indians, whom the Burmese hated as profiteers and usurers. The whole town was in confusion; the mob ransacked warehouses and shops and burnt the villas of the rich. There were sanguinary battles between the Burmese and the Karens, a minority, many of whom were Christians. Order was not restored until the Japanese moved in.

Penned up as we were and left alone to our suspense, we naturally suffered from that morbid craze of all prisoners who are left in the dark about their fate for searching into the plans and motives of their gaolers. We asked ourselves over and over again what was the real reason for the way the Japanese were behaving. We had every incitement to indulge in this tormenting occupation, and as we had no other sources of information we subjected every chance remark, every action and measure of the Japanese, to a rigorous analysis, either to endorse or to invalidate one or other of our theories. Sometimes we pointed, in explanation of the long delay, to the lavish expenditure of time common to the whole East; what, elsewhere, would be cleared up and acted upon in three hours, would take as many months east of Suez. In view of this, it was mere folly on our part to press for a decision, we told ourselves, and led to nothing but bad feeling. Sometime we put the delay down to the fear of responsibility; no one wanted to risk accepting spies as Germans, nor on the other hand would anyone risk treating citizens of an allied power as enemies. On this theory we might hope that, as nobody cared to act on his own responsibility, our case might finally reach Tokyo. And there was one thing we could say that was beyond dispute: the Japanese treated us well from their own standpoint. They gave us officers' rations, bearable accommodation, and left us physically in peace. All that annoyed us might be put down either to their peculiar mentality or to lack of means.

Six weeks perhaps had gone by since our arrival in Rangoon when we had unexpected news. Orders had been received to hand us over to another authority, which would take over all further responsibility for us. We were to be ready to set off on the following morning. Although we felt quite sure that the new authority would reopen our case from the very beginning and go into it with the usual expenditure of time, we were glad all the same to get free of the Kempetai, whose embrace might so easily have been fatal. Probably we should now be handed over to the civil arm, perhaps to the Japanese Embassy in Rangoon, as seemed likely from earlier indications and the recent visit of a mysterious civilian, who was presumably a member of the Consular Service.

Next morning we were waiting in front of the main entrance at the appointed time and already congratulating ourselves on our safe escape from a place where life was so cheap, when an orderly from the officers' quarters on the second floor came up to us. He informed us that the order had been countermanded at the last moment. We were not now to be removed, but to be kept in custody as before.

"If they're going to go putting it off at every turn, we may not be free for years," Have said in disgust.

And so our intercourse with the outside world was once more confined to the view from the window of our room, a depressing view which showed us nothing but the utterly derelict port of Rangoon. Before the war, steamers had berthed there stem to stern, and now there was not a single seagoing vessel to be seen. Possibly the Japanese were landing their reinforcements at some place less exposed to air-attack, but that was unlikely, judging from what we had seen. No; if our allies had been able to keep up the flow of men and supplies, Rangoon was the only place to land them, and if they could not make use of it, Burma must be cut off by sea.

From the very first day we made contact with the Japanese, we had come to the conclusion that their Indian campaign was starved of supplies. They had, we felt, overtaxed their resources and exceeded the limit of what was possible. This suspicion was now fully confirmed. It was obviously impossible to feed their war-machine from the enormous territories they had overrun without, in the first place, access to an ample supply of shipping. As though they wanted to show us how they made up for their lack of the munitions of war, they used to train their men in bayonet-fighting for hour after hour in the now derelict dockyards. Every day we saw the men hurl themselves in a frenzy of rage on straw dummies. What a farce, we thought, to pretend that in modern war you can make up for inferior equipment by superior animal ferocity or contempt of death.

Day after day went by. The second month was at an end. Then things unexpectedly began to move. We were sitting reading in the room next to the office, thinking of nothing less than any change in our prospects, when the one-eyed interpreter burst in and told us to follow him at once up to the second floor. Aha, we thought, something's up. Visits to the second floor had never been for nothing.

One of the worst features of imprisonment is that one gets accustomed to it. We had come to feel it was quite right to be hidden from human sight, as though locked away in a cupboard. But no account whatever was taken of our retiring natures on this occasion.

We were put in through a door and found ourselves in the full glare of publicity, faced by a semicircle of reporters, with pencils hungrily poised above their pads. Interviewed by the Press! Surely a great step forward. There were two vacant chairs in the crowded room, which were intended for us. As we walked to them someone asked if we were sick. We certainly looked it. No, Glass-eye replied for us, no; we had enjoyed the best of health throughout.

We were painfully conscious that every word we said might have world-wide publicity, and would certainly come to the ears of the British. We had therefore to be on our guard against saying anything that might damage anybody inside our old camp or outside it.

"We'll have to be damned careful," Have whispered into one of my deaf ears.

To start the interview, an officer, whose function it was to put the curb on the reporters, called upon us, through Glass-eye, to tell the reporters about our escape. I had to speak first, and I tried to suppress such matters as how we procured money, and might have succeeded if it had not been for the presence of Glass-eye. But he, having been present at my examination, was familiar with all the details; and so detecting my omissions at once, he was able to defeat them either by the questions he put or by filling in my account himself. Have had the same experience.

So we asked the officer who was acting as censor to see that the reporters omitted certain specified details. This was agreed to, but the next day, when we read the account in the Rangoon paper, where it was splashed across the front page with a sensational write-up, we found that nothing but our names had been left out. This we had not asked for, as our names were the only facts about our escape of which the British were definitely certain.

The interview as far as it went was a turning-point for us. It meant that we had emerged from hiding. Our existence was no longer a secret, and we had good reason for thinking that the Japanese would not introduce spies to the Press. They must therefore have finally come to believe what we said, and to have achieved this was a great thing in a situation like ours. If we were tempted to deduce from it that our isolation was at an end, we were being much too hasty, because after this brief inspection we were put back in our case and locked away.

And yet the wheels, once they had begun to turn, kept on turning. Our custody this time was brief. Some days after being interviewed by the Press we were summoned to the presence of the lieutenant-colonel with the powdered neck, who, making full use of the element of surprise, gave us some very important news. Orders had been received from high up to despatch us to Tokyo by air. Our seats were reserved and the plane was due to leave on the next day but one. The long suspense, which had begun four months ago when we broke out of Dehra Dun, had ended.

He did not say a word as to how this decision had come about, or what had caused the Japanese to drop the suspicions they had had of us; nor have we ever heard since to what we owed our lives. At the time we thought it was reports received from persons we had named as references, but later we heard that they had never even been approached. We were thus provided with a fresh proof that the Japanese were masters of mystification.

The lieutenant-colonel told us also that our wish to take the quickest way back to Germany was not dealt with by present arrangements.

Outlying commands like Rangoon were not competent to decide that. We should make a fresh application in Tokyo. And, finally, would we say which of his Kempetai men we should like as a travelling-companion, because he had to send someone with us. We named our room-mate, a choice which the colonel endorsed.

Events now crowded on each other.

We went several times to have injections; we were issued far too small army shorts, although they were the largest stocked anywhere in Rangoon; we were introduced like dancing bears to all senior officers and their staffs, and our lieutenant-colonel even went so far as to give us advice. He also allowed us to accept an invitation from Sabhas Chandra Bose, the Indian revolutionary, who then had his HQ as commanding officer of the INA in Rangoon. We spent the whole evening with him and his closest associates and did not leave until nearly dawn. Bose, for whom, even on first acquaintance, we felt a high esteem, had good reason to sympathize with us, because he too had had to flee from India to escape from the British. He suffered as we had from the suspicions of the Japanese and made no secret of it. He seemed to be fighting a relentless but, as we thought, hopeless battle with them for independence. It did us good to talk to these Indians. It helped us to regain our capacity for normal contact with other men. We were allowed to visit Bose without an escort, but a man had been detailed to wait for us at the gate of the Kempetai building, and he seemed to be very much upset when we did not turn up until a little before sunrise.

We had a continuous flow of visitors to receive in our room. They were mostly soldiers who wanted us to take something to their families in Japan. Besides letters, there was very characteristically a box of cigarettes adorned with the Imperial chrysanthemum, one of those which the Tenno had distributed among his troops and which the fortunate possessor wished to send home as a tangible emblem of his sovereign's favour to take its place on the domestic altar.

Our travelling-companion was almost out of his mind during these last days. He had not been to Japan for three years, and suddenly he was going, and in an aeroplane, he who had never been in one. He did not close his eyes those last nights; he wanted to know everything about Bangkok, Saigon and Taihoku, where we should land on the way; he went over all the old tears and patches in his uniform with assiduous needle; packed and repacked his kit, and occasionally cast an eye on his two charges, for whom he would now have let himself be hacked to pieces. His orders were to conduct us unharmed to Tokyo; and if he had

had the responsibility laid on him by the Emperor in person, he could not have shown a more religious determination to carry it out.

We had already felt on more than one occasion what it was to be free. The first time was when, dazed and astounded, we found ourselves outside the camp – in the free air, but not yet free. Then in Calcutta, where we joined in the life of a large town, the illusion of freedom was almost complete, although we knew it was surreptitious and might be short-lived, at best only an anticipation of a future state. And then later when we penetrated the Japanese positions we tasted the joys of freedom once more, with justification this time, even if our claim was not accepted; we were free, but could not make use of our freedom. The first time we could really call ourselves free men was on the last morning in Rangoon, when we left the Kempetai Headquarters. We were therefore in the highest spirits by the time we reached the aerodrome.

The engines roared, the machine which was to take us to Tokyo gathered speed. The lieutenant-colonel of the Kempetai and a colonel on the General Staff of the Burma Army, who had come to see us off, stood like statues with their hands to their caps. We waved back.

As the heavy aircraft left the ground and gradually gained height, we sat in our seats and said nothing. So much had happened, so much we hadn't expected, so much nobody could have expected – we felt utterly dazed when we thought of it.

Our escape had turned out to be no common experience, no adventure in the usual sense – it was something which took one over into another life as another person. It had disturbed rooted ideas, shaken inborn principles – for what did reality mean now? What was real and what was dream? Where was the line to be drawn?

Have interrupted the train of my thoughts by saying:

"I'm reconciled with the past again. The insult of imprisonment has been wiped out."

Chapter Twelve

FINALE IN THE FAR EAST

Anyone who has once handed himself over to uncertainty, as we did when we broke out of the routine of Dehra Dun camp, must not expect everyday life to resume its sway all at once; the spell of the unusual, once invoked, will persist for a time. It seemed to us fantastic, irresponsible, and yet also a matter of course to be on our way to Japan, the island of blossom and sword. We, who had seemed to be condemned to stay where we were for the rest of the war, were now flying through the fathomless blue of the tropics to a country which in our wildest moments we had never expected to reach.

The Gulf of Martaban was below us, but soon the strip of coast which becomes, further south, the Malay Peninsula was visible. The cloudless sky was utterly transparent, and below we saw a scene of unimaginable beauty – the turquoise sea transparent to the bottom, the whitish-yellow edge of the land in curve after curve, which the green luxuriance of mountain-jungle parts from the mirrorlike expanses of the Bay of Bengal. We could recognize every detail in spite of our great height, every palm-hut on the beach, every canoe. Now we flew over primaeval forest, forbidding mountain-ranges and uninhabited valleys. How alluring they looked from that height! Strange impulses overtake civilized men who have become estranged from nature. We would have liked to dive down into the vast healing stillness below, and begin, down there, all over again.

Now the clearings became more frequent, with tree-dwellings here and there. The first rectangular patches of cultivation could be seen; then we passed quickly to the plains, where the villages were surrounded by irrigated rice-fields, gleaming like mirrors. We were approaching the delta of the Menam, on which Bangkok is situated.

As we were not flying on to Saigon until next morning, we had half a day to spend in Bangkok, the capital city of Siam. Our escort conducted us past stupas and temple-enclosures, through a maze of canals, crowded with houseboats, a scene of brilliant colours in the blazing sun, to our quarters in the Kempetai barracks. It was then early in the afternoon, and he requested us to join him again in barracks by ten at night. We at once rang up the German Legation to announce our arrival. We were given the welcome of the Prodigal Son. A few people were invited to meet us and hear our adventures. Many other invitations followed. We were thoroughly spoiled. The Minister's family took the lead, and must have had a shock when at a sitting we ate them right out of ham and asparagus.

We continued our journey in the early morning in the twin-engined Mitsubishi, flying high above impenetrable jungle eastwards to Indo-China. Range after range of densely-clothed heights and peaks rose from the morning haze which filled the valleys. On our left, too far off to be visible, Angkor, the town of temples, was hidden in the jungle. These temple-buildings of Cambodia date from the days, five hundred years ago, when the Khmer ruled the country.

Some time before Saigon we came down and flew low through the steaming heat of the thickly-populated delta of the Mekong. We were close above the watery rice-fields and marshes, and the ground across which our shadow swept was clay-coloured, diversified by the yellow straw-thatch of the buildings. One could feel how the poisonous miasma of the marshes seeped into them.

The Japanese did not want the French in Saigon to know of our arrival. A Japanese met us at the aerodrome and took us in a closed car to an hotel the Japanese had requisitioned. Before leaving, he asked us to keep to ourselves and avoid contact with the French. We did as he wished, and saw only one or two Germans who were living in Saigon.

I had a shock when I entered my bedroom. There before my eyes was myself at full length in a looking-glass. This was an experience I had not had for years. In camp we only had small hand-mirrors. Now suddenly I saw myself in one piece! I went to tell Have of my encounter, but when I opened the connecting-door I saw him seated in front of his two-winged shaving-mirror, enjoying the delightful view of his own profile, of which he had been so long deprived.

Our next hop was to Formosa, quite close to Japan. The mainland of Asia was behind us and we were crossing the South China Sea. We were thankful to have been sent by air, as communication by sea had become very uncertain. But now while we flew over the open sea, in a region where fighters from aircraft-carriers might well have dived on us, I did not feel much safer than if we had been on a ship. I spied out anxiously, and was annoyed that the curtains were kept drawn over the windows.

185

We landed on a small island to refuel. We could not find out its name. The curtains were kept drawn until we were far out of sight of the fuelling-station.

After we had flown for several hours through cloud the curtains were drawn back, and we landed at Taihoku, the capital of Formosa. A car took us rapidly to the outskirts of the town, whence our escort conducted us to a hostel run by the Kempetai. It was a charming Japanese house, without chimney or cellar, empty rooms with clean mats made from rice-straw, latticed sliding panels, covered with transparent paper, instead of windows. We were waited on by Japanese girls. They were quite round and very merry. At the sight of us huge giants striding about in their doll's house, they laughed till they could laugh no more. When they laugh they hold their hands in front of their mouths as if they were yawning.

On the next and fourth day of our flight we trod at last the sacred soil of Japan, the island of the gods. We came down at Fukuoka, on Kiushu, the southernmost island of the empire.

There is not a land on earth to compare with Japan in beauty. We fell under the spell of it at once when we resumed our journey to Tokyo by train. For a long distance the railway followed the rocky east coast, along peninulas, promontories, large and small bays, sprinkled with tiny rocky islets on which there was scarcely room for an umbrella-beetle. The train tore through gorges, opening up romantic and unexpected glimpses of crags and waterfalls. Before sundown we saw the regular cone of holy Fuji, an extinct volcano, appear over the mountains. Its summit was now in late summer free of snow, and in the light of the setting sun it took on a pale violet colour.

It was not far now to Tokyo. Representatives of the German Embassy and two German officers attached to the Japanese General Staff were on the platform. Our Kempetai escort from Rangoon made us a last, very low, very long bow in the station-hall and withdrew for good.

But what we took to be a short stop, merely to change planes before continuing our journey home, turned out to be a three-year visit to Japan. Our return to Germany was at that time impracticable.

We were the guests first of two attachés, whose houses were next door to each other, and later of the Embassy. Everyone called us "the two escaped prisoners", and treated us with the greatest kindness. The Japanese too were friendly, although they were a little hurt that we had penetrated their lines without being shot by their soldiers. Up to that point our experiences delighted them, but apparently our survival was a national insult.

186

We arrived in Tokyo at the beginning of September, 1944, when Japan was suffering her first serious defeats. The Americans had broken through the outer perimeter of her defences, and were jumping from island to island to close in on the mother-country. Japan lost command of the air and the sea throughout the whole of her extensive conquests. It was a time of increasing difficulty.

We had therefore to prepare for a long stay and to look out for work. German firms had nothing to offer, not even the I.G. Farben Industrie, which was overstaffed for what little business it still had left. On the advice of the German Embassy we went to Shanghai in search of suitable jobs, but found nothing. But we saw something of China.

We were back in Tokyo in February, 1945, and rented a small house, with an amah to look after us. We had now found work with the Embassy and were fixed up for the time being.

The Americans, meanwhile, had approached Japan so closely on the south-east that they were able to launch heavy air-attacks from the island of Saipan. The sirens were heard continually for the next weeks and months, and air-attacks became more and more frequent. Crowded quarters of Tokyo went up in flames. Fire-bombs were used, because the wooden Japanese houses burned like tinder; and this was the best way of reducing the town to ashes. Hundreds of thousands lost their lives.

The day came when we heard the news of Germany's surrender. The Japanese Government accused Germany of disloyalty and was not sparing in her comments on her ally. But the man in the street showed more sympathy, and even sorrow. A German married couple, who lived out in the country, were sent a spray of lilac by some Japanese acquaintances as a token of their sympathy. It was accompanied by a message which would only occur to Japanese, "This is the time when the lilac blooms in your country."

Every race has many faces and, in war, it shows its worst. We had known Japan's unkind face in the Burmese battle-zone, and now we discovered by degrees a more friendly and amiable one. We admired and liked the simple, good-hearted peasants and fishermen who lived close to nature, the well-mannered girls and the gentle women, that clear and ringing tone characteristic of Japanese life, and the patina which is the hallmark of all that is genuinely Japanese.

Japan now entered her period of hard trials. The Americans intensified their bombardment from the air and, at the end of May, Tokyo was the target of an air armada, flying in from the Pacific. That night the German Embassy was burned to the ground.

It was now a desolate and half-deserted city. All civilians moved out by degrees. Have and I spent our days in the Embassy grounds, where there was a large air-raid shelter. One warm tropical August day, when we were sitting there as usual, an official of the Japanese Foreign Office, a good friend of ours, came hurrying out to us in our improvised office beneath the ruins. As soon as he entered I saw unmistakable signs of dismay for the first time on a Japanese face. Yet he forced himself to smile as he got the words out:

"Something terrible has happened. The Americans have dropped a new type of bomb on our town of Hiroshima. The whole town is destroyed. I have just heard Truman on the radio. He says it is the atom bomb."

Then came the 15th of August, 1945. A radio message to the nation from the Tenno Heika, the Emperor, was announced for noon. He had never before spoken on the radio, and all expected news of decisive importance. When the short speech was over we asked a former interpreter of the Embassy what the Tenno had said, "The Emperor has ordered us to stop fighting." Japan had surrendered.

It was fortunate that it happened in the season of severe storms, when typhoons occur. This compelled the Americans to postpone their landing for some weeks and gave the Japanese time to compose themselves and prepare to meet the conqueror. It was the first time that Japan had been occupied by an enemy.

The arrival of the Americans altered our lives in many ways. Our shelter was required for their troops, and we were sent first to Hakone and then to Atami, an enchanting and unspoilt country town on the east coast, about thirty-five miles south of Tokyo. We lived in a Japanese hotel there for the next eighteen months.

The Americans announced immediately after they landed that they were going to send most of the Germans in Japan back to Germany, but the date of repatriation was left uncertain. Rumour followed rumour, but hope was always deferred. Have and I, a small party of Germans and a few recalled Axis diplomats stayed on at Atami, where we lived with full board in the Hotel Mampei at the charge of the Japanese Government. By order of the occupying Power, we were guests of Japan. Food rapidly became scarcer.

We got to know the real, unspoiled Japan during our enforced idleness at Atami, and made the astonishing discovery that there still existed on the earth a great nation living in the service of beauty, bound by strict aesthetic laws in the building of its houses, the make of its domestic implements, in its dress and its manners. It could be said without exaggeration that in the real Japan nothing tasteless or ugly ever met the eye.

In time there were indications that the day of our departure for Germany was within sight. Finally, 17 August 1947 was fixed on. We had many affectionate proofs that the Japanese were attached to us and would keep their feeling of friendship even after we had gone.

There was a crowd of Japanese at the station to wish us all a happy voyage. Then the American officer in charge gave the order to take our seats and our special moved off. We boarded the *General Black* at Yokohama. As we steamed along the island, the top of Fuji was visible – a sign that we should see Japan again.

We reached home after a journey of forty-five days, thus achieving the task we had set ourselves at Dehra Dun over three years before. How unlike our expectations it had all turned out! And how ironical it seemed that our fellow-prisoners had got home nearly a year before us, in spite of the hurry we had been in.

"Barbed wire seems to exert a strong pull on us," Have said with a laugh when we were put in the repatriation camp at Ludwigsburg, an American reception-camp for Germans returning from abroad. Once more we were on the inner side of a prison enclosure.

So you might say the British had the last word after all.

POSTSCRIPT

Initially, I only wrote this report for myself because I wanted to find out why this lunatic undertaking involving an escape route right across southeastern Asia succeeded at all. Why did the long chain of fortunate circumstances remain unbroken right to the end? There is no rational explanation. For once the die had been cast, we were all entering into competition with the unknown. And after we had taken our first step into freedom we were inevitably at the mercy of fate. Anything might happen. Our destiny was to go for the most outlandish option that would help our endeavour, to overcome the odds that were stacked against escaping. We staked all. But why we succeeded remains a mystery to this day.

Of course, bluff played a big part in our success. The bluff was that we passed ourselves off as members of the British ruling class. This enabled us to assume the unassailable status of colonial officers. Bluff was to be our passport across India.

It was different in the jungle. There you had to draw on your innermost resources of strength. Muscle power rather than brains drove us forward. We never made a mistake because we were in a permanent state of heightened concentration. This gave us lightning reactions and protected us automatically against the Sword of Damocles that was constantly hanging over our heads. Our escape went something like this: cautious progress – then imminent crisis – successful circumvention – a look into the abyss – astonishment at having avoided the fatal fall – deep breath – and continuation on our way. This happened countless times.

Heins von Have was something else. My companion on the long journey to Tokyo was a daredevil. He was a man without fear, confident of winning through in the end. He revelled in the thrill of danger. It enhanced his powers. Heins von Have overcame obstacles with a smile, just as if it were a game. He got bored if the atmosphere wasn't electric.

Without him – my blood brother – and his driving force, I would still be sitting in Dehra Dun today.

My daily contact with Heinrich Harrer in the camp also energized my internal resources. We kept fit together, doing exercises for months on end, and became close friends. His wild spirit drove him inexorably to break the shackles of captivity.

When I look back on my life from today's vantage point, my successful escape appears to me as the zenith of my existence. Nothing has the power to match that achievement. Everything else seems pale and second-rate by comparison. When I returned home, my standards for my own accomplishments became more stringent. I was probably also expected to rise to greater heights. When I was competing with others and the going got tough, I could always draw on an inner reserve of strength in the background: my memory of the terrible conditions in those far-off mountain jungles.

I too believe that the deeds we hold most dear are those of which we never thought we were capable.

Rolf Magener,
Heidelberg
March 2000

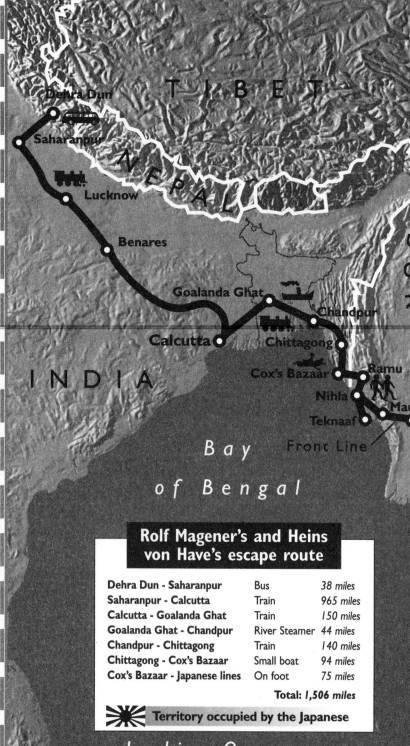

TIBET

NEPAL

BURMA

INDIA

Dehra Dun

Saharanpur

Lucknow

Benares

Goalanda Ghat

Chandpur

Calcutta

Chittagong

Cox's Bazaar

Ramu

Nihla

Maungda

Teknaaf

Tau

Front Line

P

Bay

of Bengal

India Ocean

Rolf Magener's and Heins von Have's escape route

Dehra Dun - Saharanpur	Bus	38 miles
Saharanpur - Calcutta	Train	965 miles
Calcutta - Goalanda Ghat	Train	150 miles
Goalanda Ghat - Chandpur	River Steamer	44 miles
Chandpur - Chittagong	Train	140 miles
Chittagong - Cox's Bazaar	Small boat	94 miles
Cox's Bazaar - Japanese lines	On foot	75 miles
	Total:	**1,506 miles**

Territory occupied by the Japanese